"Peter Rudnytsky has long been in the forefront of Ferenczi scholarship. By bringing Ferenczi together with Fromm, and through his compelling readings of Shakespeare and Milton, he opens new vistas on the history of psychoanalysis and shows what it means to be resolutely independent in theory and genuinely interdisciplinary in practice."

Franco Borgogno, Training and Supervising Analyst, Italian Psychoanalytic Society; author of *The Girl Who Committed Hara-Kiri and Other Clinical and Historical Essays*

"*Formulated Experiences* brings Erich Fromm back to public awareness as well as to the attention of the psychoanalytic community. Peter Rudnytsky's excellent and original essays invite a new generation of readers to discover why Fromm's social psychoanalysis is more urgently needed today than ever."

Rainer Funk, literary executor of Erich Fromm, author of *Life Itself Is an Art: The Life and Work of Erich Fromm*

Formulated Experiences

In *Formulated Experiences*, Peter L. Rudnytsky continues his quest for a "re-vision" of psychoanalysis by coupling his revival of the unjustly neglected figure of Erich Fromm with his latest groundbreaking research on Ferenczi and Groddeck.

Committed at once to a humanistic and to a literary psychoanalysis, Rudnytsky explores the subjective roots of creativity and critiques the authoritarianism that has been a tragic aspect of Freud's legacy. Through his clinically informed interpretations, he brings out both "hidden realities" and "emergent meanings" of the texts and authors he examines, including Shakespeare's *Othello* and *Macbeth*, as well as Milton's *Paradise Lost*.

A preeminent scholar of the history and theory of psychoanalysis, Rudnytsky displays an interdisciplinary expertise that makes *Formulated Experiences* truly *sui generis* and unlike any existing book. Bridging the artificial divide between the academic and clinical worlds, his eloquent championing of the interpersonal and relational traditions will captivate contemporary psychoanalysts and psychotherapists, while his insightful close readings provide a model for psychoanalytic literary critics.

Peter L. Rudnytsky is Professor of English at the University of Florida and Head of the Department of Academic and Professional Affairs of the American Psychoanalytic Association. He maintains a private practice in psychoanalysis and psychotherapy in Gainesville.

Psychoanalysis In a New Key Book Series
Series Editor
Donnel Stern

When music is played in a new key, the melody does not change, but the notes that make up the composition do: change in the context of continuity, continuity that perseveres through change. Psychoanalysis in a New Key publishes books that share the aims psychoanalysts have always had, but that approach them differently. The books in the series are not expected to advance any particular theoretical agenda, although to this date most have been written by analysts from the Interpersonal and Relational orientations.

The most important contribution of a psychoanalytic book is the communication of something that nudges the reader's grasp of clinical theory and practice in an unexpected direction. Psychoanalysis in a New Key creates a deliberate focus on innovative and unsettling clinical thinking. Because that kind of thinking is encouraged by exploration of the sometimes surprising contributions to psychoanalysis of ideas and findings from other fields, Psychoanalysis in a New Key particularly encourages interdisciplinary studies. Books in the series have married psychoanalysis with dissociation, trauma theory, sociology, and criminology. The series is open to the consideration of studies examining the relationship between psychoanalysis and any other field—for instance, biology, literary and art criticism, philosophy, systems theory, anthropology, and political theory.

But innovation also takes place within the boundaries of psychoanalysis, and Psychoanalysis in a New Key therefore also presents work that reformulates thought and practice without leaving the precincts of the field. Books in the series focus, for example, on the significance of personal values in psychoanalytic practice, on the complex interrelationship between the analyst's clinical work and personal life, on the consequences for the clinical situation when patient and analyst are from different cultures, and on the need for psychoanalysts to accept the degree to which they knowingly satisfy their own wishes during treatment hours, often to the patient's detriment.

A full list of all titles in this series is available at: www.routledge.com/series/LEAPNKBS

Vol. 51 Formulated Experiences: Hidden Realities and Emergent Meanings from Shakespeare to Fromm
Peter L. Rudnytsky

Vol. 50 The Emergence of Analytic Oneness: Into the Heart of Psychoanalysis
Ofra Eshel

Vol. 49 Homosexuality, Transsexuality, Psychoanalysis and Traditional Judaism
Edited by Alan Slomowitz and Alison Feit

Formulated Experiences

Hidden Realities and Emergent Meanings from Shakespeare to Fromm

Peter L. Rudnytsky

LONDON AND NEW YORK

First published 2019
by Routledge
2 Park Square, Milton Park, Abingdon, Oxon, OX14 4RN

and by Routledge
52 Vanderbilt Avenue, New York, NY 10017

Routledge is an imprint of the Taylor & Francis Group, an informa business

© 2019 Peter L. Rudnytsky

The right of Peter L. Rudnytsky to be identified as author of this work has been asserted by him in accordance with sections 77 and 78 of the Copyright, Designs and Patents Act 1988.

All rights reserved. No part of this book may be reprinted or reproduced or utilised in any form or by any electronic, mechanical, or other means, now known or hereafter invented, including photocopying and recording, or in any information storage or retrieval system, without permission in writing from the publishers.

Trademark notice: Product or corporate names may be trademarks or registered trademarks, and are used only for identification and explanation without intent to infringe.

British Library Cataloguing-in-Publication Data
A catalogue record for this book is available from the British Library

Library of Congress Cataloging-in-Publication Data
A catalog record has been requested for this book

ISBN: 978-0-367-19058-3 (hbk)
ISBN: 978-0-367-19059-0 (pbk)
ISBN: 978-0-429-20011-3 (ebk)

Typeset in Times New Roman
by Apex CoVantage, LLC

To James P. Bednarz

"Something too much of this."
　　—Shakespeare, *Hamlet*

Contents

Acknowledgments   xi

Introduction   "One Man Cannot Be the Same as Many": Glimpsing New Paradigms through Old Keyholes   1

PART 1
Discovering Fromm   37

1   Freud as Milton's God: Mapping the Patriarchal Cosmos in Psychoanalysis and *Paradise Lost*   39

2   The Indispensability of Erich Fromm: The Rehabilitation of a "Forgotten" Psychoanalyst   70

3   Freud, Ferenczi, Fromm: The Authoritarian Character as Magic Helper   104

PART 2
Ferenczian Inflections   115

4   The Other Side of the Story: Severn on Ferenczi and Mutual Analysis   117

5   Trauma and Dissociation: Ferenczi between Freud and Severn   137

6   Groddeck's Lessons   152

PART 3
Basic Faults   165

7 *Othello* and *Macbeth*: Complementary Borderline
   Pathologies at the Basic Fault   167
8 "I Am Not What I Am": Iago and Negative Transcendence   187
9 Did Freud Masturbate?: The Folly of Élisabeth Roudinesco   205

   References   215
   Index   231

Acknowledgments

As will be clear from the Introduction, I am indebted to Donnel Stern not only for including this book in the New Key series but also for the intellectual stimulation afforded by his work. Crowning both of these has been the gift of his friendship.

Also in the front rank of those to be thanked are Rainer Funk, infinitely generous and supremely knowledgeable custodian of the legacy of Fromm, and Franco Borgogno, whose exemplary psychoanalytic journey attests that Ferenczi's spirit lives on in our time.

Out of the Fromm world Sandra Buechler has arisen to answer my every call, while among Ferenczians the bounty of Giselle Galdi knows no winter and Aleksandar Dimitrijević has proven himself no less reliable than resourceful. Lewis Aron and Adrienne Harris personify all that is good about relational psychoanalysis. Vera Camden has pointed me toward the wicket gate. Warren Poland continues to enlighten me from the Clinician's Corner. John Auerbach is my indispensable interlocutor in Gainesville. Robert M. Galatzer-Levy stands *primus inter pares* among those who have helped me to find a home in the Chicago Psychoanalytic Institute.

I was privileged to study Shakespeare and Milton at Columbia with the late Edward W. Tayler. I grapple Kathie Plourde, James Bednarz, Peter Greenleaf, and Matthew Santirocco to my soul with hoops of steel. Best of all is Cheryl, my Loyalty Lion.

* * *

In addition to these personal words of thanks, I would like to express my appreciation to all those who have played a role in the gestation of the essays in this book, for which Charles Bath at Routledge and Autumn Spalding at Apex CoVantage have served as the guardian angels behind the scenes.

Chapter 1 was published in *American Imago*, 71(2014):253–87; shorter versions were presented at a session sponsored by the American Psychoanalytic Association, moderated by Vera Camden, "The Living Self and the Literary Self," at the Modern Language Association convention in Chicago in January 2014, and at the Tampa Bay Psychoanalytic Society in September 2015. Chapter 2 was given in October 2016 as the first annual Erich Fromm Lecture at the International Psychoanalytic University in Berlin and published in *Fromm Forum*, 20(2016):5–23. Chapter 3 was presented at a panel, organized by Aleksandar Dimitrijević and sponsored by the Committee on Psychoanalysis and the University, at the Boston Congress of the International Psychoanalytical Association in July 2015; it, too, was published in *Fromm Forum*, 19(2015):5–10, as well as in a Spanish translation by Hugo Bleichmar, "*Freud, Ferenczi, Fromm: el carácter autoritario como ayudante mágico,*" in *Aperturas Psicoanalíticas: Revista Internacional de Psicoanálisis*, 51(2015), available online at *aperturas.org*.

In the Ferenczi section, Chapter 4 began life as an invited paper at "Legacy of a Psychoanalytic Mind," an international conference of the Sándor Ferenczi Society in Toronto in May 2015, and has been previously published both in *The Legacy of Sandor Ferenczi: From Ghost to Ancestor*, edited by Adrienne Harris and Steven Kuchuck (New York: Routledge, 2015), pp. 134–49, and as the introduction to my edition of Elizabeth Severn's *The Discovery of the Self: A Study in Psychological Cure* (New York: Routledge, 2017), pp. 1–19. Chapter 5 was presented at the most recent conference of what is now the International Sándor Ferenczi Network, "Ferenczi in Our Time and A Renaissance of Psychoanalysis," this time in Florence in May 2018, and is forthcoming in a French translation by Judith Dupont in *Le Coq-Héron*. I was honored to deliver Chapter 6 in German as the only American speaker at "*Das Es in Zeiten von Unvernunft*" (The It in Times of Unreason), a conference celebrating the 150th anniversary of the birth of Groddeck, organized by Beate Schuh and Michael Giefer and sponsored by the Georg Groddeck Society, held at the International Psychoanalytic University in Berlin in October 2016. The German text of my paper, translated by Michael Giefer under the title "*Groddecks Lehren*," is available on the website of the Groddeck Society at *http://www.georg-groddeck.de/de/GGzum150DieVortraege/*.

Of the two chapters on Shakespeare in the final section, I presented the first at the invitation of James W. Anderson at the Chicago Psychoanalytic Society in April 2017, and is heretofore unpublished, while an abridged version of the second was delivered at the Second Erich Fromm Research Symposium, held in June 2018 at the International Psychoanalytic University in Berlin, and at a session sponsored by the American Psychoanalytic Association at the convention of the Modern Language Association in Chicago in January 2019; it is now published in *Fromm Forum*, 22(2018):21–37. My critical essay on Élisabeth Roudinesco's biography, *Freud in His Time and Ours*, was commissioned by Phyllis Wentworth for a Special Book Review Section, "Freud's Long Shadow," in the *Journal of the History of the Behavioral Sciences*, 54(2018):219–25, where interested readers will also be able to find Roudinesco's response to my review, along with my rejoinder.

Introduction

"One Man Cannot Be the Same as Many"

Glimpsing New Paradigms through Old Keyholes

> "The advantage of the emotions is that they lead us astray, and the advantage of Science is that it is not emotional."
> —Oscar Wilde, *The Picture of Dorian Gray*

Scope of the Book

If, as the distinguished editor of this series has written somewhere, there is truth to the saying that every author writes only one book, that book may at least have several chapters.[1] The present volume harvests what Milton would call the choicest fruits of my "left hand" from the past five years, during which time I have been working with my right on two other projects, *Mutual Analysis: Ferenczi, Severn, and the Origins of Trauma Theory* and *Facing the Facts: The Case for Freud's Affair with Minna Bernays*. In extenuation of the unfinished state of these more ambitious undertakings, I can again only invoke Milton's words in *The Reason of Church Government*, published in 1642, a full quarter-century before he bequeathed to posterity the original, ten-book edition of his immortal epic: "Neither do I think it shame to covenant with any knowing reader, that for some few years yet I may go on trust with him toward the payment of what I am now indebted" (Hughes, 1957, pp. 667, 671).

The major impetus for the transformations in my thinking transcribed in the essays that follow is my belated discovery of, and increasing immersion in, the work of Erich Fromm, a story I tell in Chapter 2. My admiration of Fromm dates back to my reading years ago of *Sigmund Freud's Mission* (1959b), but it did not take off until Adrienne Harris's (2014) review of Lawrence Friedman's (2013) biography of Fromm spurred me to pluck from the shelf my Avon Books edition of *Escape from Freedom* (1941), and everything has snowballed from there. At the heart of my esteem for Fromm is his critique of authoritarianism and, above all, his courage and brilliance in laying bare the consequences of this authoritarianism for psychoanalysis itself, a theme I pursue in Chapter 3 by using his concept of the "magic helper" to examine the relationship between Freud and Ferenczi. It was an uncanny experience to realize that Fromm had anticipated me in championing Rank, Ferenczi, and Groddeck as the torchbearers for a vision of psychoanalysis with the potential to emancipate us from the baleful aspects of the legacy of Freud.

Beyond that, I have gravitated toward Fromm because of his espousal and embodiment not simply of a relational but of a *humanistic* psychoanalysis, which was unfashionable even in his own day and continues to be disparaged in many quarters in our postmodernist and, indeed, "posthumanist" era. At the same time, as his seminal concept of the "social character" attests, no psychoanalyst has done more than Fromm to highlight the importance of social and cultural factors in psychic life, and his work thus serves as an inspiration for anyone who seeks an antidote to the "social constructionism" that postulates that an awareness of these differences makes it impossible to speak of essences or universals where the human condition is concerned. As Fromm writes in "Humanism and Psychoanalysis" (1964b), a paper presented at the dedication of the building of the Mexican Society of Psychoanalysis—Fromm lived and worked in Mexico City for twenty-five years—the humanist movement that arose in the Renaissance and has continued through the Enlightenment to the twentieth and now also the twenty-first centuries dares to affirm that there is an "*essence of man*," but in doing so its proponents "do not imply by the word 'essence' a fixed substance which exists in man and which does not change" in heterogeneous times and places. Instead, this "essence" refers "to the *potentialities* and *possibilities* existing in all men"—meaning all human beings—that can only be unfolded, or thwarted, through their own choices and actions in the "process of history" (p. 72).

As Fromm further remarks, "humanism has always been a reaction to the threat of dehumanization, to a threat to the existence, even, of the human race" (p. 72). How can one not be awed by the wisdom of a man who, in his late masterpiece, *The Anatomy of Human Destructiveness* (1973), warned not only about the dangers of an arms race in which "the two super-powers are constantly increasing their capacities to destroy each other, and at least large parts of the human race with them," but also against the perils posed by a species that, "in the name of progress, is transforming the world into a stinking and poisonous place," and "is doing this to a degree that has made it doubtful whether the earth will still be livable within a hundred years from now" (pp. 389–90)? To be sure, the threat of a nuclear holocaust, which continues to loom today, was widely recognized in the aftermath of World War II and the Cuban missile crisis, but for Fromm to have also envisaged the ravages of climate change and the extinction of all the precious forms of life on earth as early as he did is agonizingly chilling and prophetic.

Although my passion for Fromm is of comparatively recent date, my love affair with Ferenczi has stood the test of time for more than a quarter-century. Thus, whereas the chapters in the first section of this book, "Discovering Fromm," record my adventures on a new intellectual continent, those in the second, "Ferenczian Inflections," offer transformed vistas of more familiar territory. Here, the springboard for my conceptual leap was the realization that Ferenczi's most important patient, Elizabeth Severn, who became his partner in mutual analysis, included disguised case histories not only of Ferenczi but also of herself and her daughter in her third and last published book, *The Discovery of the Self* (1933). By giving us "the other side of the story" of their mutual analysis, Severn's almost completely forgotten book can henceforth be seen to be an indispensable companion to Ferenczi's *Clinical Diary* (Dupont, 1985), as well as a landmark contribution to the psychoanalytic literature in its own right. The gist of what I have been able to glean from Severn is distilled in Chapter 4, while Chapter 5 uses what I have very recently come to understand about the links between trauma and dissociation to cast Ferenczi as torn between his conflicting loyalties to Freud and Severn, and in the end turning decisively away from the former and toward the latter.

The attentive reader will notice that there is an "outlier" in both of these first two sections. My opening chapter, on the parallels between Freud and the God of *Paradise Lost* as narcissistic and authoritarian patriarchs, was written just prior to my encounter with Fromm, but all the ingredients of a Frommian critique of both Freud and Milton can be found there in incipient form. Similarly, Chapter 6 is on Groddeck not Ferenczi, but it, too, constitutes a return to, and reassessment of, one of my most beloved psychoanalytic authors, and I hope that the friendship between these two kindred spirits suffices to justify the placement of an essay on the healer from Baden-Baden cheek by jowl with my Ferenczian forays.

The third and final section, "Basic Faults," follows from the second inasmuch as Michael Balint was not only Ferenczi's literary executor and foremost representative in British psychoanalysis but also because, as Arnold Rachman (2018, pp. 255–59) has recently observed, Balint's delineations of the benign and malignant forms of therapeutic regression in *The Basic Fault* (1968) constitute a response to the lessons he believed that he had learned from witnessing Ferenczi's "grand experiment" with Severn—although Balint never names her in his book—more than a half-century earlier. In Chapter 7, I deploy Caroline Polmear's contemporary understanding of Balint's dichotomy between "ocnophilic" and "philobatic" character structures as a lens through which to view Othello and Macbeth as incarnations of these complementary borderline pathologies. Then, in Chapter 8, I return to Fromm and attempt to pluck out the heart of Iago's mystery by considering him not in terms of individual psychology but as a "social character" and a case study in necrophilia. Finally, in Chapter 9, I come full circle back to Freud's authoritarianism and show how Élisabeth Roudinesco's acclaimed biography, in addition to being riddled with factual errors, exhibits an arrogance and idolatry that epitomizes everything that is wrong in Freud studies, most notably in her whitewashing of the problematic aspects of Freud's sexuality.

In describing the scope of the book as extending "from Shakespeare to Fromm," I mean in the first place to suggest the temporal horizon of the authors with whom I am engaged here. Yet my opening chapter deals with Milton and Shakespeare does not appear until the third section, just as I take up Fromm before Ferenczi, so my argument unfolds in a conceptual rather than a chronological sequence. Above all, by coupling the names of Shakespeare and Fromm, I seek to evoke the interpenetration of the realms of literature and psychoanalysis that informs my thinking. Rather than segregating my clinical experience and sensibility from my forays into what is customarily designated as "applied psychoanalysis," a term that invariably carries a note of condescension, I embrace the spirit of what Fromm (1992b) has called "literary psychoanalysis," which includes not only the study of authors' works in the context of their lives—to the extent that biographical inquiry may be feasible and appropriate in a given instance—but also the close reading of psychoanalytic texts as literary productions, a skill that I believe has everything to do with cultivating a stance of attentive and empathic listening in a therapeutic dialogue with patients.

Homage to Stern

Beyond suggesting the chronological and disciplinary scope of the book, both my title and subtitle are an homage to the work of Donnel Stern, especially to his first book, *Unformulated Experience* (1997). What Stern calls "unformulated experience" is the "uninterpreted form of those raw materials of conscious, reflective experience that may eventually be assigned verbal interpretations and thereby brought into articulate form" (p. 37). Hence, "if we are asked exactly *what* is unformulated in unformulated experience, then, we can say that is meaning," so "when we accomplish a new formulation, we have created a new meaning" (p. 48). In other words, once hitherto inchoate experiences become "formulated" or interpreted, they can be seen for the first time as imbued with meanings or perspectives that must necessarily coexist with myriad other meanings or perspectives, among which it becomes possible to choose, rather than being taken for granted as immutable truths or simply the way life is for the person who had formerly been enmeshed in them.

By calling this book *Formulated Experiences*, in the plural, therefore, my aim is to highlight how each chapter constitutes an attempt to "create a new meaning" by capturing in words the "raw materials of conscious, reflective experience" when I immerse myself in the authors and works in question, and how the process of articulating my "verbal interpretations" helps me come to see them, and psychoanalysis, and ultimately life itself in an altered and enhanced way. As in *Rescuing Psychoanalysis from Freud* (Rudnytsky, 2011), my quest can be summed up as one of keeping alive my capacity for "re-vision" or, in the phrase from T. S. Eliot's essay on Andrew Marvell that I took as the epigraph to the introduction to that book, cultivating "an awareness, implicit in every experience, of other kinds of experience which are possible" (p. xxi)—a defining feature of metaphysical poetry just as it should be one of the primary aims of every psychoanalytic treatment.

The pairing of the terms "hidden realities" and "emergent meanings" in my subtitle alludes to a fundamental principle of Stern's (1997) thought, namely that what the philosopher Herbert Fingarette has called the "hidden reality" view of the mind, where "fully formulated experience is hidden" away in the unconscious, "like the prince in the frog" (p. 54), must be rejected in favor of a conceptual framework in which "psychoanalysis is not a search for the hidden truth about the patient's life, but is the emergence, through curiosity and the acceptance of uncertainty, of constructions that may never have been thought before" (p. 78). This polestar of Stern's vision leads him to contend that "a perspectivistic, socially constructed psychoanalysis must do without personal idiom and the true self, too" (p. 20)—the former term being Christopher Bollas's and the latter, of course, Winnicott's—and to opine not only that "the archaeological metaphor has outlived its usefulness" (p. 205) but also, and even more emphatically, that "the era of psychic geography"—like, I suppose, that of big government—"is dead" (2010, p. 3).

In responding to Stern's provocations, let me begin by reiterating my gratitude for the intellectual stimulus I have derived from reading his work. As I explain in Chapter 5, it was only when I thought I had finished the manuscript of my book on Ferenczi's mutual analysis with Severn that it dawned on me that the necessary corollary of a return to trauma theory in psychoanalysis is a shift from repression to dissociation as a model of the mind. It was this realization that led me to want to familiarize myself as quickly possible with the essential texts in the vast literature on trauma and dissociation, including the books of Stern himself and those of his equally distinguished colleague at the William Alanson White Institute, Philip Bromberg. Although, as Ferenczi wrote in Groddeck's guest book in Baden-Baden, I have come away from this latest stage in my psychoanalytic journey "wholly smitten" but only "half-converted" (see Chapter 6), I have no doubt that their writings are among the most important and generative in the field today and a vital point of reference for all manner of contemporary debates.

My first debt of gratitude to Stern is for helping me to appreciate just how central the "hidden reality" view of the mind was to Freud, and specifically how it undergirds his appropriation of the Oedipus myth as a paradigm for psychoanalysis. When Freud writes in one of the most frequently quoted sentences from *The Interpretation of Dreams* (1900),

> The action of the play consists in nothing other than the process of revealing, with cunning delays and ever-mounting excitement—a process that can be likened to the work of a psycho-analysis—that Oedipus himself is the murderer of Laius, but further that he is the son of the murdered man and of Jocasta,
>
> (pp. 261–62)

what is this but to equate the psychoanalytic process to a detective story, in which not one but two mysteries are to be solved? In all the controversy that has swirled about the status of the Oedipus complex in psychoanalytic theory, very little attention has been paid, as far as I can tell, to the way that Freud's appeal to Sophocles' *Oedipus Rex* as a proof text for psychoanalysis rests on the "unformulated" assumption of a "hidden reality" conception of the unconscious, and by extension the assumption that clinical work involves bringing buried truths to light. Thanks to Stern, what I had previously unreflectively taken for granted comes into focus for the first time as a constructed "figure" that stands out against its "ground," and this change in my own perspective has allowed a new meaning to emerge in my understanding of Freud's deployment of Sophocles' tragedy as a prototype for "the work of a psycho-analysis."[2]

This shift in my understanding of what is implied by Freud's account of *Oedipus Rex* as "nothing other than the process of revealing" the truths that Oedipus had presumably repressed from himself has in turn led me to rethink one of the most notable features of the play. As it begins to dawn on Oedipus that he may indeed have killed Laius—his predecessor on the throne of Thebes and the former husband of Jocasta, though he does not yet suspect him of having also been his own father—at the crossroads at Phocis, he clings to the hope that he may be innocent because the Herdsman who was the sole surviving witness to the massacre of Laius and his retinue reported at the time that the deed had been committed not by one wayfaring man but by a band of marauders.[3] As Oedipus says to Jocasta:

> You said that he spoke of highway *robbers* who killed Laius. Now if he says the same number, it was not I who killed him. One man cannot be the same as many. But if he speaks of a man traveling alone, then clearly the burden of guilt inclines toward me.[4]
>
> (ll. 843–45)

It is a masterstroke of Sophocles' artistry that the same Herdsman who was initially summoned by Oedipus to testify about the murder of Laius was also the man who had taken Oedipus as an infant from Jocasta to expose him to death on Mount Cithaeron, only to save his life by giving him to a shepherd from Corinth (who also does double duty as the Messenger bringing the news of the death of Oedipus's adopted father), who then gave the abandoned and ankle-pierced infant to the king and queen of Corinth to be raised as their child. Thus, at the climax of the play, the Herdsman who is supposed to clear up the mystery surrounding the death of Laius never reveals whether he was killed by many men, as he alleged originally, or by Oedipus acting alone, but instead simply confirms that Oedipus is indeed, in Freud's words, "the son of the murdered man and of Jocasta." In response to learning the truth about his origins, Oedipus, in a display of what the deconstructionist critic Sandor Goodhart (1978) terms "oracular logic" (p. 67), jumps to the conclusion—or, if one prefers, draws the logical inference—that he must also be guilty of the murder.

The reason that my reading of Stern and Bromberg caused me to think of this crux in *Oedipus Rex*, and to contemplate it from a new angle, is the insistence of these authors that the replacement of repression with dissociation as a model of the mind perforce entails an acceptance of the idea of what Stern (2010) calls a "multiple self" or, in other words, that "the self is not simple and unitary but a more or less cohesive collection of self-states" (p. 48). In Bromberg's even more famous version of this same precept, from which he derives the title to his book *Standing in the Spaces* (1998), "there is no such thing as an integrated self—a 'real you,'" and psychological health is defined as "*the capacity to feel like one self while being many*" (p. 186). With these pronouncements ringing in my ears, I had to wonder: maybe the lesson of Oedipus, the son and husband of Jocasta and father and brother to his children, in whom not only the distinction between generations but also the three stages of the life cycle delineated in the Sphinx's riddle are confounded because he presumably walks with the aid of a staff—and thus on three legs—as a mature man, is precisely that "one man *is* the same as many," so that we have to go all the way with our brilliant relational-interpersonalists and throw out at once the "hidden reality" view of the unconscious as well as the traditional humanistic belief in an "integrated self" or individual mind?

Bones of Contention

It is here that my twinges of uneasiness reach the point of acute discomfort and cause me to question whether the positions espoused by Stern and Bromberg are really sustainable in an extreme form. In mounting my rebuttal, I think it is helpful to situate the debate in the context of the fraught relationship between Fromm and Harry Stack Sullivan, the two intellectual giants of the interpersonal tradition. Sullivan, for his part, does not cite Fromm anywhere in his lectures or writings.[5] Fromm, on the other hand, refers appreciatively to Sullivan several times in *Escape from Freedom* (1941), affirming in his concluding chapter that "we believe that individual psychology is fundamentally social psychology or, in Sullivan's terms, the psychology of interpersonal relationships," so that "the key problem of psychology is that of the particular kind of relatedness of the individual toward the world, not the frustration or satisfaction of single instinctual desires" (p. 318). By the time of *The Sane Society* (1955b), however, while he continues to laud Sullivan as "one of the most profound and brilliant psychoanalysts of our period," Fromm now chastises him for having been unduly "influenced in his theoretical concepts by the all pervasive alienation" of mid-twentieth-century capitalist society in America. Fromm elaborates:

> Sullivan took the fact that the alienated person lacks a feeling of selfhood and experiences himself in terms of a response to the expectations of others, as part of human nature, just as Freud had taken the competitiveness characteristic of the beginning of the century as a natural phenomenon. Sullivan called the view that there exists a unique individual self the "delusion of unique individuality."
>
> (p. 193)

This, then, is the nub of the matter. Whereas Fromm shares with Sullivan an interpersonal or relational sensibility, such that the individual cannot be considered in isolation from his or her environment—in the spirit of Winnicott's (1960) dictum that "there is no such thing as an infant" because "whenever one finds an infant one finds maternal care, and without maternal care there would be no infant" (p. 39n1)—he parts company with Sullivan when the latter goes so far as to deny that "there exists a unique individual self." The phrase Fromm quotes from Sullivan is taken from his best-known work, *The Interpersonal Theory of Psychiatry* (1953, p. 140), but the same view is expressed in what Stern (1997) calls Sullivan's "most mature and seminal paper" (p. 147), "The Illusion of Personal Individuality" (1950), where he proclaims:

> You will find that it makes no sense to think of ourselves as "individual," "separate," capable of anything like definitive description in

isolation, that this notion is just beside the point. No great progress in this field of study is possible until it is realized that the field of observation is what people do with each other. . . . When that is done, no such thing as the durable, unique individual personality is ever clearly justified. For all I know every human being has as many personalities as he has interpersonal relations.

(pp. 220–21)

Sullivan moves from an eminently sound starting point, with which both Fromm and Winnicott would have concurred, namely, that it is impossible to give a "definitive description" of a person "in isolation," to a conclusion they would both have rejected—that it is therefore impossible to speak of a "unique individual personality"—and to the even more extravagant contention that "every human being has as many personalities as he has interpersonal relations." Fromm's critique of his erstwhile comrade-in-arms is that Sullivan, like Freud before him, has mistaken what is in actuality a particular type of "social character" for an immutable truth of the human condition. What is worse, since Sullivan is unwittingly swayed by his cultural milieu to posit the "alienated person" as his norm, his error goes beyond confusing the ephemeral with the eternal to elevating a pathological deformation of the human spirit—a symptom of what happens when something goes seriously awry either in individual development or in society at large—to the benchmark of mental health, or, rather, to make it impossible to distinguish between illness and health in the psychological realm altogether.

Sullivan's fallacy, from this standpoint, is exactly the same as Lacan's (1949) in his theory of the mirror stage, a purported delineation of "the ontological structure of the human world" (p. 2) according to which it is incumbent on analysts to acknowledge "the *function of méconnaissance* that characterizes the ego in all its structures" as well as "the alienating function of the *I*, the aggressivity it releases in any relation to the other" (p. 6). As I have previously argued in defense of Winnicott against Lacan in *The Psychoanalytic Vocation* (Rudnytsky, 1991), if one pays adequate attention to the role of the environment in fostering or thwarting the development of the infant and growing child, "the idea that the ego originates in misrecognition—assumed by Lacan to be a universal truth—is shown to be rather a *breakdown phenomenon* that comes to pass only when the mother does not perform her mirroring function adequately" (p. 79). Coming from the side of an overemphasis on putative endogenous factors, Klein (1930), too, falls into a similar trap when she posits an innate sadism—or, later, a death instinct—in the baby nursing at its mother's breast, which leads her to make such absurd statements as that "the sadistic phantasies directed against the inside of her body constitute the first and basic relation to the outside world and to reality" (p. 221).

There is a clear line from Fromm's critique of Sullivan to my bones of contention with Stern and Bromberg. Stern, as we have seen, insists that a "socially constructed psychoanalysis must do without . . . the true self," whereas Fromm, as I show in Chapter 2, posits in *Escape from Freedom* an antithesis between the "original self" and the "pseudo self" that parallels Winnicott's far more famous opposition between the True Self and the False Self, while I note in Chapter 3 Fromm's alignment not only with Ferenczi and Winnicott but also with the entire Independent tradition of British object relations theory epitomized by his quotation in *The Anatomy of Human Destructiveness* (1973) of Harry Guntrip's declaration that psychoanalysis should be a "'theory and therapy that encourages the rebirth and growth of an authentic self in an authentic relationship'" (p. 110). In addition to holding that "the self is not simple and unitary but a more or less cohesive collection of self-states," Stern (2010) adds that his readings in anthropology have convinced him that "people are simply not the same everywhere" (p. 197). But this truism about cultural differences does not preclude the existence of a shared essence of the human condition, a position that Fromm eloquently defended on both philosophical grounds as well as those of natural science and evolutionary psychology.

In no uncertain terms, Stern seeks to repudiate as unjust the criticism that his social constructivist position requires us "to deny the uniqueness of each self" (2010, p. 77), or that "field theory does away with the conception of the individual mind" (2015, p. 45), arguing, on the contrary, that "no theory of psychoanalysis can do without the individual mind" (p. 184n4). But it is difficult to see how these sentiments can be squared with Stern's frequent approving quotations of Sullivan's dismissal of the idea of a "durable, unique individual personality" or with the premise that the "self" is simply a patchwork of interpersonally generated "self-states" with no innate component that propels what Winnicott (1965) called the "maturational processes." Indeed, in the same breath that he affirms "the uniqueness of each self," Stern (2010) rejects the assertion of Benjamin Wolstein that "'we all have a unique sense of self that is inborn,'" again contending that "the self is a social construction" (p. 77). But if nothing is inborn and everything is socially constructed, then we are left with a theory that ostensibly continues to uphold a "conception of the individual mind" but in which, in reality, there is no stable figure but only an ever-shifting ground.[6]

A hard-hitting rejoinder from an ethical perspective to the "multiple self-state" theory as it has been espoused by Bromberg has been mounted recently by Donna Orange (2018). Her main point is that "such talk implies that no central, organizing, or responsible personality exists" (p. 157), and this absence precludes one from ever being able to say, with Luther, "'Here I stand, I can do no other'" (p. 164). If "personal individuality" is an "illusion," furthermore, then what becomes of Heidegger's existentialist credo in *Being and Time* (1927), "No one can take the Other's dying away from him. . . . By its very essence, death is in every case mine" (p. 284)?

On a more empirical level, Orange acutely observes that many of the researchers to whom Bromberg (1998) appeals to support his claim that "there is now abundant evidence that the psyche does not start as an integrated whole, but is nonunitary in origin" (p. 244)—including Lewis Sander, Daniel Stern, and Beatrice Beebe and Frank Lachmann—in fact disagree with him on this fundamental point. She cites Sander (1995) on how a "moment of meeting" between a child and his or her therapist fosters "a new coherence in the child's experience of both its inner and its outer worlds of awareness," and how from this "it is a small step to Erikson's definition of identity as 'an accrued confidence that inner sameness and continuity are matched by the sameness and continuity of one's meaning for others'" (p. 590). One could not be further away from Sullivan's alienated conviction that "every human being has as many personalities as he has interpersonal relations." Lachmann (1996), too, in diametric opposition to Bromberg, adheres to a clinical theory that rests on "a process model of self as singular, striving for integration, and temporally continuous" (p. 610). Even more telling, as Orange (2018) does not fail to mention, is that Bromberg proceeds to "cite the studies by Frank Putnam of extreme dissociation that would now be diagnosed as Dissociative Identity Disorder and Complex Post-Traumatic Stress Disorders, and argues from these that mind is essentially multiple and self-experience illusory" (p. 159).

Here, again, we see the problems that arise when a breakdown phenomenon—something that happens when there is a disastrous failure of some sort—is presumed to be true across the board in the psychological realm.

Repeatedly, Stern (1997) posits the existence of "a kind of 'normative,' or perhaps better, *expectable*, dissociation" (p. 87), and refers (2010) to what he calls "normal dissociation, or dissociation in the weak sense" (p. 150), explaining that the way he uses the concept "is not specific to trauma," but that "dissociation and unformulated experience comprise a model of mind" (p. 20). Bromberg (2011), for his part, claims that "a flexible relationship among self-states through the use of normal dissociation is what allows a human being to engage the ever-shifting requirements of life's complexities with creativity and spontaneity" (p. 95).

Not content with normalizing dissociation, Bromberg takes the further step of alleging that trauma is universal and inescapable: "Developmental trauma (sometimes termed *relational trauma*) is always part of what shapes early attachment patterns (including 'secure attachment'), which in turn establish what Bowlby calls 'internal working models'" (p. 99). Having laid down this marker, Bromberg proceeds to argue in circular fashion that "developmental trauma is thus an inevitable aspect of early life to varying degrees" and "attachment-related trauma is part of everyone's past and a factor in every treatment experience" (p. 99).

But this line of reasoning is patently untenable. As Bessel van der Kolk has written in his magisterial work, *The Body Keeps the Score* (2014), "trauma, by definition, is unbearable and intolerable" (p. 1), while "dissociation is the essence of trauma" because "the overwhelming experience is split off and fragmented, so that the emotions, sounds, images, thoughts, and physical sensations related to the trauma take on a life of their own" (p. 66). The originator of this model of dissociation as the psyche-soma's response to trauma is Pierre Janet, who, as Van der Kolk reminds us, "coined the term 'dissociation' to describe the splitting off and isolation of memory imprints that he saw in his patients" and was equally "prescient about the heavy cost of keeping these traumatic memories at bay" (p. 182).[7] Because dissociation "prevents the trauma from being integrated within the conglomerated, ever-shifting stores of autobiographical memory," people afflicted with Post-Traumatic Stress Disorder develop a "dual memory system" and "are unable to put the actual event, the source of their memories, behind them" (p. 182).

For Bromberg to say that trauma "is always part of what shapes early attachment patterns, including 'secure attachment,'" is to eviscerate the distinction not only between secure attachment and the two types of insecure attachment originally identified by Mary Ainsworth and adopted by

Bowlby—anxious avoidant and anxious resistant (or anxious ambivalent)—but also, and above all, between secure attachment and the fourth type, subsequently introduced by Mary Main, of disorganized attachment, the most severe classification category, which arises, in Van der Kolk's words, when "the caregivers themselves were a source of distress or terror to the children" (p. 119). Whereas "infants who live in secure relationships learn to communicate not only their frustrations and distress but also their emerging selves," those who experience "maternal disengagement and misattunement during the first two years of life" are at much higher risk of developing "dissociative symptoms in early adulthood" characterized by "extreme levels of frightened arousal," against which the mind defends itself as best it can but which "cause the body to remain in a state of high alert." This state of "simultaneously knowing and not knowing," Van der Kolk continues, produces a "shutdown," the "most devastating long-term effect" of which "is not feeling real inside" (p. 123).

It is, of course, true that not all traumas come in the form of a single, cataclysmic event; most "developmental traumas" are the result of repeated, systematic acts of emotional, physical, or sexual degradation that cumulatively erode the child-victim's sense of safety, security, and ultimately self. But it remains wrong for Bromberg to insinuate that, because there are shades of gray, there is not a qualitative difference between traumatic and nontraumatic experience, or, in Winnicott's terms, between what is "good enough," even if it may be far from perfect, and what is so far beyond an individual's capacity to assimilate that it causes a lasting fissure in the psyche and leads to the formation of a "dual memory system." Just as it would be an oxymoron to speak of a "normal trauma," because trauma is inherently outside the range of normal experience, so it is self-contradictory for Bromberg to postulate that trauma is compatible with secure attachment, which would require that we create a novel category of "secure disorganized attachment."

The same problem arises with Stern's view that there is such a thing as "normal dissociation" and with Bromberg's (2011) analogous declarations that "dissociation is a healthy, adaptive function of the human mind," indeed a process that "is central to the stability and growth of personality," synonymous with "concentration, single-mindedness, task orientation, or full surrender to pleasurable experience" (p. 48). If dissociation, instead of being understood as "the essence of trauma" in which an "overwhelming experience is split off and fragmented," is equated with "full surrender to pleasurable experience," we might as well be talking to Humpty Dumpty, for whom a word means whatever he chooses it to mean. Again, there are gradations, as illustrated by Bill Clinton's prodigious capacity for "compartmentalization," which served an "adaptive function" by allowing him to continue fulfilling the duties of the office of the presidency without becoming engulfed by the personal scandals swirling about him. When Stern (1997) proposes that what he calls "dissociation in the weak sense" is "the consequence of so insistently turning our attention elsewhere that we never even notice alternative understandings," and thus is "controlled by the intention to enforce narrative rigidity" (p. 132), he unquestionably highlights a clinically important phenomenon. If my patient begins almost every session by asking me, "How are you, Peter?," ostensibly because such a greeting is customary in social situations, surely there is something more to this ritualized behavior that I would like to help her to become curious about so that we can open it up for joint exploration and reflection, and thereby begin to "create a new meaning" in place of the previously "unformulated experience."

Where I part ways with Stern, however, is in his contention that this "passive sort of dissociation," which he says is "based in selective attention," as opposed to Sullivan's concept of "selective *in*attention" that characterizes "active, defensive dissociation" (p. 132), lacks the defensive component that supposedly distinguishes "strong" from "weak" dissociation. I do not see how it makes sense to say that someone would "*insistently*" turn his or her attention away from something, or feel compelled to "*enforce* narrative rigidity," unless there were a motive for doing so, a motive that ultimately comes down to avoiding anxiety, and hence to a defensive maneuver. The outcome may appear to be "passive," but the psychic operations causing this "rigidity" or inability to "notice alternative understandings" are no less "active"—that is, defensive and motivated—than they are in what Stern considers to be "active dissociation." Thus, his attempt to posit the existence of two types of dissociation turns out to be a distinction without a difference, which leaves us with nothing that can be meaningfully termed "normal" or "healthy" dissociation.

At the root of my disagreement with Stern is his attempt to decouple dissociation from trauma, a counterpart to Bromberg's postulate that dissociation is a "healthy" function of the mind, and even manifested in "full surrender to pleasurable experience." I find it all the more surprising that Stern should use the concept of dissociation so broadly that it covers everything from what we are simply unable to notice at a given moment to what we actively resist allowing into conscious awareness—or, in the language of Freud's allegedly defunct topographical model, both the preconscious and the unconscious strata of the psyche—because he is far more circumspect in how he uses the term "enactment." Taking issue with those who hold the position that "*all* interactions are enactments," Stern (2010) objects that "the phenomenon would then have to be understood as omnipresent," and so despite his "acceptance that all interaction does indeed have unconscious aspects," he prefers "to restrict the term 'enactment' to the interpersonalization of dissociation" (p. 16), or what he also calls, following Gadamer, the interruption of "true conversation" (p. 40).

Thus, if Stern prudently cautions against using "enactment" in what might be called a "weak sense" because it would then be "omnipresent" and equivalent to "all interactions," it is puzzling that he would not be equally judicious with "dissociation," which in both his lexicon and Bromberg's is deemed to be "normal," "expectable," "healthy," and "what allows a human being to engage the ever-shifting requirements of life's complexities with creativity and spontaneity." This is truly to make dissociation "omnipresent" and hence to empty the term of any genuine meaning. Such is the upshot of either using "trauma" so loosely that it, too, is seen as "inevitable" and ubiquitous, as Bromberg does, or else of decoupling dissociation from trauma, as Stern does, so that the latter does not necessarily follow from the former. In either case, this way of thinking undermines the foundations on which the twin pillars of a credible trauma theory, as it has been expounded from Janet to Van der Kolk, must rest: (1) that trauma, in whatever form it may occur, "by definition, is unbearable and intolerable"; and (2) that "dissociation is the essence of trauma" because "the overwhelming experience is split off and fragmented" and relegated to a second "memory system" that "prevents the trauma from being integrated within the conglomerated, ever-shifting stores of autobiographical memory."

If we now revisit the Oedipus myth in light of the critique I have offered of Bromberg and Stern, it becomes relevant to note that Oedipus is indubitably a severely traumatized character, having been mutilated, abandoned, and left to die as an infant, before being rescued and raised as an adopted child without ever being informed of the truth about his origins.[8] This aspect of his fate is ignored by Freud in his elevation of the Oedipus complex to a universal truth of the human condition, but it is integral to the design of Sophocles' tragedy. Hence, to the extent that the play may be said to call into question the assumption that "one man cannot be the same as many," it would be possible to argue that this holds good only in the lives of individuals wounded by trauma, and who consequently suffer from dissociation, but not for the majority of more fortunate souls who were the recipients of "good-enough" parenting. It is striking that Van der Kolk speaks of the "ever-shifting stores of autobiographical memory" as the antithesis of the "split-off and fragmented" memories of trauma, so that a capacity for encompassing and moving freely among "multiple self-states"—as opposed to rigidly segregating them into separate "personalities"—becomes the very essence of what it means to have an "integrated self" and to be "a 'real you.'"

What, then, are we to make of Stern's dismissal of the "hidden reality" view of the mind? Certainly, in the clinical situation, there is much to persuade one that the metaphor of psychoanalysis as an archaeological dig can take us only so far. When, in "The Aetiology of Hysteria" (1896), Freud compares the psychotherapist to the archaeologist whose "discoveries are self-explanatory" because "the fragments of columns can be filled out into a temple" or the inscriptions "may be bilingual" and "reveal an alphabet and a language" that can be "deciphered and translated" (p. 192), his analogy is, at the very least, imperfect. In the realm of the psyche, unlike material objects that can be reassembled or the Rosetta Stone, on which the meaning of the hieroglyphs can be definitively established because there are also Demotic Egyptian and Ancient Greek versions of the same decree written on the stele, there is no objectively existing script, or once-intact column, that allows the analyst to conclude with certainty that his solution to the puzzle presented by the patient's symptom is correct. Similarly, Freud's claim that associations to the "manifest content" of a dream will lead back to the "latent content" that gave rise to the dream in the first place risks becoming a circular argument because there is no preexisting empirical basis against which the validity of the chain of associations can be tested. In light of these considerations, the idea that all we can have in clinical work are "emergent meanings"—meanings that arise and are "constructed" through the psychoanalytic dialogue—would seem to be difficult to refute.

Going Off the Deep End

But let us step back and examine the philosophical underpinnings of Stern's position. In his rejoinder to Adolf Grünbaum's (1984) critique of psychoanalysis, Stern (2015) makes it clear that he spurns "objectivist schemes," according to which "data exist prior to and independently of their interpretation" (p. 171). He underscores the point: "Facts are given in this scheme, and interpretation is limited to the meanings we assign to those facts" (p. 168). In contrast, he proffers his own "constructivist vantage point," which holds that "the data are inevitably *constituted* by interpretive acts. It is impossible for the data to precede interpretation, because it is interpretation that creates them" (p. 171). Although Stern does not cite any sources for his view, this is an almost verbatim echo of Nietzsche, who wrote in 1888, "Against the positivism which stops before phenomena, saying 'there are only *facts*,' I should say: no, it is precisely facts that do not exist, only *interpretations*" (Kaufmann, 1954, p. 458).

Here, I think, we must take a deep breath and ask ourselves whether this is not to go off the deep end. Although I have no doubt Stern would be horrified by the comparison and reject it as unfair, I do not see how this brand of postmodernism does not lead us into an Orwellian nightmare in which the propagandists for the Trump administration would seek to persuade a gullible public that there are "alternative facts" (Kellyanne Conway) and "truth isn't truth" (Rudy Giuliani). As Michiko Kakutani has recently argued in *The Death of Truth* (2018), the guiding thread of the postmodernist tradition that runs from Nietzsche and Heidegger to Foucault and Derrida is an enshrining of "the principle of subjectivity" and the concomitant denial of "an objective reality existing independently from human perception." Quoting Oxford English professor Christopher Butler, she adds that

> even the arguments of scientists can be seen as "no more than quasi narratives which compete with all the others for acceptance. They have no unique or reliable fit to the world, no certain correspondence with reality. They are just another form of fiction."
>
> (pp. 47–48)

The reason I think that Stern (2015) would reject this criticism as unfair is that the position he espouses is not merely constructivist but also hermeneutic, and he avers it does not mean that "anything goes." Although "there are multiple valid versions of reality," he explains,

> that does not mean that truth can be whatever we claim it to be. Hermeneutics is not relativistic. In the hermeneutic view, reality is "there"

and must be respected. But it cannot be perceived in an unmediated way. Instead, reality is revealed only in the constraints that it imposes on our interpretations.

He elaborates:

> *Any phenomenon can become meaningful only within reality's constraints.* If we shape an interpretation that falls outside these constraints, we are either lying or demonstrating poor judgment (*in extremis*, crazy). As they define the range within which an interpretation can be valid, these constraints simultaneously exclude from consideration a much wider array of (invalid) interpretive possibilities.
>
> (p. 169)

This sounds promising, but I am afraid that Stern's denial that his position is relativistic falls apart under closer examination. He acknowledges that "reality is 'there'" and imposes "constraints" that allow one to conclude that a person is either "lying" or "crazy" if he or she asserts something to be true that defies these criteria of "valid" interpretations. But even though "reality cannot be perceived in an unmediated way," if reality is "there," it would seem incontrovertible that its *existence* must be independent of human perception, so the question then becomes how we can come to know this reality as accurately as possible so that we have a basis that is not purely arbitrary for deciding what constitutes "truth." This conclusion seems to follow inexorably from Stern's premises, yet he undercuts his own position by repeatedly denying, in Nietzschean fashion, that "data exist prior to and independently of their interpretation," insisting, on the contrary, that "it is interpretation that creates" the facts in question.

If we try to understand how Stern, as it were, saws off the epistemological branch he is sitting on, the answer is that he does not, in the end, believe in an objectively existing natural world or universe of which humans are merely one inhabitant, but rather limits his frame of reference to the social order, which, of course, is already created by humans. He is perfectly clear on this point:

> Which valid interpretation we create on any particular occasion depends, speaking most broadly, on the era and culture in which the interpretation is made. That is, the widest possible range of valid

interpretations can be defined as the limits of meaningfulness specific to our time and place. . . . Culture mediates the relationship between reality and individual human beings. This is the doctrine of historicity, and philosophical hermeneutics is rooted in it.

(p. 170)

According to Stern, therefore, what determines whether interpretations are "valid" is "the era and culture in which the interpretation is made." But this is not to escape the pitfall of relativism, but merely to push it back from the individual to the social level, and thus to risk succumbing to the Orwellian nightmare. What if one lives in a society that tells its Winston Smiths that War Is Peace and Truth Is Not Truth? As Fromm argued in his critique of Sullivan in *The Sane Society*, if one takes an alienated society as the basis for a psychological theory, he will end up extolling the person who "lacks a feeling of selfhood" as a paragon of humanity and seriously propose that "every human being has as many personalities as he has interpersonal relations." Because he dispenses with a belief in an essence of human nature, Stern has no way of accounting for what Fromm (1955b) terms the "*pathology of normalcy*," which is not an "individual pathology" (p. 6) but rather a consequence of the realization that "the very person who is considered healthy in the categories of an alienated world, from the humanistic standpoint appears as the sickest one—although not in terms of individual sickness, but of the socially patterned defect" (p. 203).

The acid test for the dictum that "it is precisely facts that do not exist, only *interpretations*," is what one thinks about the natural world and the nonhuman universe. As Kakutani has pointed out, once one starts down the slippery slope of postmodernism, one risks reducing science to a "quasi narrative" lacking any "certain correspondence with reality" and just "one more form of fiction" competing with all the others in the cultural marketplace. And this is, indeed, where Stern ends up. Because he dispenses with the "objectivist" belief that the "data exist prior to and independently of their interpretation," he does not shy away from equating science with a "form of fiction": "Empirical research is just as thoroughly value-laden as clinical writing, although the culture of science can make it harder to acknowledge these influences" (2015, p. 183).

To be sure, empirical research is "value-laden" insofar as it believes in the indispensability of science to help us answer fundamental questions about the nature of life, disease, the cosmos, and so forth. As illustrated by the quotation from Oscar Wilde I have taken as my epigraph, whereas in the realm of what Dilthey first designated as the *Geisteswissenschaften*, or human sciences, the aim is *understanding* of meanings and the disciplined use of subjectivity—or what may be called the countertransference—is integral to the method, in the realm of the *Naturwissenschaften*, or natural sciences, the aim is *explanation* of an objectively existing reality, and this requires that the influence of subjectivity be reduced to as close to zero as possible so that our biases do not "lead us astray." Hence, of course, the importance of double-blind experiments and the need for research to be independently replicated before its findings can be considered scientifically established.

In an interview with Eric Kandel, I asked the Nobel-prizewinning neuroscientist whether "the trend in science itself that suggests that there is no objective view of a phenomenon because the phenomenon changes from the point of view of the observer"—exemplified by the uncertainty principle in physics—has called "the traditional objectivist view of science in question within the scientific world." Kandel's answer is worth quoting at length:

> No. I think the uncertainty principle, which the analysts love, is misguided. Heisenberg said that under highly selected conditions, measurement of very rapid, small events is so difficult because the mere fact of measurement interferes with the process. But we measure the phenomenon in different ways, measuring it with and without perturbation, just to control for that. We know every time we do something we're likely to screw up the system, so one of the intrinsic things built into the system are controls for the experimental manipulation. Could we be wrong under some circumstances? Of course. Science is a perpetually self-correcting process. If you were to ask, "Do you believe that there is a definite truth?," then I would answer, "In the limit, no, but after a while the evidence gets to be so strong that it's *als ob*, as if it was the final answer." So, if it's going to be modified more, chances are it's going to be a tweak. The double helix: take my word for it, it's going to be around for a *very*, very long time.
>
> (Rudnytsky, 2011, p. 163)

Because "science is a perpetually self-correcting process," Kandel concedes that there is no "final answer" or "definite truth" beyond which it will never be possible to go. For all that, however, he holds fast to an "objectivist" epistemology, and even the vaunted uncertainty principle does not shake his conviction that it is possible for scientists to build "controls for the experimental manipulation" to account for the effect of their measurements on the phenomena. As he goes on to observe, showing the penchant for Viennese Jewish humor that he shares with Freud, "So, it is true that there are certain circumstances in which there is uncertainty, but I wouldn't worry about it. I tell my friends: 'Psychoanalysis should have such problems'" (p. 163).

If we bring the discussion down from the lofty plane of quantum physics to issues of more immediate concern, what, I wonder, would Stern say about the thousands of dead fish, not to mention the manatees, crabs, and sea turtles, in the Gulf of Mexico, due to the toxic algae known as "red tide"? Of course, one can debate the "meaning" of this catastrophe, or how best to respond to it, but of the "facts" themselves can there be any question? To say that "the data are inevitably *constituted* by interpretive acts," rather than that the "data exist prior to and independently of their interpretation," is tantamount to saying that the death of the fish is not an objectively existing reality, but is rather somehow "constituted" by the "interpretive acts" of those who choose to think of them that way.

The same question can be posed with respect to climate change. When, in 2015, Senator Jim Inhofe of Oklahoma, chair of the Environment and Public Works Committee, threw a snowball on the floor of the Senate in support of his long-held belief that climate change is "the greatest hoax ever perpetrated on the American people," on what basis can one assert he is wrong? As Paul Krugman (2018), from whom I have taken the quotation from Inhofe, has pointed out, "the Orwellification of the G.O.P."—that is to say, the collapse of "the party's belief in objective reality"—"didn't start with Trump." When climate change can be dismissed as "a vast international conspiracy involving thousands of scientists, not one of whom dares to speak out," as became the default position in the Republican party long before Trump's rise, we are already in a dream world of "alternative facts," or rather a nightmare where "truth isn't truth." If "empirical research is just as thoroughly value-laden as clinical writing" and what constitutes a "valid interpretation" depends "on the era and culture in which the interpretation is made," we might as well surrender and admit that we have no way of knowing whether climate change is real or not. But the frightening sight of the dead fish serves as a reminder, to adapt the words of St. Paul in

Galatians, "Nature is not mocked, for whatsoever human beings sow, that shall we also reap" (6:7).

I have thus far been considering the competing epistemological positions of objectivism and constructivism as they pertain to the *Naturwissenschaften* in order to make two arguments. First, since, by Stern's own admission, there is a "reality" that reveals itself "in the constraints that it imposes on our interpretations," it is illogical for him to accept Nietzsche's postmodernist axiom that "it is precisely facts that do not exist, only *interpretations*." Second, notwithstanding his protestations to the contrary, his version of hermeneutics does end up mired in the quicksands of relativism because the reality that supposedly determines the limits of valid interpretation does not refer to any objectively existing realm but is rather simply "the era and culture in which the interpretation is made," and is thus a house built on sand, subject to the ever-shifting winds of ideology and fashion, and not anything that can be meaningfully described as "reality" at all.

What, then, are we to make of the *Geisteswissenschaften*, where hermeneutics indeed reigns supreme? When it comes to understanding meanings, as opposed to explaining facts, we are perforce in the endlessly proliferating fields of subjectivity and intersubjectivity, and there is no objectively existing reality to which it is possible to appeal to settle disputes. It might be possible for a modern reader to be mistaken about the meaning of a word, as it was used in Shakespeare's time, for example, so to that extent even here there is a limited place for right or wrong answers, but when it comes to determining the meaning of the word in its context, to say nothing of an entire line or of a play as a whole, it is all up for grabs, with only the constrains imposed by the community of scholars to decide what constitutes a "valid," or plausible, or a "crazy," or completely implausible, interpretation. Insofar as clinical psychoanalysis, like literary criticism, is a hermeneutic enterprise, therefore, Stern is unquestionably right that our stock-in-trade is emergent meanings, that is to say, "the emergence, through curiosity and the acceptance of uncertainty, of constructions that may never have been thought before."

But does this mean that we must therefore dispense entirely with the "hidden reality" view of the mind, according to which "psychoanalysis is not a search for the hidden truth about the patient's life"? Much as I admire and am indebted to Stern for expanding my conceptual horizons, I would like to argue that it can be "both/and" rather than "either/or" when it comes to hidden realities and emergent meanings.

Having It Both Ways

Let us come back to *Oedipus Rex*, and to Freud's use of Sophocles' tragedy as a touchstone of psychoanalysis. As Stern has helped me to see for the first time, in a beautiful illustration of an emergent meaning, Freud's assumption that "the action of the play consists in nothing other than the process of revealing . . . that Oedipus himself is the murderer of Laius, but further that he is the son of the murdered man and of Jocasta," may be an even more enduring legacy than his extrapolation of the concept of the Oedipus complex, and one that needs to be subjected to critical scrutiny. Certainly, his summary that "the action of the play consists in *nothing other*" than these twin revelations can be faulted for being an overstatement, and a characteristic piece of reductionism in that it renders invisible everything else that might be significant from a different perspective—Oedipus's infantile traumas, his having been adopted, etc.[9] But does that warrant the conclusion that Freud must therefore be wrong in saying that Oedipus's discovery of these "hidden realities" is the mainspring of Sophocles' masterfully constructed plot, and that this process of self-discovery provides a model for "the work of a psycho-analysis"?

I think not. For all its ingenuity, the deconstructionist reading of Sandor Goodhart that, because the Herdsman never explicitly addresses the question of whether Laius was killed by one man or by many, about which he was initially summoned, but testifies only as to what he knows of Oedipus's origins, Oedipus may actually be innocent of the murder of Laius falls into the category of the "crazy" and collapses under the weight of the mountain of evidence to the contrary. To suppose that Teiresias, the blind prophet, did not speak the truth in cursing Oedipus as the "fellow sower in his father's bed / with that same father that he murdered" (ll. 458–59), or that Oedipus committed incest with his mother but somehow avoided killing his father, is simply nonsense, though Goodhart has performed an important service by calling attention to the role of "oracular logic" and to the paradoxes of identity in the play. But, as has been clear at least since Aristotle analyzed the plot in terms of its peerless utilization of the devices of reversal and recognition, the greatness of *Oedipus Rex* turns on the fact that it is a detective story in which the investigator is unwittingly in search of himself, and that in the course of solving one mystery—who killed Laius?—Oedipus inadvertently stumbles on another—who am I?—which leads him ineluctably from the present increasingly further back to the past.

With its "cunning delays and ever-mounting excitement," therefore, *Oedipus Rex* provides a template for the psychoanalytic process inasmuch as it involves uncovering not one but two interconnected "hidden realities" that lay "fully formulated" but repressed or dissociated—the terms can be used interchangeably here—"like the prince in the frog," in the unconscious of the protagonist himself. Teiresias may have revealed the truth to Oedipus, but he did not implant it in his mind. It was not a creation of the intersubjective field. It was already there, at the start of the play, only Oedipus did not know it consciously, which is why he angrily repudiated the prophet's accusations, and had—painstakingly and agonizingly, against his own inner resistances—to find it out for himself.

I sometimes ask my students, how is reading a text both similar to, yet different from, solving a crime? It is different in that, with a crime, there is a perpetrator, whose identity may not be known at the outset but who, with sound detective work, can be caught and his guilt proven beyond any reasonable doubt. Thus, in solving a crime, there is an unambiguously correct answer to the riddle, as well as no end of wrong answers, much as there is in reconstructing an ancient column or deciphering the inscription on the Rosetta Stone, both of which are indeed "self-explanatory" once all the pieces of the jigsaw puzzle have been properly assembled. In contemplating a literary text, on the other hand, especially if it has the enduring fascination of a classic, there is no preexisting answer that solves the mystery once and for all, but rather a continuously unfolding network of "emergent meanings," because, in the memorable phrase of I. A. Richards (1934), it is "inexhaustible to meditation" (p. 133).

Despite this fundamental difference, however, there is also a profound similarity between literary criticism and detective work. And that is in the methodology, which consists in following the evidence, or paying attention to the clues, whether these are found in a text or at the scene of a crime, rather than imposing one's preconceptions on the material and charging off blindly in what might seem to be the obvious direction. As Pip is told by the lawyer Jaggers, after he discovers to his dismay that not Miss Havisham but the convict Magwitch has been the source of his "great expectations" in Dickens's novel (1861): "'Take nothing on its looks; take everything on evidence. There's no better rule'" (ch. 40). Or, as Dickens the narrator himself declares concerning the investigation by the bumbling Bow Street detectives into the attack on Mrs. Joe earlier in the story, "They took up several obviously wrong people, and they ran their heads very hard against wrong ideas, and they persisted in trying to fit the ideas to the circumstances, instead of trying to extract ideas from the circumstances" (ch. 16).

Thus, even though there is no "definite truth" or "final answer" in the realm of hermeneutics, it to a great extent shares with detective work what might be termed a *forensic* stance, which means reading or listening with a minimum of preconceptions and an authentic openness to the encounter with the other. The quests of Oedipus or Pip for self-knowledge within their respective texts, which involve coming to terms with the objective conditions of their existence, are paralleled by the quest of the reader to bring his or her own subjectivity to bear in a way that illuminates the independently existing work under discussion, and thereby elucidate meanings that other open-minded people can agree enrich their understandings because it thenceforth becomes possible to see them "in" the text. As Winnicott (1953) has remarked of transitional objects, it is the hallmark of a skillful interpretation that *"we will never ask the question: 'Did you conceive of this or was it presented to you from without?' The important point is that no decision on this point is expected. The question is not to be formulated"* (p. 12).

If the reader is a detective in search of meanings that cannot be known in advance, but who may nonetheless succeed in bringing to light "hidden realities," this is true *a fortiori* in clinical work, where the analyst is dealing not with fictional characters but with real people. Although what emerges—or is prevented from emerging—through the analytic dialogue is, of course, a function of the "field" created by the interpenetrating subjectivities of analyst and patient, this does not mean that what comes into focus are always and only "constructions that may never have been thought before," and never memories that may already have existed in the patient's mind, albeit outside of conscious awareness, like Oedipus's knowledge of his guilt for the murder of his predecessor on the throne of Thebes, and, at a deeper level, of the truth of his origins, of which not only his name of "Swollen Foot" but also, in the words of the Messenger from Corinth, his "ankles should be witnesses" (l. 1033).

That analysis has the potential to unearth "hidden realities" is shown above all by the treatment of severely traumatized patients, who, like Oedipus himself, carry with them the scars of emotional, physical, or sexual abuse and neglect. As Van der Kolk (2014) has written, in connection with his patient Marilyn, who "said she guessed that she 'must have had' a happy childhood" but could "remember very little from before age twelve," and whose drawing of her family depicted "a wild and terrified child, trapped in some kind of a cage and threatened . . . by a huge erect penis protruding into her space," "it takes time to allow the reality behind such symptoms to reveal itself" (pp. 126–27). After more than a year of group therapy, in response to hearing another member speak of having been raped by her brother in her childhood, Marilyn began to wonder for the first time whether she herself had been sexually abused. She then began individual therapy with Van der Kolk, as well as to practice allied healing techniques including mindfulness training and breathing exercises, in the course of which she "finally began to access her memories." These "emerged as flashbacks of the wallpaper in her childhood bedroom," which, she realized, "was what she had focused on when her father raped her when she was eight years old" (p. 133).

As with Oedipus and Teiresias, it goes nowhere to try to claim that Marilyn's memories of being raped by her father in childhood were first "created" or "constructed" by her experiences in therapy. On the contrary, she had been carrying these around for some thirty years in her mind and body, as evidenced by the drawing the meaning of which she herself was oblivious, and it was the support she received both from other incest survivors and from her therapist that allowed, in Stern's words, the "hidden truth about the patient's life," or, in Van der Kolk's, "the reality behind such symptoms to reveal itself" for the first time. It should be clear, but needs to be underscored, that a major implication of the line of argument I am advancing here is that it shows the limits of field theory, especially in the extreme form propounded by Sullivan, and the indispensability of preserving the humanist belief in a "unique individual self."

But though the analyst in one of his guises may indeed be a forensic scientist, as well as a creative artist and a thaumaturge, this does not mean he should emulate Oedipus in the relentlessness of his pursuit of the truth. As Van der Kolk (2014) cautions, what is important for the therapist is not "to know every detail of a patient's trauma," but rather for patients themselves to "learn to tolerate feeling what they feel and knowing what they know" (p. 127). He reiterates, "As a therapist treating people with a legacy of trauma, my primary concern is not to determine exactly what happened to them but to help them tolerate the sensations, emotions, and reactions they experience without being constantly hijacked by them" (p. 176). In adopting this Wordsworthian attitude of "wise passiveness," Van der Kolk is at one with Stern (2015), who defines the virtue of analytic curiosity not as "a seeking after anything in particular," or as "looking *for* something," but rather as the capacity "for quiet and contemplation in the midst of engagement," which allows the analyst's own "unformulated experience" of the session to "cast up tendrils" into his consciousness (p. 27). Truth, like love, is more likely to come to us if we stop chasing it.

The inseparability of "hidden realities" from "emergent meanings" can likewise be illustrated by an example from Bromberg. In *The Shadow of the Tsunami* (2011), Bromberg courageously shows how a review of his previous book, *Awakening the Dreamer* (2006), by Max Cavitch, a Professor of English at the University of Pennsylvania, "reached back to a trauma" in his own past "about which [Cavitch] could not have known but which was always 'sort of known' by me" (2011, p. 176). Cavitch had observed that, in quoting poems by Emily Dickinson, Bromberg had omitted almost all of Dickinson's dashes, one her principal ways of flouting literary conventions. But rather than censuring Bromberg for this apparent carelessness, Cavitch proposed that he seemed thereby "*to participate with the poet in a dissociative enactment,*" since the notoriously reclusive Dickinson was clearly a massively traumatized woman and, in Cavitch's estimation, "there may be no other writer in the English language who engages readers so relentlessly and so powerfully in the intersubjective experience of dissociative states" (qtd. p. 176).

Cavitch's sensitive and insightful review caused Bromberg to recollect a traumatic experience from his years as a graduate student of English literature, when he was "shamed in front of the class by a professor" who told him he "didn't belong in the field" because he had had the temerity to write a paper analyzing the personality of Prince Hal in Shakespeare's *Henry IV, Part 1*, which was considered to be an illegitimate way of approaching literature by the critical authorities of the day. What Bromberg realized, thanks to Cavitch, was that by misquoting Dickinson as he did, he was influenced by "the dissociated presence of a determination to never submit to the arbitrary imposition of using literature in some 'right' way," and as a result he "did to her poetry my own version of what she did in writing it," that is, he "challenged the system . . . by obliterating without acknowledgment an important piece of what had been her own challenge to the system: her signature use of dashes as *her* violation of orthodoxy" (p. 177).

This interaction between the poet, the critic, and the psychoanalyst is a tour de force of "literary psychoanalysis," to invoke Fromm's phrase, not least because Bromberg was able "to process a dissociated residue of past trauma" in a way that he found "personally healing" (p. 178) solely by reading Cavitch's review and without ever having met him personally. As Bromberg elaborates, "It was healing because it activated the shadow of the trauma with the other professor, while holding it in a relational context where I felt cared about as a person" (p. 178). But just as we have seen in the case of Marilyn and Van der Kolk, although Bromberg's ability to integrate his previously dissociated experience came about through his textually mediated encounter with Cavitch, and in all likelihood would never have taken place without it, the traumatic memory was in no sense *caused* by this fortuitous event. What transpired was, in other words, at once the construction of an "emergent meaning" that had "never been thought before" *and* the uncovering of a "hidden reality" that had lain dormant for decades in Bromberg's mind. Or, in Wallace Stevens's lines from *Notes Toward a Supreme Fiction* (1942), with which one imagines Winnicott would have agreed, "He had to choose. But it was not a choice / Between excluding things. It was not a choice / Between, but of" ("It Must Give Pleasure," sec. vi).

Final Thoughts

Some final thoughts by way of a conclusion. I have acknowledged that there is a danger of circularity in Freud's argument that one can proceed backward via free associations from the manifest content of a dream to the latent content that presumably gave rise to the dream in the first place, just as there is no absolutely foolproof test to check the accuracy of the way that psychological symptoms are "deciphered and translated." But this does not mean that we do not have an epistemological leg to stand on. Even if it can never be proven that the associations to a dream unveil the thoughts that instigated the dream, it would be rash to conclude that there is *no* connection between the associations and the dream-thoughts, just as we have ample reason to be satisfied that the traumas uncovered by Marilyn and by Bromberg through their therapeutic encounters really did happen and were at the root of their dissociative symptoms. Thus, without succumbing to the delusion that there is ever a "final answer" or "definite truth" in the realm of hermeneutics, any more than there is in the natural sciences, there may still be an *als ob* with respect to clinical work, if our interventions are "good enough" that they help our patients to lead productive and fulfilled lives and to pacify—if not lay to rest altogether—the ghosts of the past that have haunted their psyches.

Inherent in Stern's constructivist position is a rejection not only of the "hidden reality" view of the mind but also of the distinction between latent and manifest content as it has been classically set forth by Freud in his theory of dreams. But can we not agree that this dichotomy should be treated gingerly without discarding it altogether? What do we do whenever we wonder about a person's motives—ask *why* someone has said or done something—if not try to infer or deduce the *causes* of the action, which may be outside the awareness of the agent himself? This is the bedrock of the theory of a dynamic unconscious, which surely retains its cogency even if we also find immense value in Stern's way of thinking about unformulated experience. The examples are legion, and the explanations often not far to seek. One has only to open *The Psychopathology of Everyday Life* (1901) at random to find splendid cases in point. A woman says at a party that men are better off than women, who must be beautiful to attract men, because as long as a man has "'his *five* straight limbs he needs nothing more!'" (p. 76). As Freud comments, the woman has condensed the expression "four straight limbs" with the "five wits" or senses, and her allusion to the erect male member "could pass just as well for a capital joke as for an amusing slip of the tongue," depending on "whether she spoke the words with a conscious or an unconscious intention" (p. 77).

The same principle holds when it comes to the interpretation of texts. To illustrate only briefly something that could be argued at much greater length, as I hope to do when *Facing the Facts* finally sees the light of day, why does the name of Minna Bernays, alone of all his close relatives and indisputably one of the most important people in Freud's life, never appear in any of his published writings? And why, as Peter Swales (1982) was the first to emphasize, did Freud in 1907 shift a footnote, which in the first edition of *The Psychopathology of Everyday Life* (1901) was attached to the first sentence of Chapter 2, to the body of the newly added third chapter? Chapter 2 contains Freud's analysis of the *aliquis* parapraxis, which has to do with a man's fear that he might have made his lover pregnant. The footnote recounted how he himself had forgotten the name of the brother of one of his female patients and was originally worded, "'Would my brother in the same circumstances have behaved in the same way towards a sister who was ill?'" (p. 24*n*1). In addition to moving the passage, Freud deleted the revealing words "towards a sister who was ill" and rephrased the question so that it read in anodyne fashion, "'Would my brother in the same circumstances have behaved in a similar way, or would he have done the opposite?'" (pp. 22–23).

If, as I submit should be obvious to any thinking person, especially if it could be shown that "Herr Aliquis" is Freud himself and the "sister who was ill" the sister-in-law whom he had recently deposited at a health-resort after their summer travels together, Freud is covering his tracks with respect to Minna—which he would only have felt obligated to do had there been something untoward about their relationship—then his motives for doing so would have been conscious rather than unconscious, though there would inevitably also have to be unconscious reverberations not only to the relationship itself but also to his need to keep such an explosive secret under wraps. But I adduce Freud's silence concerning Minna and his change of the passage about a "sister who was ill" in the *Psychopathology* here not to delve into the controversies surrounding Freud's life, as I do in my dismantling of Roudinesco's biography in Chapter 9, but simply to make the point that a search for "hidden realities" in the form of latent meanings and motives is perfectly possible—and indeed unavoidable—not simply in our dealings with other human beings but also in our "dialogues" with written texts.

In his expositions of hermeneutics, Stern contrasts Gadamer's approach, with which he aligns himself, with the earlier versions of hermeneutics espoused by Schleiermacher and Dilthey. He cites (1997) the commentary of Richard Palmer:

> For Schleiermacher, understanding . . . is the reexperiencing of the mental processes of the text's author. It is the reverse of composition, for it starts with the fixed and finished composition and goes back to the mental life from which it arose.
>
> (qtd. p. 210)

As Stern observes, "Schleiermacher's position that truth lies underneath or behind the text immediately brings to mind the concepts of latent and manifest content" (p. 212), adding that this a form of the "hidden reality" view that he cannot accept. "For Dilthey and Schleiermacher," he elaborates (2015), "understanding meant grasping the truth; and the truth had, in Cartesian fashion, an existence independent of the person trying to grasp it" (p. 197). For Gadamer, and for Stern himself, conversely,

> One does not understand by understanding the other person per se, but by coming to a new view of what the other person is saying. There is no support in Gadamer's views, in other words, for a psychotherapy based on a direct, empathic grasp of the other person's inner world.
>
> (p. 197)

I need to put in a word here for the beleaguered Schleiermacher, whose name, appropriately enough, means "veil-maker," and whom Nietzsche derided in *Ecce Homo* (1888) along with all of his other precursors in German philosophy:

> In the history of the quest for knowledge the Germans are inscribed with nothing but ambiguous names: they have always brought forth only "unconscious" counterfeiters (Fichte, Schelling, Schopenhauer, Hegel, and Schleiermacher deserve this epithet as well as Kant and Leibniz: they are all mere veil makers).
>
> (*"The Case of Wagner,"* sec. 3)

To me, it is undeniable that a text, like the mind of a patient in analysis, has "an existence independent of the person trying to grasp it," and that understanding therefore entails not only "coming to a new view of what the other person is saying" but also an empathic "grasp of the other person's inner world" from which the discourse emanates, whether it comes in the form of living speech or a written text. To be sure, when we possess little or no information about the life of an author, such as Shakespeare, such an endeavor becomes circular and therefore futile, because we have no way of checking the validity of our reconstructions, as we can with Freud, for example, about whom we possess vast stores of biographical data, or with patients who can recount for us the stories of their lives. But the principle remains valid: there is a truth, which may be infinitely complex, that "lies underneath or behind the text," whether or not we are able to access it in any given instance. Nor does this way of understanding entail, as Stern (2015) maintains it does for Schleiermacher and Dilthey, "subtracting preconception" completely, since even the literary critic or psychoanalyst who, like the detective, seeks to follow the clues provided by the evidence wherever they may lead is using his subjectivity in a disciplined way. All that is required is that one do one's best to be on guard against its "distorting effects" (p. 197), as occurs when unexamined bias causes the investigator to try "to fit the ideas"—or preconceived theories—"to the circumstances, instead of trying to extract ideas from the circumstances." Freud's antithesis between latent and manifest content is a linchpin of his allegiance to what has come to be known, after Paul Ricoeur (1965), as the "hermeneutics of suspicion," the conviction he shares with two other masters of modernity, Marx and Nietzsche, that the true meanings and explanations of things—a dream, a moral code, a political system—are not to be found in what is visible on the surface, which is bound to be deceptive, but only by looking "behind and beneath" these appearances to an unpalatable sexual, economic, or aggressive "hidden reality." Ricoeur himself juxtaposed the hermeneutics of suspicion, or demystification, with the antipodal view of "interpretation as restoration of meaning," grounded in a "phenomenology of symbols" animated by a numinous impulse to "greet the revealing power of the primal word" (p. 32). More recently, Orange (2011), whose synthesis of the hermeneutic tradition from Schleiermacher to Gadamer is leavened by her commitment to bearing the "infinite responsibility to the face of the suffering stranger" (p. 3) to which we are summoned by Levinas, has gone beyond Ricoeur by countering the proclivity to suspicion bequeathed to psychoanalysis by Freud with a "hermeneutics of trust." Whereas the attitude of suspicion, exemplified by Freud's demeanor toward his most famous female patient, where he assumed that "everything Dora said meant something else besides what she said it did," fosters a tendency "to shame or blame the victim," the "participatory sense of inclusion and welcome" in the hermeneutics of trust conveys to the patient that his "questions and thoughts will be treated with respect and hospitality" (pp. 32, 34). In this alternative paradigm, Orange writes, "we count on the goodwill of both participants in the dialogue as we search for meaning and truth. Furthermore, *we expect meaning to be both hidden and transparent, both there to be discovered and emergent from the dialogic process*" (p. 34; italics added).[10]

Thus, the hermeneutics of suspicion and the hermeneutics of trust are not inimical, but must become, in the evocative title of Stern's (2010) second book, "partners in thought." In analogous fashion, I have argued that there are both hidden realities to be discovered and new meanings that emerge from the dialogic process. Anyone lucky enough to escape the worst ravages of trauma has an enduring sense of self, a relatively stable character structure that is molded both by nature and nurture. But which of the manifold facets of a person's being will be activated at a given moment will be a function of the forces at play in the intersubjective field—or fields—in which he finds himself. Exemplifying what is best in both psychoanalysis and hermeneutics, Stern (2015) has called for a "genuine conversation" between "the practitioners of conflicting theories," out of his conviction that "the existence of multiple conceptions of practice is a sign of a field's vigor" (p. 167). He hopes, in particular, that such an exchange can occur "between the parties committed to both perspectives, the hermeneutic and the systematically empirical, a conversation that takes place very seldom in our field today" (p. 204).

As I have tried to demonstrate in this prolegomenon, I think it is possible to reconcile "objectivist" and "constructivist" epistemologies. Strikingly, Stern's rejection of empirical methods is not shared by Bromberg, whose most recent book has a foreword by Allan Schore (2011), whose lifetime of work has been devoted to the proposition that "the problem of early developmental trauma and dissociation and their enduring impact on the mind/brain/body's capacity to interpersonally regulate affect" (p. x) can be studied not only clinically but also scientifically. It is out of a desire to heed Stern's call for a "genuine conversation" that I have taken up the gauntlet both he and Bromberg have thrown down in their brilliant and generative writings. In the humanist tradition of Fromm, I have striven to make the case that there *is* "such a thing as an integrated self—a 'real you,'" and it is in the elastic spirit of Ferenczi that I would venture to redefine psychological health as *"the capacity to feel like many selves while being one."*

Notes

1 Whether it should be deemed "familiar chaos" or "creative disorder" (Stern, 1997, p. 76), it is unquestionably ironic that while I remember reading this passage in his work, and he remembers writing it, neither of us has been able to locate it.
2 On meaning as the outgrowth of an ongoing interplay between form, field, and the standpoint of the observer, see John C. Foehl's arresting paper, "The Phenomenology of Depth" (2014).
3 See my more detailed discussion of this issue in the Appendix to *Freud and Oedipus* (Rudnytsky, 1987, pp. 350–57).
4 My quotations from Sophocles here and in the following discussion are to David Grene's translation.
5 I am grateful to Donnel Stern for confirming this point.
6 The quotation from Wolstein is taken from a posthumously published interview with Irwin Hirsch (2000, p. 199). For a comprehensive overview of

Wolstein's contributions to the interpersonal tradition of psychoanalysis, see the paper by Sue A. Shapiro (2000).
7 See also Van der Hart, Nijenhuis, and Steele (2006), who argue that "the essence of trauma is *structural dissociation of personality*," a definition they propose in order "to reinstate the original meaning of the terms *dissociation* as formulated by Pierre Janet" (p. vii).
8 See my discussion of Oedipus's "preoedipal" traumas in my chapter, "The Birth of Oedipus," in *The Psychoanalytic Vocation* (Rudnytsky, 1991).
9 Compare the full-blown hubris of Freud's boast in "Psychopathic Characters on the Stage" (c. 1905) that "the conflict in *Hamlet* is so effectively concealed that it was left to me to unearth it" (p. 310).
10 Juxtaposing the Persian carpet on Freud's couch with the antique statues on his desk, Jean-Michel Rabaté (2014) analogously observes: "If archaeology betrayed Freud's belief in a hidden truth rising from the psychic depths, the process of weaving suggests a continuous intermeshing of the patient's psyche with the psychoanalyst's own" (p. 204).

Part I

Discovering Fromm

Chapter 1

Freud as Milton's God
Mapping the Patriarchal Cosmos in Psychoanalysis and *Paradise Lost*

> "Our voluntary service he requires,
> Not our necessitated..."
> —Milton, *Paradise Lost*

Theological vs. Romantic Readings

In keeping with its depiction of a cosmic conflict between God and Satan, no work in the Western canon has given rise to more polarized critical responses than has *Paradise Lost*. The essential division has been between those readers who see Milton as having been successful in his avowed aim to "justify the ways of God to men" (1.26) and those readers, beginning in the Romantic period, who maintain, in Blake's (c. 1790) famous apothegm, that Milton "was of the Devil's party without knowing it" (p. 211)—that is, that he unwittingly sabotaged this conscious intention, and indeed that his greatness cannot be disentangled from the unresolved tensions between his theology and his poetry.[1] To be sure, some recent commentators have sought to move beyond such established positions—arguing, for instance, that the poem contains only a series of "unreliable narrators," starting with God himself, and that the destabilizing of meanings is accordingly deliberate on Milton's part (Herman, 2005, p. 125), or that Milton portrays God as a tyrant because he wishes to overthrow all forms of heavenly as well as earthly kingship (Bryson, 2004, p. 29)—but these displays of ingenuity by representatives of the "new Milton criticism" (Herman and Sauer, 2012) have not succeeded in altering the fundamental terms of the debate as it has taken shape since the epoch of Blake and Shelley (1821), the latter of whom boldly affirmed that "the most decisive proof of the supremacy of

Milton's genius" lay in the fact that he imputed "no superiority of moral virtue to his God over his Devil" (p. 1107).

Perhaps the most remarkable feature of the theologically oriented critics of *Paradise Lost* is their confidence that the poem must be read in a way that accords with what they understand to be its true meaning, which in turn reflects Milton's intentions as the author. In his classic monograph, *A Preface to "Paradise Lost,"* C. S. Lewis (1942) quotes Addison's declaration that "'the great moral which reigns in Milton is . . . that Obedience to the will of God makes men happy and that Disobedience makes them miserable'" and appends the comment: "there can be no serious doubt that Milton meant just what Addison said: neither more, nor less, nor other than that. If you can't be interested in that, you can't be interested in *Paradise Lost*" (p. 71). Lewis reiterates in his conclusion, "After Blake, Milton criticism is lost in misunderstanding," and "the critics and the poem were at cross purposes" because "they did not see what the poem was about" (pp. 133–34).

As Lewis sought to restore Milton criticism to the proper path from which it had strayed since the Romantics, so, too, in his epoch-making *Surprised by Sin: The Reader in "Paradise Lost"* (1967) Stanley E. Fish combated the intervening quarter-century of doubters whom he collectively termed "anti-Miltonists" by arguing that the responses of those who found inconsistencies in the poem simply revealed their status as fallen readers in need of education and correction, and thus were actually "the surest guide to the poet's method" (p. 31). Even more categorically than Lewis, Fish affirmed that "there is . . . only one true interpretation of *Paradise Lost*" (p. 272), and that the aim of criticism should be to uncover "the truths that God and Milton have proclaimed" (p. 234). Although the subtitle of Fish's book announces a focus on the reader, his approach paradoxically depends on a recovery of Milton's authorial intention, which he equates with the perspective of God in the poem. As he insists with respect to God's disclaiming of any responsibility for the Fall of Man, we must be guided by "our understanding of the situation as God and Milton have instituted it" (p. 211).

Thus, although Lewis was able to dismiss modern "misunderstandings" without feeling threatened by them, whereas Fish had to devise a strategy to incorporate them into his argument, they end up reading *Paradise Lost* in nearly identical fashion. Both want to go back before everything was turned upside down in the Romantic period to the eighteenth century, which had not forgotten that Milton was first and foremost a Christian poet.

As Lewis quotes Addison on the poem's inculcation of the "great moral" of obedience to God, so, too, Fish (1967) writes of the "all-inclusive virtue of obedience" (p. 161), declaring that his own conception of the poem "accords perfectly" with that of Milton's eighteenth-century commentator Jonathan Richardson, who admonished that the mind of the reader of *Paradise Lost* must be prepared "'to receive Such Impressions as the Poet intended to give it'" (p. 54). And just as Lewis (1942) celebrated Milton's commitment to a "hierarchical conception" according to which "degrees of value are objectively present in the universe" and "the goodness, happiness, and dignity of every being consists in obeying its natural superior and ruling its natural inferiors" (p. 73), calling this metaphysical principle "the indwelling life of the whole work" (p. 79), so, again, Fish (1967) observes that Satan finds himself confounded by "the superstructure of a God-centered universe" (p. 79), and when Adam counsels Eve with his "superior wisdom," the result is "the strengthening of the hierarchical relationship which is the basis of their happiness" (p. 224).

As Lewis and Fish are the leading representatives of a theological approach to *Paradise Lost*, so their counterparts on the other side of the critical divide, A. J. A. Waldock and William Empson, are the most prominent heirs to the Romantics. Published five years after Lewis's *Preface*, to which it serves as a rejoinder, Waldock's *"Paradise Lost" and Its Critics* (1947) loomed large enough to be singled out two decades later by Fish (1967) as "the most forthright statement" of the "anti-Miltonism" that he takes it upon himself to refute in his book. Indeed, Fish goes so far as to say that it is his aim to "defend the poem in the same detailed and specific manner in which it has been attacked" by Waldock (p. 2*n*1).

At stake in Fish's dispute with Waldock is whether *Paradise Lost* is an internally consistent or self-contradictory work of art. According to Waldock (1947), an "embedded ambiguity" permeates Milton's epic, as a result of which "there is a fundamental clash" between "what the poem asserts, on the one hand, and what it compels us to feel, on the other" (p. 145). As the centerpiece of his thesis, Waldock adduces Adam's decision in Book 9 to disobey God and fall along with Eve. "If we push analysis to the limit," he writes, we find that "the poem asks from us, at one and the same time, two incompatible responses," namely, to believe "with the full weight of our minds" both that "Adam did right" and that "he did wrong. The dilemma," he summarizes, "is as critical as that, and there is no way of escape" (p. 56).

In his rebuttal of Waldock, Fish (1967) agrees that *Paradise Lost* continuously gives rise to conflicting responses in the reader's mind, but he contends that this is deliberate on Milton's part, and that all such discords are overcome as soon as the reader realizes the errors of his ways and assents "to the authoritative interpretation of the poem" (p. 245) as it is promulgated by God and his representatives, including the divinely inspired narrator. Denying that "any fit reader would resolve the problem, as Waldock does," by giving at least as much weight to what he is made to feel by the poem as he does to its doctrinal assertions, Fish insists that Milton expects the reader to place this clash "in a context that would resolve a troublesome contradiction and allow him to reunite with an authority who is a natural ally against the difficulties of the poem" (p. 47).

For Waldock, therefore, there is an inescapable contradiction at the heart of *Paradise Lost*, whereas for Fish the "true interpretation" of the poem reveals it to be perfectly harmonious and consistent. Since "all values proceed from and are defined in terms of God," Fish (1967) elaborates, "the assumption of a clash between any two of them"—as when Waldock posits a conflict between Adam's love for Eve and his obedience to God—"is possible only if the situation is considered from a point of view that excludes God" (p. 264), which means that the fault lies in the distorted perception of the reader rather than in the flawless design of the poem. When Fish refers to Waldock and the other critics with whom he disagrees as "anti-Miltonists," he intimates that they have failed to appreciate the sublimity of *Paradise Lost*, which he has made manifest by his theory of the fallen reader. Although Waldock is by no means so unsympathetic to Milton as is John Peter in *A Critique of "Paradise Lost"* (1960), for example, he does regard the "embedded ambiguity" he detects in the poem as the symptom of an aesthetic failure. Because of the "fundamental clash" Milton has unwittingly imported into his text, Waldock (1947) concedes in his closing pages, "that is why we are uneasy, as at something wrong, deep down in the treatment. That is why *Paradise Lost* does not profoundly trouble, profoundly satisfy us, in the manner of great tragedy" (p. 145).

But even if we were to grant for the sake of argument that a literary work could be devoid of contradictions, why should such a work be deemed superior to one that is not? It is among the merits of Empson's *Milton's God* (1961) that he calls into question the assumption—shared by Waldock and Fish, although they disagree as to whether *Paradise Lost* is coherent—that consistency is preferable to ambiguity and even contradiction. For Empson, "the poem is not good in spite of but especially because of its moral confusions," and he encourages Milton's readers to adopt "the manly and appreciative attitude of Blake and Shelley, who said that the reason why the poem is so good is that it makes God so bad" (p. 13).[2] Thus, although Empson goes further than Waldock in asserting that *Paradise Lost* contains not simply "embedded ambiguity" but "moral confusions," he would reject Fish's aspersion that this makes him an "anti-Miltonist," because such tensions and complexities are precisely the hallmarks of great works of art.

Milton's God is justly renowned as the most distinguished openly atheistic work of English literary criticism, and Empson (1961) pays tribute at the outset to Lewis, the Christian apologist, for having "let in some needed fresh air" when he opined that "many of those who object to Milton's God only mean that they dislike God" (p. 9; see Lewis, 1942, p. 130). According to Empson, "the poem must be read with growing horror unless you decide to reject its God," though he again concurs with Lewis that what Milton has given us is "merely the traditional Christian God" (p. 25), only palliated by Milton's unwillingness to "dirty his fingers with the bodily horror so prominent in the religion" (p. 128) by being sufficiently explicit about "the Neolithic craving for human sacrifice" that is built "into its basic structure" (p. 241) with the crucifixion. Notwithstanding Milton's soft-pedaling of the agony of Christ's death on the cross, however, there can, by Empson's reckoning, be no denying that God is an implacable sadist. "Only if this God had a craving to torture his Son could the Son bargain with him about it. In return for those three hours of ecstasy, the Father would give up the pleasure of torturing a small proportion of mankind, Empson insists, though only such a "tiny proportion" are to be spared from the torments of Hell that "his eternal pleasure can scarcely be diminished" (p. 246) even by this consummate sacrifice.

The two major twentieth-century representatives of the "Devil's party" thus differ in the following fashion: whereas Waldock (1947) concentrates on delineating the tensions in *Paradise Lost* that show Milton to have reached "a result the exact opposite of what he had intended," namely, "to justify man's ways against God's ways" (p. 57), Empson's (1961) commentary on the poem is stoked by his conviction that "the Christian God the Father . . . is the wickedest thing yet invented by the black heart of man" (p. 251), and is ultimately in the service of his assault on Christianity. The formal nature of Waldock's analysis renders him a more formidable antagonist to Fish (1967), who mentions Empson's "brilliantly perverse" book only in passing, singling out as its most important idea that "'all the characters are on trial in any civilized narrative,'" adding that Waldock would doubtless "include the epic voice in that statement" (p. 46; see Empson, 1961, p. 94). For the rest, Fish treats Empson as simply one of the many critics who fallaciously assume that "'God was determined to make man fall'" (pp. 175, 210; see Empson, 1961, p. 112)—as when Gabriel guided by a heavenly portent allows Satan to escape from his custody at the end of Book 4—but who otherwise does not require extended refutation.

If we now seek to take stock of the critical debate over *Paradise Lost* in the modern period, it seems clear that the neo-Christian duo of Lewis and Fish have gained the upper hand over the Romantic scions, Waldock and Empson. Although Waldock convincingly demonstrated that the poem demands "two incompatible responses" from its readers, he regarded this state of affairs as a defect rather than a virtue, a disappointing verdict that Fish was able to overturn by arguing it to be integral to Milton's conception that makes *Paradise Lost* a masterpiece of Christian art. Whatever uneasiness we may feel at Fish's assumption that a great work of literature should do away with "troublesome contradictions" and lead us to identify with the authority figures who are our allies "against the difficulties of the poem," his reading appears to be unassailable on its own terms. For if, as Lewis (1942) has written, *Paradise Lost* "is a poem depicting the objective pattern of things, the attempted destruction of that pattern by rebellious self love, and the triumphant absorption of that rebellion into a yet more complex pattern" (p. 132), then it does seem plausible that all apparent contradictions should be exposed as illusions from the standpoint of eternity, and must be abolished if we are to understand *Paradise Lost* as Milton intended it.

Empson, for his part, cannot be said to depreciate the greatness of *Paradise Lost*, and, unlike Waldock, he regards the "moral confusions" of the poem as virtues rather than defects. His unsparing critique of Christianity is courageous and his frontal assault on God the Father certainly focuses our attention where it belongs if the stranglehold of the theological school is ever to be broken. But despite its inimitable panache, his reading is too idiosyncratic and diffuse to be able to hold its own against Fish (1967), who has no difficulty in countering that, like Waldock, Empson is not a "fit reader" because "Milton assumes a predisposition in favor of the epic voice rather than an eagerness to put that voice on trial" (p. 47), and he has thus failed to do justice to *Paradise Lost*, whatever may be said about the metaphysical truth claims of Christianity.

What is required to turn the tables on the theological critics, therefore, is an interpretation capable of synthesizing Waldock's emphasis on structural contradictions in the poem with Empson's insistence that God the Father must be "put on trial" in *Paradise Lost*, rather than being given a free pass as the putative "essence of Truth," as Fish (1967, p. 83) would have it. By effecting such a synthesis, a reinvigorated Romantic perspective ought to be able dialectically to absorb and subsume Fish's theory of the "fallen reader," just as Fish succeeded in transmuting the objections raised by Waldock into an argument for perceiving Milton as a stalwartly Christian poet, when such a view could no longer be sustained in the traditional form in which it had been articulated by Lewis and by the neoclassicists of the eighteenth century.

The Supreme Narcissist

An excellent starting point for resuscitating the Romantic reading of *Paradise Lost* is afforded by Waldock's (1947) observation that the Fall story is inherently "a bad one for God," and if "the story in Genesis was like a stretch of film minutely flawed," then the effect of Milton's "tremendous enlargement" was "that every slight imperfection would show, that every slight rift would become a gulf" (pp. 18–19). Milton was unable to "detect the problems in his basic fable," Waldock continues, because its scriptural provenance meant that for him this "fable was God's own truth" (p. 19). This belief in the truth of the creation story in the Bible would have been shared by what Lewis (1942) calls "the ordinary educated and Christian audience in Milton's time" (p. 91), and it was not seriously questioned in England until the crisis of faith brought to a head by Darwin's propounding of the theory of evolution in the mid-nineteenth century.

The chief reason why the Fall story is a "bad one for God" is that it seeks to absolve God of responsibility for the disobedience he knows will occur, but which is nonetheless held to be due entirely to acts freely undertaken by his creatures. In the classic line from God's speech to the Son in Book 3 of *Paradise Lost*, man was created "Sufficient to have stood, though free to fall" (99). From a theological standpoint, this conundrum whereby God's foreknowledge not only coexists with absolute free will in Adam and Eve before the Fall—as well as in the angels who preceded them in their revolt—but also "had no influence on their fault" (117), is an axiom that must be granted if the story is to be understood correctly. As Milton presents the same argument in Book 1, Chapter 3 of *The Christian Doctrine*, the Latin treatise he probably completed by 1660 but that was not discovered until 1823: "Thus God foreknew that Adam would fall of his own free will; his fall therefore was certain but not necessary, since it proceeded from his own free will, which is incompatible with necessity" (Hughes, 1957, p. 915).

It follows from the premise that the Fall is caused solely by man's free will that all the incidents Milton has packed into his "tremendous enlargement" of the "stretch of film" in Genesis that might seem to foreshadow the catastrophe in Book 9—Eve's gazing at her "smooth wat'ry image" (4.480) in the lake following her creation, her dream of eating the forbidden fruit in Book 5, Adam's yielding to her plea to garden separately in Book 9, and so forth—should not be seen as prefigurations, but are rather harmless occurrences that acquire their ominous quality only in retrospect. The Fall, in short, was not inevitable, and man's decision to transgress what God calls "the sole Command / The sole pledge of his obedience" (3.94–95) is radically discontinuous with everything that precedes it in the state of innocence.

Although this paradoxical reconciliation of God's foreknowledge of the Fall with man's free will is orthodox Christian doctrine, and indispensable to understanding Milton's poem on its own terms, it remains susceptible to a critique to which I first called attention in an essay published more than a quarter-century ago (Rudnytsky, 1988). Drawing on the work of Jean Laplanche (1970), I employed the concept of "deferred action" (*Nachträglichkeit*), as originally formulated by Freud, to argue that the relation of unfallen to fallen experience in *Paradise Lost* has the structure of a trauma, in which the initially innocuous "presexual" events take on new, fully sexual meanings after the Fall, and thus the quality of foreshadowing simply cannot be eliminated from our response to the poem, however unacceptable this may be theologically.

To Laplanche's exposition of deferred action I soldered Kenneth Burke's (1961) distinction between a theological and a "logological" approach to the Genesis story. By "logological" Burke means an analysis of the language used to talk about God, wholly apart from the question of God's existence. A logological approach to religious topics is thus a rhetorical or narrative approach, as opposed to the God-centered approach of theology.

In discussing the consequences of this shift in focus, Burke explains that while in most respects the theological and logological interpretations of Genesis exist on "different planes, so that they neither corroborate nor refute one another," there is one point on which "there does seem to be a necessary opposition" (p. 252). That point is the pivotal one of the conflict between the determinism implied by God's foreknowledge and the postulate that Adam and Eve possessed free will, so that the Fall could have been avoided. To illustrate why the belief in free will is unsustainable from a logological perspective, Burke uses an example that is bound to resonate with psychoanalytic readers:

> Theologically, Adam could have chosen not to sin. He could have said yes to God's thou-shalt-not. But logologically, Adam necessarily sinned. For if he had chosen not to sin, the whole design of the Bible would have been ruined. . . . Logologically, to say that Adam didn't have to sin would be like saying that Oedipus didn't have to kill his father and marry his mother, except that in the case of Adam it looks like more of a choice.
>
> (p. 252)

Burke's analysis turns on the recognition that if the Fall story is considered as a narrative, then the outcome is known to the reader in advance—for "the whole design of the Bible" depends on it—and any suggestion that Adam "could have chosen not to sin" and remained in Eden forever is nothing more than a mirage. In reality, Adam and Eve are just as fated to disobey God as Oedipus is to fulfill the curse imposed on him by the oracle. The only difference between Genesis and the tragedy of Sophocles from this standpoint is that the biblical narrative requires the reader to turn a blind eye to this exigency of the plot and to entertain the illusion that Adam and Eve had free will, whereas Oedipus did not.

To borrow Waldock's terminology, because this "embedded ambiguity" in the Fall story is passed over in silence in Genesis, it constitutes no more than a "minute flaw" in the biblical account. In the vast canvas of *Paradise Lost*, however, where Milton takes it upon himself to write an apologia for God, it receives a "tremendous enlargement" to the point where it haunts the reader at every turn. All Waldock's difficulties with the poem become intelligible when they are seen as inchoate expressions of a logological objection to the hegemony of the theological perspective. From start to finish, the poem does indeed demand "two incompatible responses" from the reader—one based on the axiom that the Fall was not inevitable and the result of man's free will, the other on the awareness that the Fall is determined by the structural requirements of the narrative—and "there is no way of escape" from this ubiquitous dilemma.

Placing Waldock's analysis of *Paradise Lost* on the foundation laid by Burke's logological outlook, moreover, provides the necessary leverage to push back against Fish's theory of the "fallen reader." Although Waldock's analysis uncovered tensions everywhere in the poem, he failed to provide an overarching explanation for the phenomena to which he called attention. Thus, Fish was able to get the better of Waldock by asserting that the divided responses evoked in the reader were intended by Milton as part of his master plan of education and that no clashes between values are possible when we align ourselves with God's point of view. But thanks to Burke, the all-encompassing theological perspective now must confront an equally comprehensive alternative perspective, which accounts no less satisfactorily for everything in *Paradise Lost*, and which restores a fundamental contradiction at the heart of the poem. Indeed, when *Paradise Lost* is seen in light of the stalemate between theological and logological interpretations, it comes to resemble nothing so much as the rabbit—duck illusion of perceptual psychology, in which the same anamorphic image can take on one contour or the other, but not both simultaneously

As an illustration of the rabbit—duck paradigm, let us take the passage in Book 1 where the narrator reports that Satan succeeded in arising from the burning lake to which he had been chained in Hell, and then in flying to dry land, because he was allowed to do so by "the will / And high permission of all-ruling Heaven," and that God's permission was granted so that "with reiterated crimes he might / Heap on himself damnation, while he sought / Evil to others" (210–15). For Lewis (1942), this incident exemplifies Milton's endorsement of St. Augustine's teaching that "though God has made all creatures good He foreknows that some will voluntarily make themselves bad and also foreknows the good use which He will then make of their badness" (p. 67). Similarly, for Fish (1967), Milton is here making the point that he "will make again and again" in *Paradise Lost*, namely, that "all acts are performed in God's service; what is left to any agent is a choice between service freely rendered and service exacted against his will" (p. 18).

For the theological critics, accordingly, there is nothing problematic about the passage. Satan is deluded in thinking he has escaped from the lake by his own power, and his apparent freedom, even in Hell, ratifies God's omnipotence and the triumph of his benevolent plan for the universe. For narrative or logological critics, however, matters are not so straightforward. For these latter-day Romantics, what Milton here tells us is that Satan's journey to Earth, which leads to the Fall of Man, would not have taken place had God not released him from the Stygian lake, and the further consequence of God's decision is that Satan "on himself / Treble confusion, wrath and vengeance pour'd" (1.219–20). Since no one disputes that these outcomes are foreseen by God, once it has been conceded that the Fall is mandated by the demands of the narrative, then Empson (1961) is justified in inferring not only that God "was determined to make man fall" (p. 112), but also that "God's actions towards Satan were intended to lead him into greater evil" (p. 42). That God, having routed the rebel angels, cannot forbear augmenting Satan's already eternal punishment to a still more incalculable degree confirms Empson's diagnosis of him as a sadist, and this brutality is what led Shelley, in *A Defence of Poetry* (1821), to conclude not merely that Milton had ascribed "no superiority of moral virtue to his God over his Devil," but indeed that

> Milton's Devil as a moral being is as far superior to his God, as one who perseveres in some purpose which he has conceived to be excellent in spite of adversity and torture, is to One who in the cold security of undoubted triumph inflicts the most horrible revenge upon his enemy, not from any mistaken notion of inducing him to repent of a perseverance in enmity, but with the alleged design of exasperating him to deserve new torments.
>
> (p. 1107)

By anchoring Waldock's awareness of the "two incompatible responses" that *Paradise Lost* demands of its readers in Burke's antimony between theological and logological approaches to the Fall, we have succeeded in turning the tables on Fish by subsuming his all-encompassing but monocular interpretation into a larger pattern in which the neo-Christian reading is simply one pole of an ever-oscillating dialectic. And since the consequence of adopting a logological perspective is to equate God's foreknowledge of the outcome with responsibility for everything that happens in the poem, a narrative analysis converges here with Empson's admonition that God, like every other character, is "on trial" in the poem. In keeping with the rabbit—duck paradigm, moreover, if the falls of both Satan and man must be laid at God's doorstep, then instead of being the "essence of Truth," he metamorphoses before our eyes into being the principal villain of the piece.

That this possibility had occurred to Milton himself is attested by *The Christian Doctrine*, where he writes in Book 1, Chapter 2 that the evidence of order and purpose in nature has "compelled all nations to believe, either that God, or some evil power whose name was unknown, presided over the affairs of the world" (Hughes, 1957, p. 905). Milton's acknowledgment that God could be indistinguishable from an "evil power" prompted Empson (1961) to comment wryly that "even Voltaire could not have written that icy sentence" (p. 203). The controversy over divine foreknowledge and human free will is taken to its logical conclusion in Book 1, Chapter 3 when Milton protests that those who oppose his position "do not hesitate even to assert that God is himself the cause and origin of sin," which renders such men "the most abandoned of all blasphemers," while "an attempt to refute them would be nothing more than argument to prove that God was not the evil spirit" (Hughes, 1957, p. 916). But since, as Waldock put it, there is a case to be made that Milton in *Paradise Lost* reached "a result the exact opposite of what he had intended," namely, "to justify man's ways against God's ways," then might it not ironically be Milton himself who has proved that God is simply another name for the "evil spirit" who rules the world?

In putting forth his argument that "God was determined to make man fall," Empson (1961) makes many scintillating observations, as when he compares God to a parent who sets his children up for failure, which goes beyond simply imagining what the future holds in store for them: "But a parent who 'foresaw' that the children would fall and then insisted upon exposing them to the temptation in view would be considered neurotic, if nothing worse; and this is what we must ascribe to Milton's God" (p. 116). Similarly, of God's speech in Book 7 saying he can make up for Satan's having "dispeopl'd Heaven" (151) by creating "out of one man a Race / Of men innumerable" (155–56), Empson remarks, "As usual, God is making the necessary excuses without admitting that there is anything to excuse" (p. 175). Finally, Empson notes, "Milton insists throughout the poem, whenever he pronounces about the motives of God, even when the incidental effects might be good, that God acted for his own glory" (p. 155).

But though Empson scores points with each of these jabs, they are too glancing to deliver a knockout blow because he does not grasp that

God's desire for glory furnishes the key to an analysis of his character in *Paradise Lost*. Just as Waldock's delineation of the "fundamental clash" between doctrine and narrative in the poem could not withstand Fish's neo-Christian appropriation until it was reinforced by Burke's explanation of the dichotomy between theological and logological perspectives on the Fall, so, too, the implications of Empson's insights into the character of God can be fully appreciated only when they are placed within a more capacious psychological framework.

As his title promises, John Rumrich's *Matter of Glory: A New Preface to "Paradise Lost"* (1987) deals learnedly with the theme of glory in the poem, and there is much that is of value in his book. In his opening pages Rumrich states with refreshing candor, "Milton's God wants glory and uses his power to get it" (p. 4). Despite setting Milton's treatment of glory in the contexts of both Greek epic and the Hebrew Bible, however, and thus—like Lewis in his original *Preface*—endeavoring to address "the meaning of the whole poem as well as its cultural basis" (p. 6), Rumrich does not succeed any more than did Empson in providing an analysis of the character of Milton's God as a glory-seeking being that would make it possible comprehensively to reinterpret *Paradise Lost* from this angle.

Immediately after his observation that God desires glory, Rumrich (1987) writes perceptively that

> from a psychoanalytic perspective, the usual emphasis of Milton scholars on oedipal issues of law, obedience, and punishment has resulted in the corresponding neglect of the epic's primary, pervasive concern with negotiations between narcissistic longing for perfect recognition and the recalcitrance of an unresponsive reality.
>
> (p. 4)

But Rumrich does not make it clear that Milton's God is the supreme embodiment of "the narcissistic longing for perfect recognition" in the poem. Quite conventionally, Rumrich speaks of "the narcissism of the rebel angels, which contrasts with yet prefigures the innocent self-love of the newborn Eve" (p. 94), but nowhere does Rumrich expressly identify God himself as a narcissist.

But where both Empson and Rumrich fall short, Bernard J. Paris succeeds with aplomb. In *Heaven and Its Discontents: Milton's Characters in "Paradise Lost"* (2010), Paris goes beyond his predecessors not simply in his analysis of God as a narcissist who "is not sufficient to himself but is extremely dependent on others" (p. 43), but also in unmasking Heaven as a "glory system" (p. 11). Echoing Empson, Paris begins by pointing out how God makes possible the chain of events that lead to the Fall of Man by releasing Satan from the burning lake in Hell, and also by entrusting the keys to Hell's gate to Sin, Satan's daughter, with "instructions that she should let no one out," even though "Sin's loyalty to her father instead of to him is something God must have foreseen" (p. 2). In a tour de force, Paris then reconstructs the state of affairs in Heaven prior to the rebellion fomented by Satan. When Gabriel captures Satan in Paradise, he responds to Satan's taunt that he and the other dutiful angels "cringe" (4.945) before the throne of God with the following retort:

> And thou, sly hypocrite, who now wouldst seem
> Patron of liberty, who more than thou
> Once fawn'd, and cring'd, and servilely ador'd
> Heaven's awful Monarch? wherefore but in hope
> To dispossess him, and thyself to reign?
> (957–61)

Despite being part of an "exchange of insults," Paris contends that Gabriel's "charge of hypocrisy rings true, for Lucifer's adoration was clearly insincere" (p. 14). What is more, Lucifer's discontent must have been perceived by God even before it broke out into the open since, as the narrator explains in Book 3, hypocrisy is "the only evil that walks / Invisible, except to God alone" (683–84).

This account of how God could read Satan's mind even while Satan as Lucifer outwardly seemed to be united with the rest of the heavenly host provides a psychologically compelling explanation for the action that sets in motion the entire cosmological drama of *Paradise Lost*, namely, God's announcement that he has "begot" Christ as his "only Son" and the "Head" over the other angels, to whom "shall bow / All knees in Heav'n" (5.603–8). Although God promises that everyone who obeys the Son will "abide / As one individual Soul / For ever happy" (609–11), he warns that those who refuse will be thrust "Into utter darkness" (614) for eternity. In Paris's (2010) scenario, God cleverly elevates the Son as a strategy "for penalizing the ungrateful angels with what they feel to be demotion on the pretext of making them happy, while preparing to cast them out should they disobey an edict that is calculated to make them rebel" (p. 16). God is narcissistically injured by Satan's recalcitrance; Satan is enraged by God's promotion of the Son; God is further enraged by Satan's rebellion, with the result that *Paradise Lost* has the structure of "a double revenge plot," in which "each side is outraged at having been injured by the other, each injury provokes retaliation, and each retaliation intensifies the craving for revenge," while Adam and Eve are merely "pawns in the struggle between God and Satan that begins with their discontent with each other in Heaven" (p. 1).

From Paris's analysis of Heaven as a "glory system," it follows that although it appears to be based on freedom—as when Raphael explains to Adam, "freely we serve / Because we freely love" (5. 538–39)—in actuality God's rule is based on coercion and the threat of punishment for disobedience. A few lines earlier Raphael informs Adam, "Our voluntary service he requires, / Not our necessitated" (528–29). Although, in a theological reading, the word "requires" could bear the meaning "justly expects," if taken at face value the statement that God "requires" the angels' "voluntary obedience" is self-contradictory, and it exposes the bad faith on which his sovereignty depends. In Paris's (2010) words, God "seems to need to feel that their love is free so it can give him pleasure and at the same time to behave coercively so as to be sure of receiving the adoration he requires" (p. 12). As God himself exclaims, "What pleasure I from such obedience paid" (3.107), if it be not freely proffered by those in his service.

Because of his insatiable need for praise from his underlings, God's places first angels and then humans in a double bind, in which they can choose either to submit and remain "For ever happy" or else to rebel and suffer the consequences. As Abdiel metaphorically expresses this dilemma to Lucifer on the eve of the War in Heaven: "That Golden Scepter which thou didst reject / Is now an Iron Rod to bruise and break / Thy disobedience" (5.886–88). Fish (1967) encapsulates the offer that cannot be refused in his previously quoted comment, "all acts are performed in God's service; what is left to any agent is a choice between service freely rendered and service exacted against his will" (p. 18). But the message, reiterated throughout the poem, that obedience is rewarded and disobedience punished becomes ominous when it is seen to be a manifestation of God's narcissism. Raphael concludes his recitation of the War in Heaven by admonishing Adam, "let it profit thee to have heard / By terrible example the reward / Of disobedience" (6.909–11), while Adam sums up Michael's history lesson in the last two books, "Henceforth I learn, that to obey is best" (12.561). Although obeying the "Golden Scepter" earns God's favor, it comes at the cost of accepting a position of inferiority, while the display of strength that comes with defiance is met with the "Iron Rod" that "bruises and breaks" any claimants to power or even autonomy.

Paris compares the hypocrisy of Satan's worship of God before his rebellion to that of Iago, who confides to Roderigo in the opening scene of Shakespeare's tragedy that he is one of those unscrupulous servants "Who, trimmed in forms and visages of duty, / Keep yet their hearts attending on themselves" (1.1.49–50). The analogy between Iago and Satan extends to what Heinz Kohut (1972) has taught us to recognize as the narcissistic rage experienced by both characters when they are passed over for promotion in the prehistories of their respective works. The narrator describes Satan as having been "of the first, / If not the first Arch-Angel" (5.659–60), implying that he is elder by birth, until he is superseded when God adopts Christ as his spiritual Son, while Iago is infuriated by Othello's disregarding of the "old gradation, where each second / Stood heir to th' first" (1.1.36–37) by preferring the upstart Cassio to the rank of lieutenant while he must remain "his Moorship's ancient" (32).[3]

Although *Othello* provides the obvious antecedent for Satan's relationship with God, Paris's (2010) argument that God's edict is motivated "by his appetite for glory and his desire to punish those who have disappointed him," and that it allows him to replace Lucifer "with a favorite who will give him exactly what he wants" (p. 15), likewise enables us to see his proclamation as a variation on the love test imposed by *King Lear* on his daughters. Both rulers place their subjects in a double bind, although in Milton it is Christ, the loyal "younger" son, who wins his father's love by telling him what he wants to hear and Satan, his disloyal "elder" counterpart, who defies God and is cast out, whereas in Shakespeare the disloyal elder daughters are rewarded for flattering the king and the loyal Cordelia tells him the truth and is banished. Despite Milton's inversions, the common dominator between Lear and God is the narcissism that governs the actions of both authoritarian fathers.

Like King Lear, God the Father possesses a dissociated awareness that he is acting in bad faith, although any attempt by another character to make this knowledge conscious leads to execration and retribution. God's mental state comes out, to recall Empson's formulation, in the way that he keeps "making the necessary excuses without admitting that there is anything to excuse." On no count is God more defensive than that of his responsibility for having set Satan loose when he was already imprisoned in Hell. As Paris (2010) underscores, "he keeps obscuring the fact that he freed Satan and thus set up the fall of Adam and Eve because at some level he is aware that this is what he did" (p. 104). God's inability to admit consciously what he knows unconsciously, moreover, places him in exactly the same position as Milton with respect to the question of whether "God is himself the cause and origin of sin."[4] For if, in Fish's reading, God and Milton are aligned as spokesmen for the "essence of Truth," then one cannot reverse the rabbit—duck paradigm by putting God on trial without also indicting Milton as his co-defendant.

To impugn God as the "evil spirit" of *Paradise Lost* is simultaneously to apprehend the poem as a projection of his inner world. "Because everything that happens is an expression of his will," Paris (2010) writes, "Satan's rebellion, the fall of Adam and Eve, and the subsequent history of humankind can all be seen as manifestations of his psyche" (p. 101). The female characters, Sin and Eve, accordingly, are not simply the incarnated fantasies of their immediate begetters, Satan and Adam, but also disavowed scapegoats for God's own narcissism. Because God is the quintessential controlling parent, to whom all his offspring are attached by a primal bond even though he does not love them for their own sakes, there is no place in the universe where one can escape his gaze. In an exemplification of the dictum of W. R. D. Fairbairn (1952b) concerning the child's need to maintain a tie to a bad object, "it is better to be a sinner in a world ruled by God than to live in a world ruled by the Devil" (pp. 66–67), Satan cries out on Mount Niphates, "Be then his Love accurst, since love or hate, / To me alike, it deals eternal woe" (4.69–70). Even the hatred of the devils in Hell, as Rumrich (1987) has observed, constitutes "an attempt somehow to continue relations with [God]," and "although the devils talk as if they have entered a power struggle and couch their discussions in military idiom, at the heart of their machinations is a failed love" (pp. 96–97).

The effect of the theological premise that the Fall is the result of free will is to induce Adam and Eve to accept responsibility for their own suffering, as well as that of all their descendants. Death is transformed from a natural part of the life cycle into a punishment for sin, for which human beings are expected to feel a crushing burden of guilt. In his anguished introspection after the Fall, Adam concludes that he is "forc'd" to "absolve" God (10.829), whereas "all the blame lights due" (833) on himself. But this assessment grievously inverts the true situation, because it is God who "is himself the cause and origin of sin," but who succeeds in convincing human beings that they have brought on their own loss of innocence. In keeping with Ferenczi's understanding that trauma, as Donna Orange (2011) has expounded, "always included two moments if it were to become pathogenic: the original shocking repetitive abuse or neglect"—God's series of actions that leads to the Fall—"followed by the disavowal, hypocrisy, and rejection both by the perpetrators and by others to whom the devastated child might have turned" (p. 79)—the brainwashing of Adam and Eve by God and his deputies into believing that they are the guilty ones—God in *Paradise Lost* is not simply a narcissistic but an abusive parent, compounding his violation with denial, while the human characters exhibit the self-blame regularly found in trauma victims. As Paris (2010) sums up Adam's predicament, "He seems to be in such a state of helplessness and terror that he has been rendered abject and clings to his abuser" (p. 96).

Like the Oedipus myth, the story of the Fall has been accorded canonical status in the Western tradition as a source of truth about the human condition. But if the doctrine of original sin taken over by Milton from St. Augustine wrongly blames Adam, the child-victim, for the trauma inflicted by his father God, then might not the same be said of Freud's "shibboleth" of the Oedipus complex? For, as revisionist scholars have argued, when Freud in 1897 repudiated his so-called "seduction" theory, which was on the right track even though he gave too much emphasis to sexuality instead of recognizing the shattering effects of the violation of trust on the nascent psyche, and ascribed neurosis instead to universal fantasies of incest and parricide, he scotomized the consequences of the abuse too often experienced by children at the hands of parental figures, while deeming children to be culpable for wishing to have sex with and kill their parents.[5] It is emblematic of the revolution in contemporary psychoanalysis, which has left Freud behind in many respects while retaining those of his contributions that are truly seminal—the dynamic unconscious, the indelible effects of early experience, free association as a clinical method—that Kohut (1982) could ask, "Is not the most significant dynamic-genetic feature of the Oedipus story that Oedipus was a rejected child?" (p. 404).

Freud as God

The creator of a universe over which he presides with unfettered sway. A deep-rooted insecurity leading to demands for unconditional love and obedience from his followers. The imposition of a double bind on those in his orbit, who must choose between accepting his authority while remaining in a subordinate position or asserting their autonomy and being cast out from his presence. A patriarchal order organized around father—son conflicts, in which females are defined as narcissistic creatures and the objects of masculine desire. All these statements about Milton's God and the cosmos of *Paradise Lost* also pertain to Freud and his domain of psychoanalysis. Having completed my synthesis of a logological argument concerning the contradictions inherent in the theological premise that the Fall was solely the result of man's free will with a psychological profile of God as a narcissist, and thereby placed the Romantic approach to *Paradise Lost* on a doubly reinforced theoretical foundation, I propose to conclude by using what we have gleaned about Milton as the basis for a reading of psychoanalysis, which I here take to mean the theoretical system fashioned by Freud and the organized movement that even today remains to no small degree an extension of his personality.

Concerning God's "begetting" of Christ as his Son in Book 5, which precipitates the War in Heaven and everything that ensues in *Paradise Lost*, Rumrich (1987) quotes the observation of J. M. Evans that Milton's decision to make this proclamation the reason for Satan's revolt "is one of the most genuinely original things in the whole poem" (p. 148; see Evans, 1968, p. 224).[6] In his midnight speech to his legions, Satan takes umbrage at God's demand for "double" subservience, "To one and to his image now proclaim'd" (5.783–84). As Rumrich glosses Satan's protest, what he finds galling is that the Son, who had from the beginning been God's *word*, has been made into God's *image*, to whom obedience is henceforth owed by all the angels. By this primal deed, God implements his intention "to transform a naturally good order into a morally good order," with the result that "the manifestation of his glory" that is the purpose of creation "will now be accompanied by the voluntary, moral actions of his creatures, actions performed first and foremost because they are what God wants, not because they promote the advantage of the creature" (p. 162). As we have seen, God himself confirms that this new order exists for his benefit when he asks rhetorically, "What pleasure I from such obedience paid" (3.107), if he cannot persuade himself that his dependents offer their homage freely.

Although he does not say so explicitly, Rumrich's analysis makes it clear that God's designation of Christ as his Son simultaneously marks the inception of patriarchy. Until there is a Son (in Heaven, the only possibility), there can be no Father, and thus the deeper logic of God's action—as well as of Milton's unprecedented decision to make this symbolic "begetting" the mainspring of his poem—is to create a social order founded on father–son relationships, with all the consequences that this entails.

In the history of psychoanalysis, God's elevation of the Son finds an uncanny parallel in a well-known passage from Freud's letter to Jung on April 16, 1909:

> It is strange that on the very same evening when I formally adopted you as eldest son and anointed you—*in partibus infidelium* [in the lands of the unbelievers]—as my successor and crown prince, you should have divested me of my paternal dignity, which divesting seems to have given you as much pleasure as I, on the contrary, derived from the investiture of your person.
>
> (McGuire, 1974, p. 218)

During his recently concluded second visit to Vienna, Jung had gotten the better of Freud's scoffing at his mystical tendencies by accurately predicting that a noise in the bookcase would repeat itself, and in the letter to which Freud is responding Jung had declared that this experience had "freed me inwardly from the oppressive sense of your paternal authority" (p. 217).

Whereas in *Paradise Lost* Milton separates the two poles of the son's relationship to the father into the anointed Christ and the rebellious Satan, Jung, who rebels even as he is being anointed, fuses them into a single ambivalent dynamic. Both Freud and God, however, assert their paternal authority by adopting an "eldest son," and in so doing provoke a crisis of succession by forcing the males who love and wish to work with them into an oedipal straitjacket. From a slightly altered vantage point, Satan's rage against God for bypassing him for promotion in favor of Christ has a further counterpart in psychoanalytic history in the anger unleashed against Freud at the 1910 Nuremberg Congress by Freud's Viennese Jewish followers, led by Wilhelm Stekel, for slighting them, who had been loyal to him for so long, by installing Jung—the Gentile outsider—as president (initially for life) of the newly formed International Psychoanalytical Association. As in *Paradise Lost*, what could be tolerated so long as power rested solely with Freud himself became intolerable when he proclaimed Jung to be his "crown prince" and demanded that the Viennese accept "his great Vicegerent Reign" (5.609) over the psychoanalytic movement. In the same way that God acknowledges obtaining "pleasure" from the obedience of his inferiors, Freud confesses to Jung that he derives "pleasure" from "the investiture of your person." Thus, as Rumrich (1987) has said of God's "begetting" of the Son, the "voluntary, moral actions" that Freud expects of his disciples in falling into line behind Jung as their "Head" (5.606) are to be "performed first and foremost because they are what [Freud] wants, not because they promote the advantage of the creature" (p. 162). Or, in the words of Raphael's injunction to Adam, "Our voluntary service he requires, / Not our necessitated," which means in effect that Freud—like God—will continue to love his subjects only as long as they do as he wishes, and not a moment longer.

Nowhere does Freud resemble Milton's God more closely than in his fondness for dichotomies and in his imposition of a double bind on those around him. According to the law that governs the universe in *Paradise Lost*—epitomized in Abdiel's antithesis between the "Golden Scepter" and the "Iron Rod"—either creatures must submit to God voluntarily and reap the rewards of his favor, or they must submit involuntarily, having been crushed for refusing to accept his authoritarian rule, disguised as an enlightened despotism. Similarly, as Ernest Jones (1955) writes in his biography, Freud exhibited an "obstinate dualism" and "had a difficulty in contemplating any topic unless he could divide it into two opposites, and never more than two" (p. 422). This style of black-and-white thinking was not confined to the theoretical realm, where Freud regularly resorted to such polarities as hunger and love or Eros and the death drive, but extended into his intimate life. When his fiancée, Martha Bernays, had the temerity to suggest that she might prefer to stay with her brother in Vienna because this would ease the burden on her mother, instead of allowing Freud to make arrangements on her behalf, Freud exploded, "If that is so, you are my enemy.... You have only an Either—Or. If you can't be fond enough of me to renounce for my sake your family, then you must lose me" (qtd. p. 130).[7] Just as Martha's desire to consider her mother's needs alongside his own was construed by Freud as defiance and led him to brand her his "enemy," so, too, he famously wrote in *The Interpretation of Dreams* (1900):

> My emotional life has always insisted that I should have an intimate friend and a hated enemy. I have always been able to provide myself afresh with both, and it has not infrequently happened that the ideal situation of childhood has been so completely reproduced that friend and enemy have come together in a single individual.
>
> (p. 483)

Freud's compulsive need to classify other people as either friends or enemies, but then to find both in a "single individual," who is both loved and hated, is displayed to perfection in his simultaneous adoption and repudiation of Jung, though Freud—blind to his own role in the experience—casts all the blame on Jung for having "divested" him of his "paternal dignity." But despite his gratitude to those who remained unswervingly loyal, Freud always tended to devalue such dutiful disciples because, by accepting their subordinate status, they were confessing their weakness and thus could not activate the hatred that was indispensable to stirring his deepest passions. As Samuel Rosenberg (1978) has illuminated Karl Abraham's fate of playing the role of Freud's "less-favored son" in a triangle first with Jung and then with Rank, both of whom eventually rebelled against Freud: "Abraham excluded himself from close friendship with Freud by being too much of a 'friend' and not enough 'enemy'" (pp. 239–40).

If the primal deed of God's "begetting" of the Son marks the inception of patriarchy in *Paradise Lost*, by provoking Satan's rebellion it also leads to the creation of Sin. Just as Freud quashed Martha's desire to take her mother's feelings into account and banished from psychoanalysis those who refused to place his authority above their personal quest for truth, so God's refusal to countenance any assertion of autonomy that conflicts with his creatures' overriding duty of obedience causes him to stigmatize their striving for independence as a treasonous betrayal. Thus, when Sin reminds Satan of how, having sprung Athena-like from his head at the assembly of discontented angels, "Thyself in me thy perfect image viewing / Becam'st enamor'd" (2.764–65), this equation of Satan's resistance to God with narcissism, far from being a self-evident truth, is rather the result of the imposition of an ideology—at once by God within the poem and by Milton as its author—in which it is taken for granted that subservience to the Father forms the bedrock of the natural order of things.

When the character of Sin appears in *Paradise Lost*, she does so not in the irretrievably lost form with which she had allured Satan in Heaven but as the monstrous guardian of Hell's gate, who "seem'd Woman to the waist, and fair, / But ended foul in many a scaly fold / Voluminous and vast, a Serpent arm'd / With mortal sting" (2.650–53). This bifurcation of the female body, also found in Lear's diatribe, "But to the girdle do the gods inherit, beneath is all the fiend's" (4.6.122–23), is a staple of the patriarchal tradition, and it comes complete in Milton with the fantasy of a penis "arm'd / With mortal sting." When Satan is about to fight Death, the fruit of his incestuous union with Sin, who asserts his sovereignty in Hell and whom Satan had been unable to recognize as he had not recognized his erstwhile lover, Sin thrusts herself between the combatants, pleading that they not destroy one another: "O Father, what intends thy hand, she cri'd, / Against thy only Son? What fury, O Son, / Possesses thee to bend that mortal Dart / Against thy father's head?" (2.727–30).

The structure of this allegorical scene is transparently oedipal. Satan and Death seek to kill one another in a struggle for supremacy, and Sin, who comes between them as peacemaker, is also the mother-wife over whom the father and son are contending. By the patriarchal logic of the poem, because Satan had refused to accept the authority of God, his own attempt to assert authority over Death is doomed to failure, and he is saved from being sent back to Hell only by Sin's intervention. Satan's copulation with Sin, moreover, is outdone by Death, who forcibly rapes his mother, which in turn engenders the Hell Hounds that devour Sin's womb, into which they return whenever they please. This three-generational crescendo of incest finds an echo in Book 10, where the causeway built by Sin and Death following the track taken by Satan in his journey to bring about the Fall of Man is described as leading "three sev'ral ways," one to "Empyrean Heav'n," another to "this World," and the last "on the left hand Hell" (321–23). Not only does this intersection evoke the crossroads in *Oedipus Rex* where Oedipus slays Laius, but Earth takes the place of Sin in the maternal position, at once poised between Heaven and Hell and the object of the cosmic struggle pitting God the Father against his son Satan.

Yet it would be unwarranted to conclude from the presence of these oedipal dynamics that Milton's poem furnishes evidence of the universality of the Oedipus complex. On the contrary, the isomorphism in Milton and Freud's depiction of gender relations is a byproduct of their shared allegiance to patriarchy. Just as Sin comes into being as the emanation of incestuous desire and plays the role of the prize in an oedipal rivalry, so Eve—the only other female character in *Paradise Lost*—might be a case study in Freud's paper on narcissism. Eve's first speech, in Book 4, recounts to Adam her memory of her creation, in which she is spontaneously far more attracted to her own reflection than she is to him, out of whose side she has been formed. Once again, just as Satan's refusal to submit to God is equated with Sin, so Eve's incipient strivings for autonomy are stigmatized by her identification with Narcissus. The unseen voice of

God pressures Eve to renounce her desire for her own "smooth wat'ry image" (480) in favor of her ordained role as the object of Adam's desire, "Whose image thou art" (472). But though Eve seems by the end of her speech to have learned her lesson when she acknowledges that "beauty is excell'd by manly grace / And wisdom, which alone is truly fair" (490–91), her susceptibility to Satan's flattery in Book 9 stands as proof that she is unable to efface the stigma of narcissism that inheres in femininity in a patriarchal culture.

In "On Narcissism: An Introduction," Freud (1914b) asserts that "a comparison of the male and female sexes" shows that "there are fundamental differences between them in respect of their type of object-choice" (p. 88). Whereas "complete object-love of the attachment sort is, properly speaking, characteristic of the male," Freud maintains, and features "marked sexual overvaluation" of the beloved, "women, especially if they grow up with good looks, develop a certain self-contentment which compensates them for the social restrictions that are imposed on them in their choice of object," and "it is only themselves that such women love with an intensity comparable to that of the man's love for them" (pp. 88–89). In *Paradise Lost*, not only does Eve exhibit the narcissism predicted by Freud, but Adam manifests "marked sexual overvaluation" of his partner when he confesses to Raphael that he is "only weak / Against the charm of Beauty's powerful glance" (8.532–33). As the archetype of woman in a patriarchal culture, moreover, it should not be surprising that Eve suffers from penis envy. After her Fall, Eve fantasizes that refusing to share the forbidden fruit with Adam would allow her to keep the "odds of Knowledge" for herself, and so "add what wants / In Female Sex" (IX.820–22). But rather than lending credence to Freud's theory of gender differences, Eve's desire for the "phallus" can itself once again be explained by her position of social inferiority, as Freud's feminist critics beginning with Karen Horney (1924) have argued.

In his landmark analysis of Milton's characters, Paris (2010) has observed, "we do not get a direct view of God's inner life, as we do of Satan's in his soliloquies" (p. 101). But given the remarkable series of parallels between Milton's God and Freud, and between the cosmos of *Paradise Lost* and that of psychoanalysis in its classical form, a promising strategy for tackling the psychology of God is to extrapolate from the biography of Freud, about whom surely as much is known as there is about any other human being who has ever lived. In his revisionist study, *Why Freud Was Wrong* (1995), Richard Webster writes:

> For although such secular theories as psychoanalysis and structural anthropology have evidently shed the theism of Christianity, it is not at all clear that they have repudiated the view of human nature which was once associated with creationist theology, and with Judeo-Christian doctrines of sin and redemption.
>
> (p. 7)

Webster here succinctly summarizes the deep, and troubling, affinity, between Milton's doctrine of original sin and Freud's concept of the Oedipus complex, both of which, as I have argued, fail to pay sufficient heed to the role of environmental factors, especially traumatic experiences, in shaping the human psyche, and instead seek to induce traumatized individuals to accept responsibility for the abuse inflicted on them by parental figures. With respect to the character of Freud, which he views through the lens of his outsized ambition, Webster (1995) opens an equally provocative line of inquiry:

> If we are to have any chance of understanding Freud's inner biography, we need to consider in some detail what lay behind this appetite for fame, and ask to what extent Freud's compulsive need for fame may have engendered his psychological theories, rather than, as is normally assumed, his theories generating his fame by their own profundity and intellectual acuity.
>
> (p. 34)

The inversion proposed by Webster in approaching the topic of Freud and fame precisely mirrors the shift that occurs if we replace the theological readings of Milton by Lewis and Fish, which take for granted a "hierarchical conception" of the universe in which creatures are expected to give glory to God because he is the Supreme Being, with a logological and psychological analysis that approaches God as a character who covets glory from others to fuel his own narcissism. Thus, if we can get to the bottom of Freud's "compulsive need for fame," then we will have gained a window into the mind of God that is not afforded directly in *Paradise Lost*. Webster

(1995) notes that children who, like Freud, are treated as exceptional by their parents from infancy on "tend to experience their parents' adulation not as an unconditional gift but as something much more complex" (p. 35). Indeed, "in countless subtle or not so subtle ways the affection and approval which parents give to their children tend to be conditional on 'good' behavior"—that is, on complying with parental expectations—and such children, therefore, "grow up weighed down by the sense of having incurred an essentially unrepayable debt which they must, nonetheless, spend the rest of their lives endeavoring to repay" (p. 38).

Webster's description of the "unrepayable debt" that the emotionally burdened "gifted child"—in Alice Miller's (1979) apt phrase—must nevertheless spend a lifetime "endeavoring to repay" cannot fail to remind the reader of Satan's soliloquy on Mount Niphates, in which he ruminates on "The debt immense of endless gratitude" that he feels was exacted from him by God as a condition of his existence, "So burdensome, still paying, still to owe" (4.52–53). Since there is evidence to support the hypothesis that Freud's (1900) ambition was warped by feelings of inadequacy introjected from his primary caretakers—epitomized by his father's rebuke, "'The boy will come to nothing'" (p. 216), after he had urinated in his parents' bedroom as a youngster—and Milton's God is Freud's literary double, then it may be inferred that God, by projective identification, is causing Satan to experience the same psychological conflicts that he must have suffered in what we can only imagine to have been his own childhood.[8]

Because an insatiable desire for glory stems ultimately from the oppressive conditionality of the "affection and approval" bestowed on many precociously talented children by their parents, Webster (1995) goes on, "for this very reason extreme ambition is almost always related to a sense of resentment—and perhaps above all to a desire for vengeance" (p. 38). But as Paris has shown, no one exhibits more conspicuous signs of being driven by a "desire for vengeance" than God himself, enraged as he is by the hypocrisy of Lucifer's submission to him even prior to his rebellion, and who then releases Satan from the lake of fire in Hell only so that he will have a justification for torturing him to an even more incalculable extent throughout eternity. God, therefore, must, like Freud, have been a conditionally loved child, who grew up burdened by the weight of an "essentially unrepayable debt," and who then takes out his "sense of resentment" on the universe by engaging in a feud in which he unleashes his "desire for vengeance" against Satan—and anyone else who dares to stand up to him—to his heart's content.

Webster (1995) concludes his analysis of Freud's "compulsive need for fame" by explaining how the achievement of great renown paradoxically at once fulfills the "emotional contract" entered into involuntarily by the child with his parents while also "settling old scores" with them:

> For to be revered, to be worshipped, to be loved unconditionally by strangers is to prove to the parents who, by the very intensity of their conditional adulation, made them feel unloved and unlovable, that they were mistaken. At a certain tortured extreme it would seem that it is just such a dream of exchanging intimate rejection for universal acceptance which underlies messianic fantasies.
>
> (p. 39)

In Book 3, after God and the Son have completed their colloquy in which the Son agrees to sacrifice himself to redeem humankind, God's final speech is greeted by "all / The multitude of Angels with a shout / Loud as numbers without number" (344–46). The angels then turn their attention where it most properly belongs: "Thee Father first they sung Omnipotent, / Immutable, Immortal, Infinite, / Eternal King" (371–73). It is thus not simply "messianic fantasies" but what Jones (1913) has dubbed the "God complex" that is to be explained by the "dream of exchanging intimate rejection for universal acceptance," and there could be no more graphic instance of being "revered," "worshipped," and "loved unconditionally by strangers" than this heavenly tableau in which God basks in the adulation of a faceless crowd that is by its very intensity a measure of the emotional pain to which he must at one time have been repeatedly subjected to make the craving for glory so compulsively addicting.

Beneath the more obvious "oedipal issues of law, obedience, and punishment" in *Paradise Lost*, therefore, there is in the epic, to draw on Rumrich's (1987) insight once again, a "primary, pervasive concern with negotiations between narcissistic longing for perfect recognition and the recalcitrance of an unresponsive reality" (p. 4), and the same is true of the Freudian cosmos. But neither Freud nor Milton's God—to say nothing of the apologists for either—would be prepared to admit that their visions of the human condition, or troubled history of personal relationships, are afflicted by any astigmatism or symptoms of a character disorder. For Fish

(1967), as we have seen, "God's speech represents the essence of Truth" (p. 87), and when God calls man an "ingrate" (3.97) for refusing to heed his prohibition against eating from the Tree of Knowledge, he does so without emotion because "ingrate" is "a term not of reproach, but of definition" (p. 64). God is alleged to be engaged in nothing more than "a logically necessary inquiry" so that the Fall may be "placed in the context of total reality" (p. 65). Similarly, in "On Narcissism" (1914b), Freud, aware that some might take exception to his analogy to "the charm of certain animals which seem not to concern themselves about us, such as cats and the large beasts of prey," hastens to assure the reader that "this description of the feminine form of erotic life is not due to any tendentious desire to depreciate women," and indeed that "tendentiousness" of any kind is "quite alien to me" (p. 89). Freud, that is, like God, sees himself as devoid of subjectivity and simply speaking the truth, so that what he says about women is not attributable to any bias but must be "placed in the context of total reality" as unveiled by psychoanalysis.

In the August 4, 1932, entry to his posthumously published *Clinical Diary* (Dupont, 1985), to which he gave the heading "Personal Causes for the Erroneous Development of Psychoanalysis," Ferenczi, who knew Freud more intimately than anyone else in the psychoanalytic world, sums up his analysis of Freud's character: "In his conduct Fr[eud] plays only the role of the castrating god, he wants to ignore the traumatic moment of his own castration in childhood; he is the only one who does not have to be analyzed" (p. 188). In what can also be read as a profound commentary on God the Father in *Paradise Lost*, Ferenczi sees Freud as behaving like a "castrating god," but recognizes that his autocratic tendencies are defenses designed to forestall awareness of "the traumatic moment of his own castration in childhood," which should be taken to mean the cumulative experiences of being shamed by his parents that led to Freud's "compulsive need for fame."[9] Because of his narcissistic injuries, Freud set himself up as the analyst privy to everyone else's secrets, but was "the only one who does not have to be analyzed," just as the propagandists for Milton's God seek to exempt him from Empson's law that "all the characters are on trial in any civilized narrative."

The opposition between the "Golden Scepter" and the "Iron Rod" permeates Ferenczi's relationship to Freud. As Ferenczi recalls, Freud could "tolerate my being a son only until the moment when I contradicted him for the first time" (Dupont, 1985, p. 185), when he refused to serve as Freud's amanuensis and asked to collaborate with him on the Schreber case in the course of their 1910 trip to Sicily. During Ferenczi's period as an ardent loyalist, Freud "could indulge in his theoretical fantasies undisturbed by any contradiction and use the enthusiastic admiration of his blinded pupil to boost his own self-esteem" (p. 185). For his part, Ferenczi, "of the first, / If not the first Arch-Angel" in the "glory system" of the Freudian heaven, profited from his willingness to curry favor with Freud by gaining "membership in a distinguished group guaranteed by the king, indeed with rank of field marshal for myself (crown prince fantasy)"—the same fantasy that had animated Freud's "anointing" of Jung—and likewise "learned from [Freud] and from his kind of technique various things that made one's life and work more comfortable: the calm, unemotional reserve; the unruffled assurance that one knew better; and the theories, the seeking and finding of the causes of failure in the patient instead of partly in ourselves" (p. 185). The qualities that Ferenczi saw in Freud and for decades sought to emulate—"calm, unemotional reserve," "the unruffled assurance that one knew better"—are equally attributes of Milton's God, who purports to be devoid of subjectivity and to be the last word on everything. And just as Freud "finds the causes of failure" in his patients, rather than looking to himself, when an analysis ends badly, so, too, God holds Adam and Eve to be solely responsible for the catastrophe of the Fall.

Nor is Ferenczi oblivious to the feminist implications of Freud's role as a "castrating god," commenting on "the unilaterally androphile orientation of his theory of sexuality," which Ferenczi acknowledges having followed in his own phylogenetic fantasy, *Thalassa* (1924), but which he now realizes "clings too closely to the words of the master" and would require a "complete rewriting" (Dupont, 1985, p. 187) if it were to reflect his current views. But if, as Luce Irigaray (1974) has written of Freud, "man is explicitly presented as the yardstick of the same," the "hitherto masked desire for the same" (p. 28) is also what motivates God's begetting of the Son as his "image" in *Paradise Lost*. It may therefore be said of Milton no less than of Freud that the work of both authors, in Irigaray's words, "by exhibiting this 'symptom,' this crisis point in metaphysics where we find exposed that sexual 'indifference' that had assured metaphysical coherence and 'closure,'" lays bare the fissures in the very patriarchal order they seek to legitimate, and in so doing "offers it up for our analysis" (p. 28).

In setting down his valedictory reflections on "the personal causes for the erroneous development of psychoanalysis," Ferenczi's purpose was neither to bash Freud nor to reject psychoanalysis. On the contrary, by compassionately yet with unsparing honesty arraigning Freud for the human failings that he was unable to admit to himself, and showing how these blind spots had damaged his beloved creation, Ferenczi sought to "rescue psychoanalysis from Freud" (Rudnytsky, 2011) in order to preserve what was of enduring value in Freud's legacy so that it could be passed on to future generations. In the same spirit, by undertaking to reanimate the Romantic reading of *Paradise Lost*, and to put God on trial for his crimes against humanity, my hope has been to show how out of Milton's tragically flawed vision there emerges an artistic masterpiece of inexhaustible fascination and imperishable beauty.

Notes

1 All quotations from Milton's works are to the edition of Hughes (1957), with book and line numbers of *Paradise Lost* given parenthetically in the text.
2 By contrast, Waldock (1947) dismisses Blake's "rather unhelpful paradox," which "might suggest the presence of unresolved conflicts in Milton's mind" (p. 2), and he likewise distances himself from the thesis of E. M. W. Tillyard (1930) that there are "unconscious meanings" in *Paradise Lost*. Although Waldock (1947) acknowledges that what Tillyard calls "'unconscious meanings' really are in the poem," he thinks that Tillyard's "name for them is wrong" (p. 122). But given Waldock's own premise that "it was out of the question for Milton to admit to himself difficulties in the scriptural story of the Fall—impossible for him, really, to see them," and that he "never to the end became aware of the gravest of the narrative problems he had been grappling with" (p. 21), Waldock's aversion to Tillyard's implicitly psychoanalytic terminology would appear to be purely semantic and not substantive.
3 My quotations here from *Othello*, as from *King Lear* next, are from the latest Arden editions of the plays. In Chapter 8, I subordinate the narcissistic rage that is a component of Iago's individual pathology to an analysis of his function as a prototypical "social character" in early modern capitalism.
4 See Waldock's (1947) observation, quoted in note 2, that "it was out of the question for Milton to admit to himself difficulties in the scriptural story of the Fall—impossible for him, really, to see them" (p. 21), even though he rejects, for no apparent reason, Tillyard's conclusion that there are "unconscious meanings" in *Paradise Lost*.
5 Mary Marcel (2005) has laid out a compelling case that Freud's espousal of the theory of the Oedipus complex was a defensive response to his recovery during his self-analysis of memories of abuse by his nanny during his early childhood in Freiberg. Larry Wolff (1988) has given the definitive account of Freud's concurrent neglect of the shocking stories of child abuse reported in the Viennese press in the late 1890s. On the differences between Freud's pre-1897 "seduction" theory and the prescient conceptualization of trauma put forward by Ferenczi in his final phase, see Guasto (2014).

6 To the same effect, Rumrich (1987) quotes William B. Hunter, Jr.'s remark that, prior to Milton, "the exaltation of the Son ha[d] never been related to Satan in this way by any Christian tradition" (p. 161; see Hunter, 1971, p. 118). Although Hunter denies Milton's Arianism—the heretical belief that the Son is subordinate to the Father—Rumrich argues with greater cogency the view accepted by most scholars that "Milton's understanding of the Son is categorically Arian" (p. 161) in *Paradise Lost*, just as it is in *The Christian Doctrine*.

7 After Adler's break with Freud in 1912, Freud likewise imposed an ultimatum—for which he made an exception only for Lou Andreas-Salomé—that no one who attended the meetings of Adler's Society for Individual Psychology would be admitted to meetings of the Vienna Psychoanalytic Society. As Max Graf (1942), the musicologist and father of Little Hans, subsequently recalled: "I was unable and unwilling to submit to Freud's 'do' or 'don't' . . . and nothing was left for me but to withdraw from his circle" (p. 475).

8 Freud's insecure attachment to his parents is superimposed on his treatment by his abusive nanny, who, as he reported to Fliess in his letter of October 3–4, 1897, "instilled in me a high opinion of my own capacities" but also "complained because I was clumsy and unable to do anything," memories that fueled Freud's present-day feelings of "impotence as a therapist" (Masson, 1985, pp. 268–69).

9 As Ferenczi restates his observation without resorting to phallic terminology, "Thus the antitraumatic in Fr[eud] is a protective device against insight into his own weaknesses" (Dupont, 1985, p. 186).

Chapter 2

The Indispensability of Erich Fromm

The Rehabilitation of a "Forgotten" Psychoanalyst

> "Some human beings affect you so deeply that your life is forever changed."
> —Gérard D. Khoury, "A Crucial Encounter"

A Life-Changing Experience

It always begins with an act of reading. Winnicott's *Playing and Reality* (1971), Ferenczi's *Clinical Diary* (Dupont, 1985), Groddeck's *Book of the It* (1923), Nina Coltart's "Slouching towards Bethlehem" (1986), or—to go back to the beginning—Ernest Jones's (1953, 1955, 1957) biography of Freud and, even before that, Norman O. Brown's *Life Against Death* (1959): all these have been, for me, life-changing experiences, the most passionate love affairs in my lifelong romance with psychoanalysis. To this list must now be added Erich Fromm's *Escape from Freedom* (1941). I confess that I had never read *Escape from Freedom*, and my knowledge of Fromm's work was confined to a sense of general agreement with his perspective on Freud, until quite recently when, spurred on by Adrienne Harris's (2014) review of Lawrence Friedman's (2013) biography of Fromm in the *Journal of the American Psychoanalytic Association*, I moved *Escape from Freedom* to the top of my "must-read" list. The result was the intellectual equivalent of falling in love, the familiar feeling that here was something for which I had been searching without realizing it, after which I would never look at psychoanalysis—or at life—in the same way again.

The more I immersed myself in Fromm, the more I was struck by how much my longstanding concerns have overlapped with his and how much I would have benefited had I heeded his writings sooner. Shortly before this experience, I had published the first chapter of this book in essay form. No sooner had I read *Escape from Freedom*, where Fromm sets forth his concept of the authoritarian character, than I realized that here was the indispensable missing linchpin to my comparison of Freud to the character of God in Milton's *Paradise Lost* as patriarchal fathers who impose a double bind on their followers that forces them to choose between the equally unpalatable alternatives of obedience and subordination, on the one hand, and rebellion and rejection, on the other. I then picked up my copy of *Sigmund Freud's Mission* (1959b) and saw that Fromm had actually a chapter in that book titled "Freud's Authoritarianism," so it was simply due to my not having sufficiently appreciated his importance that I had neglected to make use of him in my essay on Milton.

Similarly, although I had cited Fromm in a chapter on Little Hans in *Reading Psychoanalysis* (Rudnytsky, 2002a, p. 40), it was only on rereading his essay (1968b) on Freud's case history that I realized how closely my critique of Freud for his underrating of environmental factors as well as his patriarchal bias had been anticipated by Fromm and that I ought to have acknowledged more explicitly the extent to which I was following in his footsteps. By the same token, my sole mention of Fromm in *Rescuing Psychoanalysis from Freud and Other Essays in Re-Vision* is in the introduction where I name him as one of the "noblest spirits of psychoanalysis" (Rudnytsky, 2011, p. xxiii), but only recently did I discover that the title of my book had been foreshadowed by the volume of Fromm's (1992c) writings posthumously published by Rainer Funk as *The Revision of Psychoanalysis*.

Finally, in the course of researching my book in progress on Ferenczi's mutual analysis with Elizabeth Severn, I was led first to Fromm's (1958a, 1958b) refutation of Jones's impugning of the sanity of Rank and Ferenczi in his biography of Freud, and from there to the correspondence in the Fromm Archives in Tübingen, which was made available to me in digital form with characteristic generosity by Funk.[1] From this correspondence I could see that Fromm had been in contact not only with those who had known Ferenczi in his final years—especially Clara Thompson and Izette de Forest, both of whom became Fromm's analysands after having been in analysis with Ferenczi in Budapest—but also with those who had known Rank, including Jessie Taft, Fay B. Karpf, and Harry Bone, as well as with Carl and Sylva Grossman, who had known Groddeck in Baden-Baden. The Grossmans (1965) later published the first biography of Groddeck, while Karpf (1953) and Taft (1958) were the authors of the first books on Rank, as was de Forest (1954) on Ferenczi. I suddenly had the epiphany that Rank, Ferenczi, and Groddeck were the same figures I had brought together in *Reading Psychoanalysis* and celebrated for having inaugurated the "relational turn" in psychoanalysis in their landmark works of 1923 and 1924. It was uncanny to realize that, as early as the 1950s, Fromm had been the foremost advocate for the identical triad of first-generation analysts to whom I had independently gravitated nearly a half-century later.

It might seem perverse to claim that the reputation of a writer whose books sold literally millions of copies and who became one of America's most famous public intellectuals might be in need of rehabilitation. And yet, as Neil McLaughlin (1998a, 1998b) has documented in two seminal articles, Fromm has indeed become "forgotten" insofar as he was not only "hated within the Freudian establishment with a special passion" for being "a unique combination of a Freudian revisionist, Marxist social thinker, and popular writer" but he has also remained "far more marginal to contemporary Freudian thought" (1998b, p. 116) than have the other two leading representatives of neo-Freudianism, Karen Horney and Harry Stack Sullivan. To Fromm belongs the distinction of having been attacked on all sides, including by his former colleagues in the Frankfurt School; and in finding himself "caught in no man's land," as McLaughlin (1998a) has elucidated, the trajectory of Fromm's reputation makes him the antithesis not only of Jacques Derrida, the Pied Piper of deconstruction, who so successfully courted the centers of American intellectual power and prestige beginning in the late 1960s, but likewise of George Orwell, who "was also famous and relatively marginal to the academy," but who, paradoxically, "gained support from intellectuals who had little in common with his democratic socialism," whereas "Fromm's strongest enemies were often intellectuals who essentially shared his basic socialist political perspective" (p. 227).

Although I have borrowed McLaughlin's designation of Fromm as "forgotten," I refer to him not as a "forgotten intellectual" but rather as a "forgotten psychoanalyst." It is not to dispute Kieran Durkin's (2014) thesis that "radical humanism" constitutes the unifying principle of Fromm's thought, "irrespective of the differences that obtain between periods" (p. 3), to claim that Fromm's sense of himself as a psychoanalyst was at the core of his professional identity and stamped the successive iterations of his humanist project. Indeed, it was above all Fromm's identity as a psychoanalyst that made him a lightning rod for criticism and caused the decline of his reputation. It is not by coincidence that Max Horkheimer, on behalf of the supposed radicals of the Frankfurt School, and the psychoanalytically orthodox Karl Menninger should have come together from opposite sides of the ideological spectrum to denigrate Fromm's credentials as a psychoanalyst. Even though Fromm "considered himself a psychoanalyst," Menninger wrote in a review of *Escape from Freedom*, he was in reality a "distinguished sociologist" who with a "curious presumptuousness" had merely exercised his right to apply "psychoanalytic theory to sociological problems" (qtd. in McLaughlin, 1998b, pp. 123–24), just as Horkheimer described Fromm in a 1949 letter to the publishers of the *Philosophical Review* as "the head of one of the 'revisionist' schools of psychoanalysis" who had "tried to 'sociologize' deep psychology, thereby ... making it more superficial" (qtd. in Funk, 1999a, p. 101).

In contrast to Sullivan and Horney, who died in 1949 and 1952 respectively, moreover, Fromm was not only a leading neo-Freudian "revisionist." He was also the most acute analyst of psychoanalytic politics in the heyday of Freud-worship and someone who fought a series of courageous private and public battles with the representatives of the Freud establishment. Even more than Fromm's controversial engagements with the theory of psychoanalysis, it was his attempts to expose and counteract the ossification of Freud's legacy into a quasi-religious movement that led to his becoming a *persona non grata*. My wager in this book is that, nearly forty years after Fromm's death, the psychoanalytic profession has finally reached a point where his heroism can be recognized and the same qualities that once made him an outcast can be appreciated as those that render his rediscovery indispensable to securing our future.

Just as Fromm (1959a) recommended that in clinical work "the first thing one should do is to form an idea of what this person was meant to be, and what his neurosis has done to the person that he was meant to be" (p. 30), so, too, in undertaking what he called (1992b) a "literary psychoanalysis" of Freud he was guided by the principle that "every creative thinker sees further than he is able to express or is aware of," which makes it incumbent on a commentator to recognize how that thinker may be at once "ahead of himself" and limited by the personally or culturally determined blind spots that lead to "distortions in the author's thinking" (pp. 22–23). In applying Fromm's own method to Fromm himself, I will be seeking to disentangle what in *Escape from Freedom* (1941) he terms "the genuine growth of the self" that constitutes the "unfolding of a nucleus that is peculiar for this one person and only for him" from those places in his work where "the growth on the basis of the self is blocked," resulting in the superimposition of a "pseudo self" that is "essentially the incorporation of extraneous patterns of thinking and feeling" (p. 290). If Fromm's language here reminds us of Winnicott, that may provide a clue to the perspective from which I will be paying tribute to Fromm's enduring greatness while not failing to point out what I regard as the limitations of his thought, as he himself (1980) sought to do with Freud.

Oppositional Analysts

There is no better place to begin a study of Fromm's writings on psychoanalysis than with his paper "The Social Determinants of Psychoanalytic Therapy," published in 1935 in Horkheimer's *Zeitschrift für Sozialforschung* and not translated into English until 2000. Here we have what we may designate as Fromm's starting point and springboard, which propels him into his first period that reaches its culmination in *Escape from Freedom*.

By the time Fromm published this paper, he had moved to the United States and his first marriage, to Frieda Reichmann, eleven years his senior, had dissolved, though they were not divorced until the 1940s, and he had begun his prolonged but conflict-ridden affair with Horney, who was not eleven but fifteen years older than Fromm. As is notorious, Reichmann had been Fromm's analyst in Heidelberg when they began the affair that led to their marriage in 1926, the same year in which they became founding members of the Southwest German Psychoanalytic Working Group, a satellite of the German Psychoanalytic Society in Berlin. Other integral members of this collective, which evolved in 1929 into the Psychoanalytic Institute of Frankfurt, included Heinrich Meng and Karl Landauer. It is an indication of the extent of Fromm's dependency on Reichmann at this period in his life that he emulated her in subsequently obtaining analysis from Wilhelm Wittenberg in Munich as well as from Hanns Sachs in Berlin, where Reichmann subsidized his analytic training. Between his voluntarily undertaken analysis with Wittenberg and his required training analysis with Sachs, Fromm also had some form of therapeutic contact with Landauer in Frankfurt.

Extremely illuminating information about Fromm's experience with the German Psychoanalytic Society has recently been unearthed by Michael

Schröter. It has long been known that, after two years as an associate member, Fromm in 1932 had been elected a full member of the German Society, entitling him to membership in the International Psychoanalytical Association (Roazen, 2001, p. 9). What Schröter (2015) has gleaned from a letter of May 19, 1928, from Max Eitingon to Landauer, which he found in the Eitingon papers in the Israel State Archives in Jerusalem, however, is that even before he became an associate member Fromm lectured "as a guest" at meetings of the German Society first in 1927 and again in 1928, but neither of these presentations—"Healing of a Case of Pulmonary Tuberculosis during Psychoanalytic Treatment" and "Psychology of the Petty Bourgeois"—was well received by the triumvirate of Eitingon, Sachs, and Sándor Radó. These lectures, moreover, were manifestly efforts by Fromm to gain membership in the German Psychoanalytic Society, to which he was entitled to apply by virtue of his affiliation with the Southwest German Working Group, on the basis of his personal analyses with Reichmann, Landauer, and Wittenberg as well as intellectual immersion in the field. Fromm, however, was twice deferred and finally left with no alternative but to go to Berlin for formal training, including his didactic analysis with Sachs, which he appears to have commenced in February 1929. In September 1930—the same year in which he joined the Frankfurt Institute for Social Research—he gave a formal membership lecture, "On the Belief in the Omnipotence of Thoughts," leading to his election as an associate member of the German Society in October and at last qualifying him to practice as a psychoanalyst.

By 1935, therefore, Fromm was in impeccable standing in the world of psychoanalysis. But though he had not yet commenced the overt political battles that would result in his leading the charge against Jones and in the publication of *Sigmund Freud's Mission*, Fromm had traveled what Schröter (2015) terms a "thorny way" on his training journey, which evinced "certain parallels" (p. 4) with the obstacles encountered by Reichmann, who earlier in the decade had likewise been advised of the insufficiency of her analysis with Wittenberg (who was not a training analyst) and obligated to commute from Heidelberg to Berlin for an approved analysis with Sachs before being recognized as a psychoanalyst in 1927. As Gail A. Hornstein (2000) has written in her biography of Fromm-Reichmann, "Frieda seems to have barely tolerated Sachs," who was the personification of the unresponsive classical analyst, and she must have considered his "worshipful attitude" toward Freud—symbolized by his placing a bust of Freud on a pedestal so that it faced his patients on the analytic couch—to be "ridiculous" (p. 33). Thus, as Schröter (2015) has argued, although Fromm in "The Social Determinants of Psychoanalytic Therapy" "made reference to Freud's writings, he (also) in subterranean fashion settled the score with his own training analyst," and the new direction charted by Fromm in his psychoanalytic writings of the mid-1930s "could to that extent have been owed to a critical reflection on his analytic experiences in Berlin" (p. 6).

Indeed, Fromm's revolutionary spirit is on full display in "The Social Determinants of Psychoanalytic Therapy," and we see him here at his most farsighted and visionary, with only the slightest hint of an opacity that becomes a greater cause for concern in his later writings. But if Fromm's intellectual radicalism received a negative impetus from his struggle with Sachs and the German Psychoanalytic Society, an equally powerful motive on the positive side is not far to seek. Through his connection with Reichmann, Fromm had come into frequent contact with Groddeck (another member of the Southwest German Psychoanalytic Working Group) in Baden-Baden, where he likewise met Ferenczi. According to Grossman and Grossman (1965), who heard the story from Fromm himself, in September 1926, shortly before Ferenczi was to leave for the United States, Fromm was present "when Groddeck delivered a forthright attack on the method of psychoanalytical training," to which "Ferenczi made no defense" (p. 164). The joint influence of these master spirits, both of whom had died within the past two years, infuses Fromm's 1935 paper and largely accounts for his capacity to formulate such a lucid and trenchant critique of Freud even while the latter was still alive. Ironically, as Schröter (2015) observes, despite appearing in Horkheimer's journal, "this essay not only provoked the objection of analytic colleagues such as Fenichel and Landauer, it also marked the beginning of Fromm's scientific alienation from the Institute for Social Research" (p. 6). According to Theodor Adorno, the text was "sentimental and outright false" and it placed Adorno "in the paradoxical situation of defending Freud" (qtd. p. 6). In crystallizing Fromm's perspective on psychoanalysis, therefore, "The Social Determinants of Psychoanalytic Therapy" also cast him for the first time in his quintessential role as an independent thinker caught in the crossfire between the loyalists of the Frankfurt School, on the one hand, and of the Freudian movement, on the other.

Although Fromm (1935) praises as "one of Freud's most magnificent achievements" the creation of a "situation of radical openness and truthfulness" (p. 151) in the analytic relationship, the main thrust of his paper is to show how Freud fell short of this ideal in practice by evincing "the social taboos of the bourgeoisie, hidden behind the idea of tolerance" (p. 154). Despite his occasional willingness to criticize "bourgeois sexual morality" (p. 155), Fromm maintains, Freud expects the patient "to act according to the bourgeois norm," which "means to fulfill the ideals of the present society and to respect its taboos" (p. 157). To illustrate how Freud "regards, down to the least detail, the capitalistic attitude as the natural healthy one," Fromm cites his admonition that the patient should be required to "pay for the hours allotted to him by agreement, even when he is prevented by illness or other reasons from coming into analysis" (p. 157). In adopting this stance, Fromm continues, Freud does not take into account "that the analyst gains free time for himself by the patient's not coming" and he thereby mistakenly equates "the capitalist character in its most developed form" with a supposedly "natural and human" attitude, such that "all deviations from this norm are regarded as 'neurotic'" (p. 157). By this specious reasoning, if a person fails to behave "in the socially accepted way," such as by joining a "radical party" or by entering "upon a marriage not according in age or social class with the bourgeois norm," or "even if he questions the Freudian theory, this just proves that he has unanalyzed complexes—and resistances to boot if he contradicts this diagnosis of the analyst" (p. 157).

In addition to "questioning the Freudian theory," Fromm himself was politically radical and his marriage to Reichmann, not to mention his affair with Horney, was not in keeping with the "bourgeois norm." There may thus be a personal motive to his indictment of Freud for "the unconscious authoritarian, patricentric attitude usually hidden behind 'tolerance'" (p. 159). Not only does Fromm identify Freud as an authoritarian character, but—as I have argued is also true of Milton's God—he observes that this patriarchal constellation manifests itself with special clarity in his "attitude toward his followers, whose only choice is between complete subordination or the prospect of a ruthless fight of their teacher against them, entailing also pecuniary consequences" (p. 158).

Having introduced Freud's relations to his followers into the discussion, Fromm turns his attention to the conflict "between Freud and his closest circle on the one hand, and 'oppositional' analysts on the other" (p. 159). As "typical representatives of this oppositional attitude" (p. 159) he instances Groddeck and Ferenczi and proceeds to honor the memory of these two men whom he had personally known. Although Groddeck "despised science," refused to express himself in "systematic theoretical form," and espoused a "reactionary stance in social matters," Fromm credits Groddeck's "feudal" outlook with liberating him from "the hidden prudery so typical of Freud" and enabling him to adopt an attitude toward patients that "was not soft, but full of humanity and friendliness" (p. 159). For Groddeck, in contrast to Freud, "the patient was at the center, and it was the analyst's task to serve him" (p. 159). Fromm's antipathy to Groddeck's "lack of rational and scientific inclination and rigor" leads him to underestimate *The Book of the It* by alleging that Groddeck's "literary legacy can in no way give an impression of the importance of his personality," but he counterbalances this by testifying that "his impact was above all a personal one" and that Ferenczi's intellectual development "can only be understood in light of the strong influence Groddeck exercised on him" (p. 159).

The one paragraph that Fromm devotes to Groddeck serves as a prelude to his far more extended discussion of Ferenczi. With exquisite sensitivity, Fromm teases out how, "during the last years of his life," Ferenczi "more and more moved away from Freud," as well as how Freud's "peculiar character"—that is, his authoritarianism—"let this theoretical difference turn into a personal tragedy" (p. 159) for Ferenczi. Because Ferenczi, unlike Groddeck, was "soft and anxious," Fromm explains, "he never dared to place himself in open opposition to Freud, and the more he realized that his views on the inadequacies of the Freudian technique had to lead to a personal confrontation with the latter, the more difficult his personal situation became" (p. 159). Ferenczi's inhibition "made him hide the antagonism among assurances of his loyalty," so that "it may be scarcely comprehensible, when reading Ferenczi's works, that the slight nuances in which Ferenczi expressed his deviation from Freud could be the expression of a conflict" (p. 159). Agreeing with Ferenczi that the analyst should show the patient "a certain amount of love," Fromm argues that it is precisely "the self-evidence of Ferenczi's demands" and the diffidence with which he expressed his opposition to Freud that demonstrate most vividly "the peculiarity of the Freudian position" (p. 159).

In "The Social Determinants of Psychoanalytic Therapy," Fromm proves himself to be at once a masterful analyst of the Freud-Ferenczi relationship and authentically Ferenczian in his own thinking. Like Ferenczi, Fromm connects the "lack of . . . unconditional affirmation in the average bourgeois family" with the patient's longing "for an unconditional acknowledgment of his claims to happiness and well-being" that is "necessary for his recovery" (p. 158). Without using the word "trauma," he understands that when a person does not receive "unconditional affirmation" in childhood it must leave deep wounds, as a result of which "he needs an environment in which he is certain of the unconditional and unshakeable affirmation of his claims to happiness and well-being" (p. 158) in order to heal. If such a vulnerable patient goes to "an analyst of the patricentric character type," by whom he is treated not with love but rather with a "frequently unconscious" hostility, this "not only makes all therapeutic success impossible but also represents a serious danger to the patient's psychic health" (p. 159). In contrast to the widespread tendency to minimize the divergences between Freud and Ferenczi, Fromm accurately sees them as antithetical incarnations of a psychoanalytic identity and he takes Ferenczi's critique of Freud to its radical conclusion: "His difference with Freud is fundamental: the difference between a humane, philanthropic attitude, affirming the analysand's unqualified right to happiness—and a patricentric-authoritarian, deep down misanthropic, 'tolerance'" (p. 162).

The brilliance of this paper sets a standard against which Fromm's subsequent writings on Freud can be measured. But it nonetheless contains a "distortion" that impedes Fromm from reaching what my "literary psychoanalysis" would envision to be the full potential of his own thought. Ironically, this blind spot involves his famous concept of "social character" and it is encapsulated in the sentence: "Freud's personality and the characteristic features of his theory are ultimately to be understood not from individual but from general social conditions" (p. 163). Although this formulation has the great virtue of enabling Fromm to explain how Freud's outlook is indeed prototypical of the "patricentric-authoritarian" attitudes of bourgeois society, which are likewise an expression of "the capitalist character in its most developed form," it has the equally great defect of leaving Fromm with no way of explaining how Ferenczi, who belonged to the same social class as Freud, somehow arrived at a "humane, philanthropic" world-view that is diametrically opposed to Freud's ostensibly benevolent but "deep down misanthropic 'tolerance.'"

Fromm is aware of the problem, but his solution remains unsatisfactory. After asserting that "from a sociological point of view, Freud's attitude is the logical one," whereas "Ferenczi was an outsider" who "was in opposition to the fundamental structure of his class," Fromm asks us to believe that Ferenczi "was not aware of his opposition" (p. 163). But though Ferenczi may have been cautious about expressing his disagreements with Freud openly, there can be no doubt that he was cognizant of the extent to which they had parted ways, as can be seen not only in his *Clinical Diary* and in his correspondence with Freud but also in his final sequence of papers from "The Principle of Relaxation and Neocatharsis" (1930) to "Confusion of Tongues" (1933). The fact, as Fromm (1935) says, that "Ferenczi succumbed in this struggle" (p. 163) with Freud is irrelevant both to whether he was aware of his status as "an outsider" psychoanalytically and sociologically and to how his differences from Freud are to be explained. All Fromm can say on the latter point is that "the example of Ferenczi shows . . . that the Freudian attitude need not be that of all analysts," and that what he here calls (for what I believe to be the first time in his writings) the "social character structure" is no more than an "average standard" from which "a number of individuals" will differ to a greater or lesser extent for reasons "stemming from the individual fate of the person in question" (p. 163).[2]

Even in introducing his concept of "social character structure," therefore, which receives systematic exposition in the appendix to *Escape from Freedom*, Fromm has no alternative but to have recourse to "the individual fate of the person" to account for how two men who ought to have the same "social character" turn out not merely to show "gradual differences" but to be as "radically different" (p. 163) from each other as are Freud and Ferenczi. The problem is that while Fromm acknowledges the importance of attending to "individual fates," he does not integrate this realization into his theory, as is clear when he asserts that "Freud's personality and the characteristic features of his theory are ultimately to be understood not from individual but from general social conditions." Instead of developing his concept of social character as a further dimension of what we would define today as a relational psychoanalytic perspective, Fromm too often leaps over individual experience altogether and goes directly to a collective level of analysis. On the other hand, he acknowledges earlier in "The Social Determinants of Psychoanalytic Therapy" that "it is difficult to prove the existence of a judgmental attitude," such as we find exhibited by Freud, "since it is essentially unconscious," but "the most important source for such a proof is a study of the personality in question" (p. 154). By Fromm's own admission, what is required to understand Freud—or anyone else, for that matter—is an analytically informed biography that attends to both the individual and the social contexts of its subject, but Fromm begs the reader's indulgence by pleading, "it is not possible to make such an attempt in this paper" (p. 154).

There is so much to admire in "The Social Determinants of Psychoanalytic Therapy" that the limitations I have pinpointed in Fromm's initial deployment of the concept of social character are no more than a minor blemish on what I regard as one of the greatest papers in the psychoanalytic literature. But this defect serves as a barometer that allows us to gauge whether Fromm is living up to his potential or succumbing to a "distortion in his thinking." Whenever Fromm integrates his social level of analysis with a respect for the uniqueness of individual experience, he is magnificent, but when he subsumes the individual entirely into the social, he falls flat. We see him at his best in *Man for Himself* (1947), where he concludes by affirming that "our moral problem . . . lies in the fact that we have lost the sense of the significance and uniqueness of the individual" (p. 248), or in the previously quoted passage from *Escape from Freedom* (1941) where Fromm emphasizes that "the genuine growth of the self" means "the unfolding of a nucleus that is peculiar for this one person and only for him," whereas "the development of the automaton . . . is not an organic growth" (p. 290).

Without having read Winnicott, Fromm here soars on extended wings as an object relations psychoanalyst. By the same token, although Ferenczi has disappeared from the pages of *Escape from Freedom*, we can nonetheless sense his presence when Fromm upholds the view that "every neurosis" is "essentially an adaptation to such external conditions (particularly those of early childhood) as are in themselves irrational and, generally speaking, unfavorable to the growth and development of the child" (pp. 30–31). This Fromm, who affirms the uniqueness of the individual and the effects of traumas in "early childhood" while bringing to bear his own unsurpassed dissection of larger social formations and defense of radical humanism against the perennial perils of authoritarianism—this is the true Fromm, whose vicissitudes I shall now endeavor to chart in his subsequent works on Freud and psychoanalysis.

Fromm's Dark Twin

At the outset of "The Social Determinants of Psychoanalytic Therapy," Fromm (1935) observes that repressions take place "when an impulse is condemned not only by a single person, or even by several individuals, but by the social group" to which a person belongs, and that "the danger of isolation and of the loss of social support" is a greater source of anxiety than is "losing the love of the individual most important to the person in question" (p. 149). In 1935, as we have seen, Fromm was a member of the International Psychoanalytical Association, and he had only begun to part ways with his colleagues in the Institute for Social Research, so he still enjoyed the "social support" of both these professional communities, but his warning concerning the "danger of isolation" takes on a prophetic quality when one turns to the second phase of his writings on psychoanalysis, culminating in 1959 with *Sigmund Freud's Mission*.

The crucial facts are laid out in one of the finest papers by the late Paul Roazen (2001), where he avoids the rambling and disorganization that afflict so much of his writing. In 1936, after the forced resignation of the Jewish members of the German Psychoanalytic Society, Fromm, as an émigré lay analyst living in New York, accepted an offer from Jones that he become a "Nansen" or direct member of the IPA. So matters stood throughout the 1940s, during which Fromm participated in two acts of secession. In 1941, together with Thompson, Sullivan, and others, he joined Horney, who had resigned from the New York Psychoanalytic Society after being stripped of her position as a training analyst, in founding the American Institute for Psychoanalysis. Then, in 1943, Fromm was himself joined by Thompson, Sullivan, and others in breaking away from Horney's group and founding what became the William Alanson White Institute after Horney—in a vendetta against Fromm and a repetition of her own experience of banishment—refused to permit Fromm to teach clinical seminars on the purported grounds of his lack of a medical degree.

The turning point came in 1953 when Fromm, who had been living in Mexico since 1950, discovered, in Roazen's (2001) words, "that he had somehow been dropped from being a direct member of the IPA" (p. 31). A correspondence ensued with Ruth Eissler, Secretary of the IPA and wife of Kurt Eissler, who was then in the process of founding the Freud Archives. Eissler informed Fromm that he would have to apply for reinstatement of his membership and go before a screening committee consisting of the President of the American Psychoanalytic Association, the Chairman of the Board on Professional Standards, and an American member of the Central Executive of the IPA. Seeking clarification, Fromm replied on June 29:

> According to what principles is such a screening carried out? Would, for instance, the fact that my psychoanalytic views do not correspond

to the views of the majority be one of the factors to be taken into consideration at the screening, and a reason for denial of membership?

(qtd. p. 33)

Eissler rejoined on July 27 that she could not anticipate what the screening committee might recommend; but, speaking personally, she "would assume that anyone who does not stand on the basic principles of psychoanalysis would anyway not be greatly interested in becoming a member of the International Psychoanalytic Association" (qtd. p. 34). Having been taunted in this fashion, Fromm struck back in a letter of August 26 that ended their exchange:

I am sure you realize that the main issue is just what we mean by "basic principles" of psychoanalysis. I consider myself as sharing these principles, but the question is, how broadly or how narrowly the International Psychoanalytic Association interprets them. It is also not quite a question of wanting to become a member of the International Psychoanalytic Association, but rather, of the reasons for being dropped from membership.

(qtd. p. 34)

Fromm never disclosed this dispute with the psychoanalytic establishment, preferring to wage his personal battles behind the scenes. Nonetheless, it is clear that Fromm's involvement in the founding of two unapproved institutes in New York as well as an autonomous training program in Mexico, combined with the revisionist spirit of his writings, had made him toxic to the reigning powers of whom Ruth Eissler was the mouthpiece. Had he gone forward with his application for reinstatement, Fromm would surely have met with rejection because he did not "stand on the basic principles of psychoanalysis" as defined by the authorities. Having the courage of his convictions, the author of *Escape from Freedom* chose instead to embrace the "positive freedom" of his independent status, even at the cost of being marginalized. This experience, however, must have been traumatic for Fromm and motivated him to continue his fight against the world of organized psychoanalysis vicariously by taking up the cudgels on behalf of Rank and Ferenczi against the slanders of Jones.

Accordingly, in his first counterattack, when Fromm (1958a) deplores how the psychoanalytic movement has too often "exhibited a fanaticism usually found only in religious and political bureaucracies" and charges that Jones's labeling of Rank and Ferenczi as psychotic "introduces into science a method which thus far we have expected to find only in Stalinist 'history'" (p. 11), what might seem to be hyperbole becomes comprehensible in light of the fact that Fromm himself had been purged from the psychoanalytic "party." It is a measure of the distance Fromm has traveled since 1935 that although Ferenczi continues to figure prominently in his argument, he no longer does so because of his ideas or because he offers an alternative to Freud, but solely because Ferenczi, like Rank, was victimized by the politics of exclusion of psychoanalysis, while Groddeck drops out entirely.

With respect to the pivotal question of how psychoanalysis, in its essence "*a theory and a therapy*," could "*be transformed into this kind of a fanatical movement*," Fromm initially observes that the explanation "is to be found only by an examination of Freud's motives in developing the psychoanalytic movement" (p. 55). This is consistent with his statement in "The Social Determinants of Psychoanalytic Therapy" that one must undertake "a study of the personality in question," but Fromm in the concluding paragraph of his 1958 paper shifts the blame by saying that it is "the bureaucracy, which inherited Freud's mantle" but "little of his greatness and of real radicalism," that is responsible for causing psychoanalysis to become "sterile" and abandon "its original daring in the search for truth" (p. 56). There is a recurring tension between Fromm's perception of Freud's patriarchal character and his tendency to surrender to what Daniel Burston (1991) terms "Freud piety" (p. 1) by absolving Freud of culpability for the crimes committed in his name by his apparatchiks. Just as when Fromm skips over "the individual fate of the person" and goes immediately to a collective level of analysis, this retreat from his insight into Freud's tragic flaws into an arraignment of his followers constitutes a major blind spot that distorts Fromm's thinking.

According to Friedman (2013), *Sigmund Freud's Mission* "was more an extended philippic than a closely reasoned or well-researched manuscript," in which "conclusions were postulated without much evidence or reasoning" (p. 222), just as Fromm "often exaggerated" his "differences with Freud" (p. 81). These statements exemplify the condescending attitude that pervades Friedman's biography, depriving it of the precious quality that Fromm (1959a) calls "central relatedness," notwithstanding its utility as a professionally conducted tour through his life and works.[3] Indeed, far from lacking "evidence or reasoning," *Sigmund Freud's Mission* is a masterpiece that takes its place alongside "The Social Determinants of Psychoanalytic Therapy" as a second summit rising above the range of his purely psychoanalytic writings.

Fromm begins his monograph (1959b) by agreeing with Freud that psychoanalysis "was his creation," from which it follows ineluctably that "the origin of psychoanalysis is to be sought in Freud's personality" (p. 1). The book is, therefore, the "study of the personality in question" that Fromm in 1935 had discerned would be necessary in order to explain the "judgmental attitude" that is unconsciously present in Freud's works. By virtue of his focus on Freud's "personality," Fromm avoids the pitfall of resorting prematurely to the concept of social character when a more nuanced individual level of analysis is required. At the same time, Fromm preserves what is unique about his approach when he exposes how Freud's view of human nature relies on the assumption that people "remain basically isolated beings, just as the vendor and buyer on the market do," and how he "speaks of love as a man of his time speaks of property or capital" (pp. 104–5). Fromm drives home the implications of his earlier argument that Freud fuses a "bourgeois sexual morality" with his acceptance of "the capitalistic attitude as the natural healthy one" in the apothegm that Freud's "concept of Homo sexualis was a deepened and enlarged version of the economist's concept of Homo economicus" (p. 106).

At the heart of *Sigmund Freud's Mission* is Fromm's analysis of Freud's "intolerance and authoritarianism," of which "the most drastic example . . . can be found in his relationship to Ferenczi" (p. 68). Fromm repeatedly takes aim at "the idolizing and unanalytic approach of Jones's biography" (p. 20), highlighting the "psychological naïveté" of his denial of "any authoritarian tendency in Freud" (p. 71). As Fromm contends, it was only with "people who idolized him and never disagreed" that Freud was "kind and tolerant," so that while he could be "a loving father" to his "submissive sons," he became "a stern, authoritarian one to those who dared to disagree." Utilizing his core idea in *Escape from Freedom* of the authoritarian character as a sadomasochistic structure, Fromm argues that since neither the sadist nor the masochist is able to tolerate genuine freedom, "there is an unconscious dependence in which a dominant person is dependent on those who depend on him" (p. 52). Hence, it is precisely because Freud "was so dependent on unconditional affirmation and agreement by others" (p. 71) that he unleashed his sadism against those who did not gratify his need for complete validation, though Jones was unable to see the despotic side of Freud's character. Fromm again draws on *Escape from Freedom* (1941), where he had explained that "the authoritarian character is never a 'revolutionary'" but is rather always a "'rebel'" who seeks "to overcome his own feeling of powerlessness by fighting authority, although the longing for submission remains present, whether consciously or unconsciously" (p. 192), when he asserts in *Sigmund Freud's Mission* (1959b) that Freud "was a rebel and not a revolutionary" because a "rebel" is one "who fights existing authorities but who himself wants to be an authority," whereas a revolutionary "achieves true independence and he overcomes the yearning for domination of others" (p. 64).

To bolster his claim that Freud's relationship to Ferenczi constitutes the "most drastic example" of Freud's authoritarianism, Fromm cites a personal communication he had received from Izette de Forest as he was preparing his refutation of Jones's allegations concerning Ferenczi's and Rank's supposed psychoses. In it de Forest shared Ferenczi's account of his final meeting with Freud in Vienna prior to the 1932 Wiesbaden Congress, in which Freud advised Ferenczi against publishing "Confusion of Tongues" and icily turned his back on one whom he considered to be a faithless disciple and refused to shake his hand at the conclusion of their interview. In a footnote, Fromm hails "Confusion of Tongues" as "a paper of extraordinary profundity and brilliance—one of the most valuable papers in the whole psychoanalytic literature" (p. 70n3). Fromm, however, does not engage with the substance of Ferenczi's ideas, just as he had dealt only with the political aspect of Ferenczi's conflict with Freud in "Psychoanalysis—Science or Party Line?" Similarly, although he had written privately in 1957 to Carl and Sylva Grossman that Groddeck's "teaching influenced me more than that of other teachers I had" (qtd. in Funk, 1999a, p. 62), Fromm does not mention Groddeck in either his rejoinder to Jones or *Sigmund Freud's Mission*. Thus, although Fromm continued to revere both Ferenczi and Groddeck on a personal level and the case of Ferenczi remained central to his critique of Freud, it is clear that Fromm's theoretical views were no longer deeply influenced by these two progenitors of the relational turn, as they had been in "The Social Determinants of Psychoanalytic Therapy."

This shift away from his earlier outlook helps to explain why, even though Fromm (1959b) correctly perceives that "dependency and insecurity are central elements in the structure of Freud's character, and of his neurosis" (p. 23), he misunderstands how Freud acquired these traits. According to Fromm, "the attachment to Mother, even the very satisfactory one which implies indisputable confidence in Mother's love, has not only the positive side of giving absolute self-confidence, it also has the negative side of creating a feeling of dependency" (p. 23). But Freud's "dependency and insecurity" did not arise because he had a "very satisfactory" attachment to his mother. On the contrary, it arose because Freud's attachment to his mother was extremely *insecure*. Fromm's error goes beyond taking at face value Freud's idealized picture of his relationship to his mother and extends to his conception of motherly love in general. Fromm asserts categorically:

> Mother's love is by definition unconditional. She does not love her child, as the Father does, because he merits it, because of what he has done, but because he is her child. Motherly admiration for the son is unconditional too.
>
> (p. 21)

This dichotomy between maternal and paternal love, which forms a leitmotiv in Fromm's writings, is indebted to Bachofen. In his early essay "The Theory of Mother Right and Its Relevance for Social Psychology" (1934), Fromm appends the qualification that he is "talking about paternal or maternal love in an ideal sense" (p. 130*n*24), which goes some way to meet the objections to his formulation. But when Fromm forgets that he is trading at best in ideal types, if not essentialist stereotypes, and simply assumes that Freud's mother must have loved him unconditionally because "mother's love is by definition unconditional," he blinds himself to the frequency with which maternal love proves to be ambivalent and conditional, and even mutates into the hate analyzed by Winnicott with such acuity in "Hate in the Counter-Transference" (1949).

Fromm is remembered by Edward S. Tauber (2009) as having been "always a private person" (p. 131) and by Bernard Landis (2009) as "intensely private" (p. 137). Before his death in 1980, he directed his third wife, Annis Freeman Fromm, to destroy his personal letters, and none of his correspondence before 1934 has been preserved (Friedman, 2013, p. xxvii). Nowhere in his extant writings does Fromm engage in the kind of intimate self-analysis that we find in Freud, Ferenczi, and Groddeck. Not even in the opening autobiographical chapter of *Beyond the Chains of Illusion* (1962), where Fromm describes himself as "having been an only child, with an anxious and moody father and a depression-prone mother" and confesses his infatuation as a twelve-year-old with a painter of twenty-five who, after the death of her father, broke off an engagement and committed suicide, leaving instructions in her will that "she wanted to be buried together" (pp. 3–4) with her deceased parent, does he lift the curtain more than an inch or two on his inner world. Ironically, although Fromm confesses that he "had never heard of an Oedipus complex or of incestuous fixations between daughter and father" (p. 4), he does not address the possibility that Freud's theories might be no less pertinent to his own adolescent fascination with the painter—or his subsequent pattern of relationships with considerably older women such as Reichmann and Horney—than they are to the painter's morbid obsession with her father.

Fromm's insistence that "mother's love" and "motherly admiration" are "by definition unconditional," which is reflected in his incoherent account of Freud's relationship to his mother, is—along with his tendency to retreat from an individual level of analysis and to shift the blame onto Freud's followers for the tragic flaws in Freud's character—a third major blind spot that impedes "the genuine growth of the self" in Fromm's writings. He sums up his view of Freud near the end of *Sigmund Freud's Mission* (1959b):

> We find him a man deeply in need of motherly love, admiration, and protection, full of self-confidence when these are bestowed on him, depressed and hopeless when they are missing. This insecurity, both emotionally and materially, makes him seek to control others who depend on him, so he can depend on them.
>
> (p. 122)

In place of a self-analysis, Fromm in this character study of Freud has sketched a portrait of his own dark twin—the authoritarian double of his humanist self. For Fromm, too, was indubitably "deeply in need of motherly love," with a pronounced attraction not only to older but also to depressed women. Like the painter, Fromm's second wife, Henny Gurland, who had witnessed the suicide of Walter Benjamin when she and her son set out to cross the mountainous border between France and Spain with him in 1940, almost certainly ended her own illness-plagued life by committing suicide in their bathroom in Mexico City in June of 1952 (Friedman, 2013, p. 141).

Thus, the conclusion becomes irresistible that Fromm is projecting into his theories an excessively idealized picture of his own relationship to his mother, Rosa Krause Fromm. Although he was not tempted by power and mistrusted movements, those who knew Fromm have testified that he occasionally succumbed to the narcissistic and controlling side of his own nature. As Fromm wrote of Freud in "Scientism or Fanaticism?" (1958a), he "was—and wanted to be—one of the great cultural-ethical leaders of the twentieth century" (p. 56), and Fromm undoubtedly shared this laudable ambition, which had its genetic roots in the desire of both sons to meet the emotional needs of their mothers in order to bask in the glow of their adoration. Only in fleeting moments, as when Fromm observes in *Man for Himself* (1947) that while "an oversolicitous, dominating mother . . . consciously believes that she is particularly fond of her child, she has actually a deeply repressed hostility toward the object of her concern" (p. 131), does he recognize the true complexity of the mother-child relationship, though he was never able to connect this insight either with Freud's childhood experience or with his own.[4]

The covert personal agenda that animated Fromm's attack on Jones's "Stalinist" rewriting of history in "Psychoanalysis: Science or Party Line?" continues to be felt in *Sigmund Freud's Mission* (1959b). Critical as Fromm is of Jones's "psychological naïveté," he reserves his greatest scorn in the book for Sachs's "frankly idolizing" (p. 67) attitude toward Freud. Thus, what Schröter terms the "subterranean" current of resentment toward his training analyst, and toward his entire ordeal in Berlin, in "The Social Determinants of Psychoanalytic Therapy" here comes to the fore, compounded by Fromm's antipathy toward the international psychoanalytic establishment by which he had in the interim been rejected. Sachs's "symbiotic, quasi-religious attachment" to Freud, Fromm notes, which meant that he "never rebelled against or criticized" his deity, "becomes pathetically evident" (p. 72) in his memoir, *Freud: Master and Friend* (1944), when Sachs recalls the one time in his life when he deliberately did something that incurred Freud's displeasure, leaving Sachs feeling ashamed of himself for years. By the same token, when Fromm laments in the concluding chapter of *Sigmund Freud's Mission* (1959b) that psychoanalysis has been taken over by a "hierarchy" that "gains its prestige from the 'correct' interpretation of the dogma, and the power to judge who is and who is not a faithful adherent of the religion" (p. 112), his language echoes that in his final letter to Ruth Eissler, where he avers that the "main issue is just what we mean by 'basic principles' of psychoanalysis" and "how broadly or how narrowly the International Psychoanalytic Association interprets them." That Fromm's struggle against authoritarianism in psychoanalysis may ultimately have been an attempt to free himself from what Friedman (2013) terms the "emotional cage" (p. 218) into which he had been placed by his mother is not rendered less plausible by the fact that this interpretation could not have been offered by Fromm himself.

The Downward Slide

Whereas the second phase of Fromm's writings on psychoanalysis began with the discovery that he had been dropped from membership in the International Psychoanalytical Association, the third and final phase, conversely, is inaugurated by his participation in the founding of the International Federation of Psychoanalytic Societies, which took place in 1962. As Funk (1999b) has documented, the "strongest motive," in Fromm's view, for establishing an organization that would serve as an alternative to the IPA "was to counteract the bureaucratic attitude of the orthodox Freudians against all who did not share the libido theory" (p. 3). Ironically, however, in his 1961 paper given at a conference in Düsseldorf, "Fundamental Positions of Psychoanalysis," Fromm cautioned his dissident colleagues that "the future of psychoanalysis does not lie in new schools that have to prove that Freud was wrong" (qtd. in Funk, 1999b, p. 4). On the contrary, he continued, "the future of psychoanalytic theory and therapy lies in continuing research of the unconscious psychic reality and in developing and keeping up of Freud's radical and critical thinking" (p. 4). In the abstract to his paper, Fromm was even more effusive, insisting not only that Freud "laid the foundation for psychoanalytic theory and therapy" but also that "every development of our science is an advancement of Freud's insights and not a construction of new theories which are opposed to Freud's."

Fromm here reaches a position 180 degrees from that in "The Social Determinants of Psychoanalytic Therapy" and most of *Sigmund Freud's Mission*. No longer do we hear about Freud's authoritarianism or how "the example of Ferenczi shows . . . that the Freudian attitude need not be that of all analysts." On the contrary, Fromm warns against trying "to prove that Freud was wrong" and regards "every development" in psychoanalysis as "an advancement of Freud's insights." It is as though, having been expelled from the IPA and left with no alternative but to cast in his lot with other marginal analysts, Fromm's latent "Freud piety" came to the forefront and he continued the process begun at the end of *Sigmund Freud's Mission* of shifting the blame for the totalitarian tendencies of the psychoanalytic movement away from Freud himself and onto the bureaucrats who "inherited Freud's mantle" but "little of his greatness and real radicalism."

Fromm's nearly complete repudiation in his final phase of his earlier critique of Freud enlarges one of his incipient blind spots and compounds the "distortion in his thinking." Immediately after having decried the tendency to propose "new theories which are opposed to Freud's," he contradicts himself by affirming in the abstract to "Fundamental Positions of Psychoanalysis" that "libido theory is replaced by the different forms of being related to the world; instead of the concept of sexuality (in respect to the pleasure-unpleasure principle) the male-female polarity, its satisfaction and distortion, becomes the center of attention" (qtd. in Funk, 1999b, p. 4). On the one hand, Fromm inveighs against trying to prove that Freud was wrong and against advancing theories that are opposed to his; on the other, he argues that the libido theory must be "replaced." This confusion is compounded by the heterosexism lurking in his reference to "the male-female polarity." Although seemingly innocuous in this context, it is disturbing when Fromm posits in *The Art of Loving* (1956a) that "the male-female polarity" is "the basis for creativity," whereas "the homosexual deviation is a failure to attain this polarized union, and thus the homosexual suffers from the pain of never-resolved separateness" (p. 34). Were Fromm alive today, I have no doubt he would agree that his stigmatizing of homosexuality as a "deviation" from the heterosexual norm is one of the clearest instances in which the "radical and critical" energies of his own thought were constricted by his acquiescence in the prevalent cultural prejudices of his time.

The question of where to pin the blame for "the sterility of orthodox psychoanalytic thought" (p. 22) is central to "The Crisis of Psychoanalysis" (1970a), which forms a bridge between *Sigmund Freud's Mission* and *Greatness and Limitations of Freud's Thought* (1980), published in the year of his death. Rather than being the symptom of a virus present from its beginnings, Fromm in this essay holds that the "main reason" for the crisis of contemporary psychoanalysis lies in its "change from a radical to a conformist theory" (p. 16). This change is laid at the doorstep of Freud's "orthodox disciples," who failed to develop his "most potent and revolutionary ideas" and chose instead to "emphasize those theories that could most easily be co-opted by the consumer society" (p. 18). Although Fromm concedes that Freud elevated to leadership positions those of his followers who possessed the "one outstanding quality" of "unquestionable loyalty to him and the movement," even though they lacked "the capacity for radical criticism," Fromm does not see this behavior as casting any reflection on Freud's character but simply uses it to make the point that it resulted in the taking over of psychoanalysis by "bureaucrats," whose pettiness is exemplified by the aspersions cast by Jones on Ferenczi and Rank in what Fromm acidly terms his "'court biography'" (p. 19) of Freud.

Thus, Fromm portrays Freud in "The Crisis of Psychoanalysis" as having been at heart a "radical thinker" whose greatest defect was his inability to transcend "the prejudices and philosophy of his historical period and class" (p. 17), while Fromm faults his sycophants for their failure "to develop the theory by liberating its basic findings from their time-bound narrowness into a wider and more radical framework" (p. 18). The example of Ferenczi again figures prominently, but rather than dwelling, as he had in "The Social Determinants of Psychoanalytic Therapy," on Ferenczi's personal and theoretical differences with Freud, or, as he did in *Sigmund Freud's Mission*, on the "intolerance and authoritarianism" displayed by Freud in their relationship, Fromm trains his ire in an extended footnote on a "tortuous and submissive" 1958 letter by Michael Balint in the *International Journal of Psycho-Analysis*, where, even in attempting to set the record straight concerning Ferenczi's alleged mental illness, he treats Jones so deferentially that the missive sounds as though it "had been written in a dictatorial system in order to avoid severe consequences for freedom or life" (p. 22*n*10). Fromm's censure of Balint, to say nothing of Jones, is justified, but he pulls up the weed without getting at the root. It is no longer Freud but the Eisslers of the psychoanalytic world who bear the brunt of Fromm's scorn since "the analysts who submitted" in the way that Balint did to Jones "were not forced by anyone to do so" (p. 22). After all, he continues:

> the worst that could have happened to them would have been expulsion from the organization, and, in fact, there were a few who took the "bold" step without any harmful effect, except that of being stigmatized by the bureaucracy as not being psychoanalysts.

A barely suppressed note of self-congratulation almost drowns out the throb of lingering pain in Fromm's mockery of the threat of excommunication that had been executed on him nearly two decades earlier.

The downward slide from his magisterial earlier writings on psychoanalysis that I have tracked in Fromm's Düsseldorf paper and "The Crisis of Psychoanalysis" reaches its nadir in *Greatness and Limitations of Freud's Thought* (1980). Resuming the question of how psychoanalysis betrayed its radical inspiration and became a conformist theory, Fromm again places the blame on the "pedestrian men" who "built the movement" and "needed a dogma" in which to believe. As he summarizes, "Freud the scientist became to some extent the prisoner of Freud the leader of the movement; or to put it differently, Freud the teacher became the prisoner of his faithful, but uncreative disciples" (p. 132).[5] By depicting Freud as the "prisoner of his disciples," Fromm forgets that his concept of the authoritarian character turns on its being a sadomasochistic structure involving "an unconscious dependence in which a dominant person is dependent on those who depend on him." In place of his brilliant insight that Freud's narcissism made him "dependent on unconditional affirmation and agreement by others," so that the psychoanalytic movement became a magnified projection of his personality, Fromm substitutes a naive and one-sided view of Freud as the innocent victim of the mediocrity of his followers.[6]

As with the blunting of his formerly keen awareness that "the origin of psychoanalysis is to be sought in Freud's personality," Fromm shows himself at his least impressive in other ways in *Greatness and Limitations of Freud's Thought*. Rather than integrating the concept of social character with an analysis of what he termed in *Escape from Freedom* "the individual basis of the personality," he calls for "the transformation of individual psychology into social psychology" and claims that individual psychology can be reduced "to the knowledge of small variations brought about by the individual and idiosyncratic circumstances which influence the basic socially determined character structure" (p. 63). As I have maintained, this posture leaves Fromm with no way of explaining the vast differences between individuals belonging to the same social class, as exemplified by what he himself had at one time acknowledged to be the "fundamental" opposition between Ferenczi's "humane, philanthropic attitude" and Freud's "deep down misanthropic 'tolerance.'"[7]

Fromm's minimizing of the importance of attending to the uniqueness of every individual and his or her experience in *Greatness and Limitations of Freud's Thought* is reflected in his inconsistent stance toward childhood. On the one hand, he recommends that the analyst should aim "to reconstruct a picture of the character of the child when it was born in order to study which of the traits he finds in the analysand are part of the original nature and which are acquired through influential circumstances" (p. 65). From this it follows that "the roots of neurotic developments" and "a sense of false identity" most often lie in parental pressures, whereas "genuine identity rests upon an awareness of one's suchness in terms of the person one is born" (pp. 65–66). This is excellent and very much in the spirit of Winnicott. On the other hand, in criticizing Freud for his failure "to see that the human being, from earliest childhood on, lives in several circles: the narrowest one is his family, the next one is his class, the third one is the society in which he lives," while the fourth is "the biological condition of being human in which he participates" (p. 60), Fromm overlooks that the family is itself a system that can, in typical instances, be further subdivided into dyadic and triadic structures. For Fromm, the family is significant insofar as it "constitutes an 'agency of society' whose function it is to transmit the character of society to the infant even before it has any direct contact with society" (p. 61). This is a compelling analytic perspective, but it needs to be complemented by one that starts from the countless micro-interactions between, in Winnicott's (1967) words, "any one baby and the human (and therefore fallible) mother-figure who," with any luck, "is essentially adaptive because of love" (p. 100), and moves outward to encompass all the larger circles in which that primary dyad is embedded.

Fromm's comparative remoteness from early experience has consequences for his approach to clinical work. Unlike most analysts, Fromm does not regard transference as the mainspring of the therapeutic process. Rather, he describes it in *Greatness and Limitations of Freud's Thought* (1980) as "the voluntary dependence of a person on other persons in authority" (p. 41), and hence as something to be surmounted, if not avoided altogether. As Michael Maccoby (1996) has remarked based on his years as Fromm's analysand, Fromm's "focus on feelings about the analyst in the here and now . . . short-circuited the process of working through the transferential feelings and their origins" (p. 77). This devaluing of the transference is connected to Fromm's (1980) abandonment of the couch because it leads to the "infantilization of the analysand" (p. 40) and to his conviction that "the more real the analyst is to the analysand and the more he loses his phantomlike character, the easier it is for the analysand to give up the posture of helplessness and to cope with reality" (p. 43). Fromm here could not be further removed from Winnicott's (1955) conviction that disturbed patients must be permitted to undergo a "regression to dependence" in which the analyst temporarily takes over the functions of the ego so that their primitive anxieties can be accessed, just as he departs from Ferenczi's belief that the analyst must be prepared to enter into the patient's reliving of past traumas. Rejecting the principle that the analyst should strive to be as unobtrusive as possible with patients in a regressed state, Fromm urges the analyst to become "more real" in order to induce the analysand to renounce the "posture of helplessness" and "cope with reality" in a mature fashion.

Although my critique of Fromm for neglecting childhood experience is directed primarily at the work of his final period, it points up a weakness that dates back to *Escape from Freedom* (1941). There, Fromm defines "the ties that connect the child with its mother" as "'primary ties,'" and he argues that they "imply a lack of individuality but they also give security and orientation to the individual" (p. 40). Fromm compares this bond to that of "the medieval man with the Church and his social caste," and it leads him to celebrate achieving "the stage of complete individuation" in which "the individual is free from these primary ties" and "confronted with a new task: to orient and root himself in the world and to find security in other ways than those which were characteristic of his preindividualistic existence" (p. 40). For Fromm, any attempt to "reverse, psychically, the process of individuation" is no less futile than it would be for the child to aim to "return to the mother's womb physically," and all such retreats before the challenge of freedom "necessarily assume the character of submission, in which the basic contradiction between the authority and the child who submits to it is never eliminated" (p. 45).

The difficulties with Fromm's conceptual framework have been articulated by Mauricio Cortina (1996) from the standpoint of attachment theory. Not only, as Cortina observes, did Fromm, like Margaret Mahler, rely on the assumption that "the roots of human development could be traced to a primitive undifferentiated infant-mother bond" (p. 109), but this premise led him to suppose that the only way to achieve "individuation and growth" was "by severing the symbiotic ties to primary caregivers," which "creates a false dichotomy by conceptualizing development as a choice between progressive and regressive solutions" (p. 94). Instead of appreciating that secure attachments foster independence and autonomy so that to live a productive and fulfilled life requires the cultivation rather than the sundering of these "primary ties," Fromm saw all forms of dependence as inherently regressive. As Cortina (2015) elaborates in a subsequent paper, he therefore could not provide either his patients or his readers "with an empathic understanding of the developmental pathways that derailed their ability to develop loving relations, or explain why they became anxiously attached or panicked about being abandoned" (pp. 411–12).

Fromm's negative view of early attachments as inimical to individuation is the counterpart to his depiction of maternal love and admiration as "by definition unconditional." Once again, there may well be grounds for connecting these blind spots to an unanalyzed imperative felt by Fromm to extricate himself from his own oppressive "primary ties" to his mother. Like Nicodemus, Fromm seeks a literal answer to the question, "How can a man be born when he is old? Can he enter the second time into his mother's womb, and be born?" (John 3:4). To this, Ferenczi and Groddeck, Winnicott and Balint, would all respond by proclaiming that only by allowing for a symbolic regression to the state of "preindividualistic existence" is it possible for once-broken souls to achieve a rebirth through psychoanalysis.

Dreaming of Consilience

Following Fromm's lead, I have sought in this "literary psychoanalysis" of his writings on Freud to distinguish "what is essential and lasting" from "what is time-conditioned and socially contingent" (1980, p. 22), but with the proviso that we must be prepared to look for personal as well as social causes for his blind spots. While noting the decline that becomes evident as he moves further from his original sources of inspiration in Ferenczi and Groddeck, my focus has been on Fromm's superlative analysis of Freud's authoritarian character in "The Social Determinants of Psychoanalytic Therapy," as well as in his rebuttals of Jones first in "Freud, Friends, and Feuds" and then in *Sigmund Freud's Mission*. More than anyone else of his era, Fromm not only dissected the politics of the psychoanalytic movement on the plane of theory but he exemplified in his life what it means to be an independent psychoanalyst, and even if he had done nothing else these feats alone would be enough to make him indispensable to future practitioners of this impossible profession.

But the task of disentangling "what is essential and lasting" in human nature from what is "time-conditioned and socially contingent" is likewise central to Fromm's commitment to radical humanism. His overarching aim throughout all the phases of his thought may be defined as one of exposing false universals, as when Freud imports the "bourgeois norm" into his theoretical constructs and clinical practice, so that these may be discarded and replaced with true universals, which in turn furnish a touchstone by which we may recognize what is alienated and pathological. It is characteristic of Fromm's genius that he should have advanced this argument on two distinct but converging fronts. The first is philosophical and derives from his allegiance to Marxism, fused with a deep indebtedness to Spinoza. As he writes in "Marx's Contribution to the Knowledge of Man" (1968a), whereas "modern academic and experimental psychology" studies "alienated man" with "alienated and alienating methods," "Marx's psychology, being based on the full awareness of the fact of alienation, was able to transcend this type of approach because it did not take the alienated man for the natural man, for man as such" (p. 63). Like Freud, Fromm continues, Marx views man as motivated by "passions or drives," of which he is "largely unaware," though unlike Freud's "model of an isolated homme machine," Marx starts with a recognition of "the primacy of man's relatedness to the world, to man, and to nature" (p. 64). Although only implicit in *Man for Himself* (1947), Marx's philosophical anthropology provides the foundation for Fromm's eloquent defense in that work of "the validity of humanistic ethics" and his insistence that "our knowledge of human nature does not lead to ethical relativism" but rather "to the conviction that the sources of norms for ethical conduct are to be found in man's nature itself" (p. 7). Integral to Fromm's case is the conviction that the source of morality lies in "the character structure of the mature and integrated personality," so that neither "self-renunciation nor selfishness but self-love, not the negation of the individual but the affirmation of his truly human self, are the supreme values of humanistic ethics" (p. 7).

A corollary to Fromm's powerful and persuasive argument is that "by necessity the criteria in authoritarian ethics are fundamentally different from those in humanistic ethics" (p. 8). This dichotomy, which at one time he would have equated with the choice between Freud and Ferenczi, makes Fromm truly the George Orwell of psychoanalysis, not only because of his courage but also because Orwell (1947) took a virtually identical stand in affirming that all of his writing since the Spanish civil war had been aimed "directly or indirectly, against totalitarianism and for democratic socialism," and that "it is simply a question of which side one takes and what approach one follows" (p. 318). Indeed, there could be no better distillation of Fromm's entire body of work than Orwell's (1944) reflection that "the connection between sadism, masochism, success-worship, power-worship, nationalism and totalitarianism is a huge subject whose edges have barely been scratched" (p. 151), though had Orwell read *Escape from Freedom* (1941), where Fromm calls for "the elimination of the secret rule" of the oligarchs and its replacement by "democratic socialism" (p. 299), he might have been moved to acknowledge that Fromm had not merely "scratched the edges" of this "huge subject" but had explored it in great depth.

Both Fromm and Orwell understood that the conflict between authoritarianism and humanism is not merely an academic exercise but one in which the future of the human race and life on this planet is at stake. Just as Fromm was prepared to wager that "our knowledge of human nature does not lead to ethical relativism," so, too, Orwell (1943) took up the cudgels against "the abandonment of the idea that history could be truthfully written"—a trend he presciently detected in twentieth-century thought that became enshrined in postmodernism—and warned that "it is just this common basis of agreement, with its implications that human beings are all one species of animal, that totalitarianism destroys" (pp. 204–5). In view of their far-reaching affinity, it is fitting that Fromm (1961) should have written an afterword to *1984* in which he hailed Orwell for "brilliantly and imaginatively" unmasking "the illusion of the assumption that democracy can continue to exist in a world preparing for nuclear war" (p. 282), as well as for showing that "in a system in which the concept of truth as an objective judgment concerning reality is abolished" we are left in a fog of "doublethink" where "the person is no longer saying the opposite of what he thinks, but he thinks the opposite of what is true" (pp. 264–65)—a perfect description of the mind of Donald Trump. It is thus not surprising to learn that, in imparting to Gérard Khoury (2009) "his conviction that ideas are strong enough to move mountains, even though they may seem helplessly far from daily life concerns," Fromm should have exhorted him "to follow a very large reading program spanning writers from pre-Socratic philosophers to George Orwell" (p. 165).

But as Orwell's observation that "human beings are all one species of animal" makes plain, the claim that there is such a thing as human nature does not depend solely on philosophy, and in Fromm's later work his advocacy of radical humanism is increasingly grounded in natural science. This is nowhere more evident than in *The Anatomy of Human Destructiveness* (1973), where Fromm sets out to answer the questions, "What is man's nature? What is it by virtue of which he is man?," but instead of going down the path of "metaphysical speculations, like those of Heidegger and Sartre," he proposes to "shift the principle of explanation of human passions . . . to a sociobiological and historical principle" and thereby to demonstrate that "the essence of each individual is identical with the existence of the species" (p. 27). As he elaborates later in his treatise, it is "precisely from an evolutionary standpoint" that he seeks to resuscitate the traditional belief that "there is something called human nature, something that constitutes the essence of man," and "the main argument in favor of the assumption of the existence of a human nature is that we can define the essence of Homo sapiens in morphological, anatomical, physiological, and neurological terms," from which it follows, "unless we regress to a view that considers mind and body as separate realms, that the species man must be definable mentally as well as physically" (pp. 247–48).

It is impossible to contemplate Fromm's endorsement of a "sociobiological explanation" of human nature without being reminded of Edward O. Wilson's *Sociobiology: A New Synthesis* (1975), just as Fromm's use of the term "biophilia" (p. 406) in the *Anatomy* (1973) foreshadows Wilson's (1984) book of that title.[7] Indeed, in undertaking to define the "essence of man" from an "evolutionary standpoint," Fromm has the same lofty aim as does the great biologist in *On Human Nature* (1978), in which Wilson defines his program as "the uncompromising application of evolutionary theory to all aspects of human existence" (p. x). Regrettably, however, in chastising Fromm for his idiosyncratic reliance on Freud's concept of the death instinct, Wilson mistakenly describes him as subscribing to "an even more pessimistic view" (p. 101) of man than Korard Lorenz, and he nowhere acknowledges that Fromm has not merely predicted the main lines of his argument but coined two of his signature ideas.

In *The Anatomy of Human Destructiveness* (1973), Fromm completes his intellectual odyssey from philosophical anthropology to sociobiology. Of all his works it is the most undeservedly "forgotten" and consequently most in need of being rediscovered by a new generation of readers. Fromm's achievement is even more astonishing when one recognizes that, like *Escape from Freedom*, it is merely the torso of an even more ambitious project that he was never able to bring to completion. Complementing Fromm's meticulously detailed scholarship in an extraordinary array of fields, from ethology and paleontology to modern history, is the methodological rigor that leads him to recognize an obligation "to check my conclusions with the main data from other fields to make certain that my hypotheses did not contradict them and to determine whether, as was my hope, they confirmed my hypothesis" (p. 15). This is the proper scientific method in the service of a work of social science, and in making such a commitment Fromm is the antithesis to Freud, who hubristically chose to disregard the findings from neighboring disciplines whenever the evidence proved incompatible with his articles of psychoanalytic faith. Just as Fromm was a sociobiologist before Wilson, he again displayed his prescience when he took it upon himself to investigate "the relationship of psychology, the science of the mind, to neuroscience, the sciences of the brain" (p. 112), and thereby anticipated the emergence of the contemporary discipline of neuropsychoanalysis.

Any doubt that psychoanalysis formed the core of Fromm's professional identity and his intellectual foundation must be dispelled by *The Anatomy of Human Destructiveness* (1973). Unlike Wilson, Fromm insists that his brand of sociobiology "is based on the theory of psychoanalysis," though he uses the term to refer not to the "classic theory" of Freud but rather to "a certain revision of it" that dispenses with the "libido theory" (p. 28). Just as Fromm showed himself to be a gifted polemicist in his ripostes to Jones, as well as in his jousts (1955a, 1956b, 1970a, pp. 26–31, 1992a) with Herbert Marcuse, so, too, he opens his argument for a psychoanalytic understanding of the distinction between benign and malignant aggression with a refutation of both the "neoinstinctivism" of Lorenz and the behaviorism of B. F. Skinner. In addition to expressing his solidarity with Adolf Meyer, Sullivan, Fromm-Reichmann, and Theodore Lidz on the American side, while criticizing Horney for using "somewhat superficial categories" (1973, p. 110), Fromm explicitly aligns himself with the British school of object relations theory. Not only does he couple Bowlby in a footnote with Ferenczi (who is here mentioned for the only time in the book) as one of the "few analysts" who have gone beyond Freud's "old concept" of the Oedipus complex and "seen the real nature of the fixation to the mother" (p. 261n10; see also p. 237n21 and p. 522n34), but he likewise invokes, also for the first and only time, "the names of Winnicott, Fairbairn, Balint, and Guntrip," as well as that of R. D. Laing, as kindred spirits who have joined him in transforming psychoanalysis "from a theory and therapy of instinctual frustration and control into a 'theory and therapy that encourages the rebirth and growth of an authentic self within an authentic relationship'" (p. 110).

The latter part of the preceding sentence is a quotation from Harry Guntrip's paper, "The Promise of Psychoanalysis" (1971), published two years earlier in a Festschrift for Fromm edited by Landis and Tauber, and it appears to be through Guntrip that Fromm became aware of his affinity with the analysts of the British school, though (apart from his critique of Balint's fecklessness in answering Jones) he gives no sign of ever having read any of them with the exception of Bowlby. After hailing Fromm for having made "the most trenchant criticisms of instinct theory in order to widen the purview of psychoanalysis" (p. 48), Guntrip credits him with understanding that "it is when the parents inhibit the child's development and thwart his growth so that the child is unable to stand on his own feet" (p. 49) that the most basic issues of living arise. Accordingly, Guntrip defines the aim of psychoanalytic therapy as "the liberation of the person from the emotional traumata of the past and the development of his creative potentials," which means that "the analytic work and the analytic relationship must set about to repair the damage done by past faulty relationships day by day, often from the very beginning" (p. 49). For this to occur what is required is "not the patient's 'reparation' for his destructive impulses," as Melanie Klein would have it, but rather "the analyst's 'repairing' the mother's failure to give basic ego support" (p. 54).

By situating Fromm in the context of object relations theory, Guntrip brings out the full "creative potentials" of his thought. In light of the increasing emphasis placed by analysts on "man's struggle to be himself," Guntrip insists that this concern is indeed the "business of science," so that the "real question" becomes, "not 'Is psychoanalysis a science?' but 'What kind of science is it'?" (p. 46). Guntrip answers his own question by invoking Peter B. Medawar's "account of the scientific method and the hierarchical structure of knowledge," in which knowledge is compared to a multi-storied building where "the ground floor is physics and chemistry, the successive tiers rising above it are physiology, neurology and biology, then sociology," with "psychology as the topmost tier" and "the study of 'personal mind' as the highest phenomenon of which we know" (p. 48). Quoting Medawar's caution that "'in each plane or tier in the hierarchy of science new notions or ideas seem to emerge that are inexplicable in the language or with the conceptional resources of the tier below,'" so that "'we cannot "interpret" sociology in terms of biology, or biology in terms of physics,'" Guntrip appends the proviso—"nor, we must add, psychology in terms of any lower-tier science" (p. 48).[8] Had "this view of scientific theory" been "available to Freud," Guntrip imagines, he might have been able to jettison his model of sex and aggression as governed by "drive control apparatuses" in favor of a study "of whole persons in intensely personal relationships," such as "it fell to Erich Fromm" to undertake and that lends credence to "a more affirmative view of man than the pessimistic one of classical Freudian theory" (p. 48).

Just as Guntrip reveals Fromm to have been an object relations psychoanalyst, Fromm (1973), conversely, echoes Guntrip in recognizing that "not only the neurosciences but many other fields need to be integrated to create a science of man," which concerns itself with "man as a total biologically and historically evolving human being who can be understood only if we see the interconnectedness between all his aspects, if we look at him as a process within a complex system with many subsystems" (p. 115n3). Having confessed at the outset of this chapter how uncanny it was for me to discover that Fromm had anticipated so many of the directions I have taken in my own work, including my collocation of Rank, Ferenczi, and Groddeck as the initiators of the relational turn in psychoanalysis, I am once again startled in closing to see my own image mirrored in the arguments that psychoanalysis holds out the promise of being a comprehensive "science of man" ranging from the "ground floor" of physics and chemistry to the irreducible subjectivity of hermeneutics. For it was just such a conception of "the hierarchical structure of knowledge" that I set forth in "Psychoanalysis and the Dream of Consilience," the last chapter of my book *Reading Psychoanalysis* (Rudnytsky, 2002a), where I took the term "consilience" from Wilson's (1998) sublime blueprint of the "unity of knowledge," though I had no inkling at the time that what I thought was my dream had previously been dreamt by Guntrip and Fromm.

As announced by his title "The Promise of Psychoanalysis," Guntrip (1971) seeks to dispel the rumors of the death of psychoanalysis, which have not abated in the intervening decades, and instead to persuade his readers that "a psychoanalysis which is closely related to the realities of everyday living, that penetrates to the depths of suffering beings, has nothing to fear for the future and will flourish" (p. 45). Sharing Guntrip's optimism, I hope to have made it clear why I believe that the rehabilitation of Erich Fromm—the analyst of the authoritarian character, the spokesman for radical humanism, and my fellow dreamer of consilience—is indispensable to this renewal of the promise of our field.

Notes

1 Fromm's refutation of Jones appeared first in the form of an article in *The Saturday Review*, "Scientism or Fanaticism?" (1958a), with a response by Jacob A. Arlow (1958), and was reprinted with minor revisions under the more finely honed title "Psychoanalysis—Science or Party Line?" (1958b) in *The Dogma of Christ*. I shall quote from the original version of Fromm's article, but generally prefer the amended title, throughout this book.
2 See the review of the history of this concept by Funk (1998), who traces its roots to Fromm's doctoral dissertation under Alfred Weber at Heidelberg and notes the occurrence of the phrase "socially typical character" (p. 221) in a paper of 1937. As Funk concedes, everything that makes any particular "person different from, and unique among, other persons living under the same circumstances (his or her special and often traumatic childhood experiences) is . . . of secondary interest" from Fromm's standpoint.
3 Exacerbating his patronizing tone, Friedman (2013) erroneously claims that "there is a good possibility that Fromm met Freud" at one of Groddeck's "convivial gatherings in Baden Baden" (p. 24), whereas Freud in fact never accepted any of Groddeck's invitations that he visit him there.
4 In *The Art of Loving* (1956a, p. 61). Fromm repeats verbatim both this sentence and the one following, in which he writes that such a mother "is overconcerned not because she loves the child too much, but because she has to compensate for her lack of capacity to love him at all" (1947, p. 131).
5 Fromm here repeats verbatim not merely the final sentence but the entire final paragraph of the appendix to *The Anatomy of Human Destructiveness* (1973, pp. 527–28).
6 An analogous minimizing of the degree to which the psychoanalytic movement bears the stamp of Freud's authoritarian character can be seen in Kenneth Eisold's (1997) claims that Freud "did not enjoy veneration and he was impatient with the dependency of his followers" (p. 23), and was "able to be manipulated by the group into the role of 'aging despot'" (p. 25).
7 See also *The Revision of Psychoanalysis* (1992c), where Fromm rejects the "false dichotomy" according to which his work has been classified "as 'culturally' rather than 'biologically' oriented," and maintains, "My approach has always been a sociobiological one" (p. 4).
8 Guntrip's quotation is taken from Medawar's *Induction and Intuition in Scientific Thought* (1969), with no page numbers given.

Chapter 3

Freud, Ferenczi, Fromm
The Authoritarian Character as Magic Helper

> "The example of Ferenczi shows, however, that the Freudian attitude need not be that of all analysts."
> —Fromm, "The Social Determinants of Psychoanalytic Therapy"

To contemporary students of Ferenczi Erich Fromm is likely to be best known for having spearheaded the rebuttal to Ernest Jones's (1957) preposterous accusation, in the third volume of his Freud biography, that both he and Rank toward the end of their lives "developed psychotic manifestations that revealed themselves in, among other ways, a turning away from Freud and his doctrines" (p. 45). According to Jones, fidelity to Freud is proof of sanity, whereas to deviate from his teachings is a symptom of psychosis. In his refutation on the basis of testimony from an array of eyewitnesses, including Clara Thompson and Izette de Forest in the case of Ferenczi, Fromm (1958a) went so far as to contend that Jones's "'rewriting' of history introduces into science a method which we so far have been accustomed to find only in Stalinist 'history,'" where those who stray from officially sanctioned doctrines are condemned as "'traitors' and 'spies' of capitalism" (p. 11). In his rejoinder to Fromm, Jacob Arlow (1958) asserted on behalf of orthodoxy not only that "in psychoanalysis there is no monolithic structure with a 'party line,'" but also that Ferenczi's technical innovations "went beyond psychoanalytic concepts," and indeed he had no hesitation in anathematizing them as "not psycho*analysis*" (p. 14). That Arlow endorsed Jones's proscription of Ferenczi even while maintaining that psychoanalysis has no "party line" is an irony that is doubtless more apparent to many readers today than it was to him.

Only one year after coming to the defense of Ferenczi and Rank, Fromm published *Sigmund Freud's Mission* (1959b), a compact classic of revisionist thinking in which he sought to provide an alternative to "the idolizing and unanalytic approach of Jones's biography" (p. 20). Focusing on Freud's relationship to his mother, Fromm argues that "dependency and insecurity are central elements in the structure of Freud's character, and of his neurosis" (p. 23), a structure that manifested itself in his relationships with men by causing Freud to "repress the awareness of dependency" as long as his emotional needs were being met and then to "negate it completely when the friend failed in the complete fulfillment of the motherly role" (p. 43). As Fromm points out, it made little difference whether Freud was in the position of pupil, friend, or mentor, since there is in all these relationships not only the "obvious and conscious dependence in which a person is dependent on a father figure, a 'magic helper,' a superior, etc.," but also "an unconscious dependence in which a dominant person is dependent on those who are dependent on him" (p. 52), as Freud indubitably was on his followers in the psychoanalytic movement.

Sigmund Freud's Mission is another landmark in Fromm's championing of Ferenczi because, in his chapter "Freud's Authoritarianism," Fromm singles out Freud's relationship to Ferenczi as "the most drastic example of Freud's intolerance and authoritarianism" (p. 68). Fromm cites a personal communication from de Forest relaying Ferenczi's account of his final visit to Freud in Vienna, prior to the Wiesbaden Congress where he presented his now-classic paper "Confusion of Tongues," at the conclusion of which, in Ferenczi's words, "I reached out my hand in affectionate adieu," but "the Professor turned his back on me and walked out of the room" (p. 70). While acknowledging that "the faithful worshipers of Freud," such as Jones, "make it a point to deny any authoritarian tendency in Freud," Fromm counters that such denials exhibit a "psychological naïveté" because they fail to reckon with the fact that Freud was "kind and tolerant" only "to people who idolized him and never disagreed." Precisely because he "was so dependent on unconditional affirmation and agreement by others," Fromm elaborates, Freud could be "a loving father to submissive sons," but when he encountered any opposition, Freud became "a stern, authoritarian one to those who dared to disagree" (p. 71).

That Fromm compares Jones's questioning the sanity of psychoanalytic dissidents to a Stalinist approach to history becomes all the more comprehensible when one recognizes that both his indictment of Freud's "authoritarianism" and his use of the term "magic helper" have their intellectual—as opposed to personal—roots in the conceptual framework articulated by Fromm in his 1941 masterwork, *Escape from Freedom*, a profound analysis of the allure of fascism to so many middle-class Germans, which Fromm traces back to the existential choice faced by "modern man, freed from the bonds of pre-individualistic society" since the Renaissance, between "positive freedom," on the one hand, and the retreat into "new dependencies and submission" on the other (p. viii). Although Fromm does not mention Ferenczi in *Escape from Freedom*, and his critique of Freud is confined to a demonstration of why an adherence to drive theory caused him to view man as a "closed system" who is "primarily self-sufficient and only secondarily in need of others to satisfy his instinctual needs," instead of understanding that "man is primarily a social being," so that "the needs and desires that center about the individual's relations to others, such as love, hatred, tenderness, symbiosis, are the fundamental psychological phenomena" (pp. 317–18), that book can nonetheless be read as an incisive commentary on the Freud-Ferenczi relationship, in its personal as well as its theoretical dimensions.

As Lawrence Friedman (2013) recounts in his biography, although Fromm had been a member of the Frankfurt Institute for Social Research since 1929, and "played a central role" (p. 46) in negotiating its relocation to Columbia University in 1934, by the end of the decade his emphasis on the concept of social character led to a break with Max Horkheimer and Theodor Adorno, who continued to adhere to Freud's "biologically rooted instinct theory" (p. 61), and *Escape from Freedom* emerged from the inspiration and solidarity Fromm derived increasingly from the cultural and interpersonal visions of psychoanalysis espoused by Karen Horney and Harry Stack Sullivan, among others. A pillar of the book is Fromm's thesis that both sadism and masochism spring from "the inability to bear the isolation and weakness of one's own self," and thus have as their aim what he terms symbiosis, or "the union of one individual self with another self (or any other power outside of the own self) in such a way as to make each lose the integrity of the own self and to make them completely dependent on each other" (p. 180).

As Fromm elaborates, such a "sado-masochistic character" is not limited to those with sexual perversions but can be found in otherwise "normal" people, and might better be called "the 'authoritarian character'" (p. 186). "Authority," Fromm notes, "refers to an interpersonal relationship in which one person looks upon another as somebody superior to him," but whereas in rational versions of such relationships—as one hopes would obtain between a teacher and student, for example, or a supervisor and a psychoanalytic candidate—the aim is to foster the development of the person in the subordinate position so that "the authority relationship tends to dissolve itself" as the power differential diminishes over time and the student "becomes more and more like the teacher himself," in irrational or perverse versions of this structure—prototypically, between a master and slave—the "superiority serves as a basis for exploitation" so that the power differential is maintained, and indeed the distance between the two parties "becomes intensified through its long duration" (pp. 186–87). Fromm introduces the term "magic helper" to describe the largely unconscious dependence exhibited by people on a source of power outside of themselves, the essential function of which is "to protect, help, and develop the individual, to be with him and never leave him alone," a function that can be attributed to someone who is then "endowed with magic qualities" (p. 197), whether that seemingly godlike other be a political leader, a partner in a romantic relationship, or a psychoanalyst to a patient in the throes of transference.

Fromm's analysis of the authoritarian character precisely captures the essential dynamics of Ferenczi's relationship to Freud. Thus, when Fromm writes, "the reasons why a person is bound to a magic helper are, in principle, the same that we have found at the root of the symbiotic drives: an inability to stand alone and to fully express his own individual potentialities" (p. 198), this uncannily echoes the final entry of Ferenczi's *Clinical Diary*, where he confesses, "I was brave (and productive) only as long as I (unconsciously) relied for support on another power, that is, I had never really become 'grown up'" (Dupont, 1985, p. 212). Because Ferenczi interprets his pernicious anemia as a punishment for his attempt at emancipation from Freud, he feels he must face the bleak prospect that "the only possibility for my continued existence" lies in "the renunciation of the largest part of one's own self, in order to carry out the will of that higher power to the end (as though it were my own)" (p. 212).

A further extended passage from *Escape from Freedom* (1941) highlights the pertinence of Fromm's ideas to grasping the perversely "symbiotic" quality of the Freud-Ferenczi relationship:

> The intensity of the relatedness to the magic helper is in reverse proportion to the ability to express spontaneously one's own intellectual, emotional, and sensuous potentialities. In other words, one hopes to get everything one expects from life, from the magic helper, instead of by one's own actions. The more this is the case, the more the center of life is shifted from one's own person to the magic helper and his personifications. The question is then no longer how to live oneself, but how to manipulate "him" in order not to lose him and how to make him do what one wants, even to make him responsible for what one is responsible oneself.
>
> (pp. 198–99)

A crucial component of Fromm's analysis is the ambivalence that is bound to arise in the subordinate member of a sadomasochistic dyad. As he remarks, "this dependency, springing from and at the same time leading to a blockage of spontaneity, not only gives a certain amount of security but also results in a feeling of weakness and bondage" (p. 199). Because of the inhibition of his authentic being, "the very person who is dependent on the magic helper also feels, though often unconsciously, enslaved by 'him' and, to a greater or lesser degree, rebels against 'him.' This rebelliousness against the very person on whom one has put one's hopes for security and happiness," Fromm continues, "creates new conflicts. It has to be suppressed if one is not to lose 'him,' but the underlying antagonism constantly threatens the security sought for in the relationship" (p. 109). Since "any actual person is bound to be disappointing" if burdened with the expectations of being the magic helper, the disenchantment that must ensue upon waking up from one's dream augments "the resentment resulting from one's own enslavement to that person," and once again "leads to continuous conflicts" (pp. 109–10).

Having been in analysis not only with Ferenczi in Budapest but also with Fromm in New York, Clara Thompson was in a unique position to draw on what she had learned from Fromm in pondering Ferenczi's character. Thompson renders her verdict in "Ferenczi's Contributions to Psychoanalysis" (1944):

> Despite Ferenczi's obviously lovable qualities, he suffered during life from a need to be accepted and loved. Because of this need, his personal relationship to Freud was more important to him than his own independent thinking. He was the type of man who is happy in working for a strong person; Freud was that strong person in his life.
>
> (p. 73)

Without using the term "magic helper," Thompson makes it clear that Freud served this psychological function for Ferenczi. She continues:

> Had Ferenczi had nothing original of his own to contribute, the relationship might have been a completely satisfactory one; but his was an original mind, and, beneath his devotion to Freud, there raged a constant struggle to be himself. At the same time, he feared incurring the disapproval of Freud. This made his attitude toward Freud definitely ambivalent; and this ambivalence can be seen, I believe, in his writings.
>
> (p. 73)

Thompson specifies that many of Ferenczi's papers "give one the impression of an appeasing quality," and that he evinced a tendency to be "more Freudian than Freud." With great acuity, Thompson discerns that Ferenczi's ambivalence "manifested itself despite all his efforts for he would often develop an idea of Freud's to a fantastic degree, thus, in the end, making the situation absurd," as he did in *Thalassa*, where Ferenczi "traces the stages of libido development to the Ice Age, thus making the whole idea pure fantasy" (p. 73).

By calling attention to Ferenczi's penchant for unconsciously parodying Freud's ideas by taking them to "absurd" conclusions, Thompson underscores what Ferenczi himself had privately acknowledged in the *Clinical Diary* concerning his "total inhibition about speaking in [Freud's] presence until he broached a subject, and then the burning desire to win his approval by showing I had understood him completely, and by immediately going further in the direction he had recommended," all of which "reveals me to have been a blindly dependent son" (Dupont, 1985, p. 185). Beneath this feeling of being "dazzled and amazed," however, there always lurked a "hidden doubt" because "it was only adoration and not independent judgment that made me follow him" (p. 185). Ferenczi, too, retrospectively deems *Thalassa* to be a text that, despite its "many good points," nonetheless "clings too closely to the words of the master," a "new edition" of which "would mean complete rewriting" (p. 187). Although ultimately grounded in Ferenczi's own self-understanding, Thompson's analysis of the ambivalence stemming from the conflict between Ferenczi's "struggle to be himself" and his fear of "incurring the disapproval of Freud" is directly indebted to Fromm's explication of the "blockage of spontaneity" that affords an intimidated individual a "certain amount of security," while simultaneously exacting "a feeling of weakness and bondage," and of the ensuing tug of war between the impulses to submission and rebellion that is the hallmark of someone who subjects himself to the irrational authority of another person.

Ferenczi's entire career constitutes an enactment of his unconscious ambivalence toward Freud. In his paper, "Belief, Disbelief, and Conviction" (1913a), for example, when Ferenczi describes how many of his patients who "were not really convinced of the correctness of the psychoanalytic explanations, but had believed them blindly (dogmatically, as a matter of doctrine)" and "successfully repressed all their suspicions and objections only in order to keep secure the filial love they had transferred to the doctor" (p. 438), he voices in displaced fashion his own "suspicions and objections" concerning Freud. The same is true of "The Symbolic Representation of the Pleasure and Reality Principles in the Oedipus Myth" (1912b), in which Ferenczi interprets Schopenhauer's reference to the Oedipus myth in a seemingly worshipful letter to Goethe as showing the young philosopher's "unconscious reaction against this—perhaps rather extravagant—expression of gratitude" toward the sage of Weimar, "a reaction that allowed some display of the hostile tendencies that go to make up the fundamentally ambivalent feeling-attitude of a son towards his father" (p. 220). Even as Ferenczi seeks to pay tribute to Freud and uphold the universality of the Oedipus complex, his commentary on the "hostile tendencies" that lurked beneath Schopenhauer's professions of gratitude toward Goethe again reflects his own disavowed resentment toward Freud, although, as Ferenczi observes of Schopenhauer, while writing this paper "he was himself dominated . . . by affects that would have debarred this insight" (p. 219).

No less ironic in light of subsequent events are the following: Ferenczi's role as the founder of the International Psychoanalytical Association; his proposal for the formation of the Secret Committee by "a small group of men" who would be "thoroughly analyzed" by Freud, "so that they could represent the pure theory unadulterated by personal complexes" (Paskauskas, 1993, p. 146); his insistence that "mutual analysis is nonsense," while Freud is the "only one who can permit himself to do without an analyst" and "right in everything" (Brabant, Falzeder, and Giampieri-Deutsch, 1993, p. 449); and his leading the charge against the defections of both Jung and Rank by authoring critical reviews (Ferenczi, 1913b, 1927) of their dissident books. In all these instances, we see Ferenczi having "successfully repressed all [his] suspicions and objections only in order to keep secure the filial love [he] had transferred" to Freud, though in the end the straitjacket of orthodoxy he sought to impose on others succeeded only in pinioning his own wings.

A review of Fromm's contributions to the rehabilitation of Ferenczi's reputation also serves to enhance our appreciation of his importance to the history of psychoanalysis. No less consequential than his affiliation with Horney and Sullivan is Fromm's elective affinity with Winnicott. Although, as we have seen in Chapter 2, Fromm refers to Winnicott in passing for the first and only time in *The Anatomy of Human Destructiveness*, while Winnicott never refers to Fromm, Fromm is a crucial "missing link" in the tradition of Independent psychoanalysis that runs from Ferenczi to Winnicott and beyond. Thus, when Fromm traces the "root of the symbiotic drives" to a person's "inability to stand alone and to fully express his individual potentialities," he not only looks back to Ferenczi but also looks ahead to Winnicott (1965) and his studies of the interaction between "maturational processes and the facilitating environment." Like Winnicott, Fromm (1941) traces what happens when "the parents, acting as the agents of society, start to suppress the child's spontaneity and independence" (p. 201), and he captures the essence of Winnicott's dichotomy between creativity and compliance when he writes that "every neurosis . . . is essentially an adaptation to such early conditions (particularly those of early childhood) as are themselves irrational and, generally speaking, unfavorable to the growth and development of the child" (pp. 30–31). Winnicott's antithesis between creativity and compliance is itself an outgrowth of his core distinction between the True Self and the False Self, and Fromm again arrives at the same destination nearly two decades earlier when he affirms:

> This substitution of pseudo acts for original acts of thinking, feeling, and willing leads eventually to the replacement of the original self by a pseudo self. The original self is the self which is the originator of mental activities. The pseudo self is only an agent who actually represents the role a person is supposed to play but who does so under the name of the self.
>
> (p. 229)

When it is recognized that Horney (1942), too, postulates an antimony between the "real self" and "phony self" (p. 22), then it becomes clear how close is the kinship between the "Middle Group" of British object relations theorists and the American "neo-Freudians," and how both schools have carried forward Ferenczi's psychoanalytic legacy.

During Fromm's lifetime, the most serious damage to his reputation was inflicted by his erstwhile Frankfurt school colleague, Herbert Marcuse, in a polemical exchange in the pages of *Dissent*, the centerpiece of which Marcuse adapted for the epilogue to *Eros and Civilization* (1955). Although Marcuse was widely perceived as having gotten the better of their quarrel, a rereading of his "Critique of Neo-Freudian Revisionism" shows it to be a surprisingly lame effort. Like Adorno and Horkheimer decades earlier, Marcuse staked everything on Freud's instinct theory, claiming absurdly that because of Freud's emphasis on early infancy "the decisive relations are thus those which are least interpersonal" (p. 231). Indeed, according to Marcuse, only Freud's "hypothesis of the death instinct," and not any environmental or social factors, can explain "the hidden unconscious tie which binds the oppressed to their oppressors" (p. 247). In a further reflection of the prevailing Zeitgeist, Lionel Trilling, too, hailed "the idea of the reality principle and the idea of the death instinct" as forming "the crown of Freud's broader speculation on the life of man" (1940, p. 53), and he castigated "the tendency of our educated liberal classes to reject the tough, complex psychology of Freud for the easy rationalistic optimism of Horney and Fromm" (1946, p. 95).

In a letter to Martin Jay, the historian of the Frankfurt School, Fromm commented, "my whole theoretical work is based on what I consider Freud's most important findings, with the exception of his metapsychological findings," which is "the reverse of Marcuse's position, who bases his thinking entirely on Freud's metapsychology, and ignores completely his clinical findings, that is to say, the unconscious, character, resistance, etc." (qtd. in Roazen, 2001, p. 36). The passage of time has vindicated Fromm in his debate with Marcuse. Freud's assumption that infants exist in a cocoon of primary narcissism has been discredited by neuroscientists and attachment researchers, and it would be difficult today to find an analyst who is influenced by Marcuse. Fromm, by contrast, after decades of marginalization, is increasingly gaining recognition as a seminal psychoanalytic thinker. A bellwether of this shift is Daniel Shaw's splendid book *Traumatic Narcissism* (2014), as evidenced by Shaw's delineation of how "the traumatizing narcissist recruits others . . . into a relationship that seductively offers the promise of the bestowal of special gifts"—as Freud did with his followers—only soon to "find cause to accuse the other of insufficient concern and of selfishness" (p. 13). As we have seen, a key point in Fromm's analysis of the authoritarian character is that the "dominant person is dependent on those who are dependent on him," only the dependency needs of the oppressors in such symbiotic bonds must remain unconscious because, in Shaw's words, "they have learned to defend against their history of being shamed and subjugated by putting others in the situation they were in—by becoming the shamer and the subjugator" (p. 138). To borrow Shaw's terminology, and meld it with that of Bernard Brandchaft (Brandchaft, Doctors, and Sorter, 2010), who has contributed signally from a self psychological and intersubjective perspective to our understanding of "relational systems of subjugation," whereas Freud played the part of the *traumatizing narcissist* in his relationship with Ferenczi, Ferenczi exhibited the deformations resulting from his attempts at *pathological accommodation*, though in the end he sought to cast off the shackles of Freud's authoritarianism and to promulgate a truly emancipatory psychoanalysis.

If, in the memorable pronouncement of Michael Balint (1968), "the historic event of the disagreement between Freud and Ferenczi acted as a trauma on the psychoanalytic world" (p. 152), I hope to have shown that Fromm, in addition to being Ferenczi's stalwart champion, has with his concepts of the authoritarian character and the magic helper given us invaluable scalpels with which to dissect both the psychic roots and interpersonal dynamics of this immensely generative but ultimately tragic encounter. But it must not be forgotten, as I have documented in the previous chapter, that Fromm was not only the analyst but himself the victim of institutional trauma, having by 1953 been stripped of the "Nansen" or direct membership in the International Psychoanalytical Association that

Jones had bestowed on him in 1936 as an émigré in New York (Roazen, 2001). Having been purged from the "party," Fromm knew whereof he spoke when he took Jones to task for the "Stalinism" in his account of the fates of Ferenczi and Rank in his biography of Freud. Now that Ferenczi has at last been accorded his full measure of recognition by posterity, and the William Alanson White Institute, cofounded by Fromm in 1943, together with the American Institute—also cofounded by Fromm two years earlier before he parted ways with Horney—has become a component of the American Psychoanalytic Association, and thereby also of the IPA, let us hope that Fromm in his turn may undergo a similar rehabilitation.

Part 2

Ferenczian Inflections

Chapter 4

The Other Side of the Story
Severn on Ferenczi and Mutual Analysis

> "Is the purpose of mutual analysis perhaps the finding of that common feature which repeats itself in every case of infantile trauma?"
> —Ferenczi, *Clinical Diary*

A Ferenczian Experience

In scholarship, too, we have our Orphas. Thus it was that on December 16, 2013, I received out of the blue an e-mail with the subject line, "Ferenczi student visiting Gainesville." Its author, Kathleen Meigs, a writer and editor then living in Ojai, California, reminded me that we had spoken at the 2012 conference of the Ferenczi Society in Budapest and asked if we could meet during an impending visit to see her daughter. One week later, Ms. Meigs appeared in my office, where she produced a photocopy of Elizabeth Severn's *The Discovery of the Self* and directed my attention to a case history beginning on page 96.[1] Scanning the work, which I had to confess I had not read, I swiftly confirmed her surmise, "It has to be Ferenczi..."

Discovering Severn

Severn's importance as the patient with whom Ferenczi engaged in his experiment of mutual analysis has been widely acknowledged since the publication of the *Clinical Diary*. What has until recently been known about her life is indebted above all to the pioneering work of Christopher Fortune (1993, 1994, 1996), and Severn has also found champions in Jeffrey M. Masson (1984), Martin Stanton (1991), Benjamin Wolstein (1992), and Nancy A. Smith (1998, 1999). Special mention must now be made of Arnold W. Rachman's book, *Elizabeth Severn: The "Evil Genius" of Psychoanalysis* (2018), which is no less to be applauded for its impassioned contribution to the rehabilitation of Severn's reputation than it is to be lamented for its innumerable factual mistakes and typographical errors.[2] But these authors have for the most part relied either on Ferenczi's portrait of her as "R.N." in the *Clinical Diary* or on impressionistic readings not simply of Severn's first two books (1913, 1917) but also of *The Discovery of the Self* (1933), the distillation of her relationship with Ferenczi, which began with her arrival in Budapest in April 1925 and did not end until her departure in February 1933. Rachman, although he cites the original version of this chapter in his references, does not take its findings into account; and even Smith (1998), who perceptively discerns the muffled echoes of Severn's sexual and physical abuse in the "anesthetizingly comforting" (p. 242) rhetoric of her second book, in contrast to the "depth of healing" (p. 241) evidenced by *The Discovery of the Self*, concentrates on Severn's concept of "Orpha" as a protective shield against trauma and does not convey the landmark quality of her crowning achievement.

The realization that *The Discovery of the Self* contains a thinly disguised case history of Ferenczi, as well as of Severn herself, immediately transforms the book into one of the essential texts in the history of psychoanalysis and an indispensable companion volume to the *Clinical Diary*.[3] For the first time, Severn truly emerges as a subject in her own right whose entire body of work warrants thoroughgoing reappraisal. We can hear in her writing the patient's voice that is too often missing in psychoanalysis. *The Discovery of the Self*, by the same token, takes its place in the venerable analytic tradition—extending from Freud and Ferenczi through Horney and Kohut—of covert autobiography, while also tacitly employing material from the analysis of a colleague. As I shall document, however, Severn, unlike many others who have engaged in the latter practice, did so in an ethically responsible fashion by securing her famous analysand's informed consent and allowing him to see how she had rendered his case.

Competing Legacies

In a superlative feat of research, B. William Brennan (2015a) has established the identities of the eight principal patients referred to by code names in the *Diary*. In addition to Severn, these include Clara Thompson

("Dm.") and Izette de Forest ("Ett."). What the renewed attention that should now go to Severn makes clear is the extent to which these three formidable American women, while all were marginal from the perspective of the then-hegemonic school of ego psychology, espoused alternative versions of Ferenczi, the roots of which lay not only in their individual characters but also in the group dynamics of their time together during his final years in Budapest.

Of the three, Thompson is the most critical in her attitude toward Ferenczi. When de Forest (1942), in the first article on Ferenczi to appear in the *International Journal of Psycho-Analysis*, argued that the analyst should help the patient "to face dramatically the trauma or traumatic series by re-living it emotionally, not in its original setting but as an actual part of the analytic situation" (p. 121), Thompson published a rejoinder (1943) in which she challenged the premise that the analyst should facilitate the patient's reliving of traumatic experience by insisting on the analyst's obligation "to keep the patient in touch with reality," and that he ought therefore on no account to "make the patient believe the analyst is really involved" (p. 66) in any kind of joint enactment.

Although Thompson disputes de Forest's endorsement of Ferenczi's radical views, she does so respectfully and with an absence of rancor. Matters stand quite otherwise with Severn, whom Thompson palpably loathed. When Fromm was gathering testimonials for his rebuttal (1958a) of Jones's (1957) impugning of the sanity of Rank and Ferenczi, Thompson wrote to him that Severn was "one of the most destructive people I know" and that Ferenczi had "had the courage to dismiss" her after she "had bullied him for years" (qtd. in Fortune, 1993, p. 115). What is more, in the interview Thompson gave to Kurt Eissler on June 4, 1952, she maligned Severn as "a much better bad mother than Freud" (p. 20) and called her a "paranoid bitch" (p. 6) as well as a "'Bird of prey'" (Thompson, 1952, p. 7).

In the first entry of the *Clinical Diary*, Ferenczi discloses that Thompson "had been grossly abused sexually by her father" (Dupont, 1985, p. 3) in childhood. As Sue A. Shapiro (1993) points out, however, Thompson failed "to spread the word when she returned to America about the reality of abuse and its impact on children's lives" (p. 162). Shapiro likewise notes that in his final diary entry Ferenczi posed the question, "must every case be mutual?," and he commented that Thompson "feels hurt because of the absence of mutuality on my part" (Dupont, 1985, p. 213).

Ferenczi's reference to Thompson's history of sexual abuse furnishes a context for his statements that she had "allowed herself to take more and more liberties" with his relaxation technique by kissing him, and then boasted to patients "who were undergoing analysis elsewhere: 'I am allowed to kiss Papa Ferenczi, as often as I like'" (p. 2). As Brennan (2015b) has emphasized, one of those to whom Thompson spoke was Edith Jackson, who was in analysis with Freud, and it was by this route that Freud heard about Ferenczi's supposed "kissing technique," which evoked Freud's condemnation and has led orthodox analysts, such as Arlow (1958) in his response to Fromm, to dismiss Ferenczi's technical innovations as "not psycho*analysis*" (p. 14). At least indirectly, therefore, Thompson is responsible not only for exacerbating the conflict between Ferenczi and Freud but also for much of the damage to Ferenczi's posthumous reputation.

Compelling evidence that Ferenczi's indulgence of Thompson's behavior did not stem from any erotic desire on his part may be found in Thompson's posthumously (and only partially) published manuscript, "Ferenczi's Relaxation Method" (1933). There, Thompson writes of a woman "who had grown up in an intolerant small-town community" where she had been ostracized for her "childhood sexual activities with boys," for whom it became important in her analysis not only "to talk of whether her body was repulsive to the analyst, but to test it" (p. 67). Accordingly, she was encouraged by the analyst "to try a natural expression of her feelings," which made it seem "necessary for her to kiss the analyst not only once but many times and to receive from her not simply passivity but an evidence of warm friendliness and a caress in return before she could be conscious of the degree of degradation she had felt" (pp. 67–68).

In her case report, Thompson makes it seem that the patient and analyst are both women and she professes to wonder whether the procedure would have been different had the analyst been a man. But multiple clues make it obvious that Thompson, like Severn in *The Discovery of the Self*, is giving a disguised account of her own experience with Ferenczi, which she proceeds to justify by arguing that "the technique of not touching the patient except in the most formal way might easily act as a permanent reliving of the childhood experience so that an abreaction of the experience and change of attitude might remain permanently impossible" (p. 68). According to the biographical sketch by Maurice R. Green (1964), Thompson grew up "on the outskirts of Providence," Rhode Island, where the family attended a Baptist church with "strict religious observances" (pp. 348–49) favored by her mother. This fits with the reference to "an intolerant small-town community," but even more striking is that Ferenczi, in the *Clinical Diary*, mentions that Thompson "does really have a very unpleasant odor, and people with a fairly acute sense of smell are repelled by her" (Dupont, 1985, p. 87), a compelling explanation for her need to test the repulsiveness of her body in the analysis.

Despite this veiled confession, however, and the intimation that Ferenczi's "warm friendliness" permitted an "abreaction" of her childhood trauma—an aim seen here as desirable, in contrast to her later writings—Thompson did not get what she needed from her treatment with him. The bitterness of this disappointment must have heightened Thompson's antipathy to Severn, who took up so much of Ferenczi's time and emotional energy and who cast the spell that led him to embark on the experiment in mutual analysis that Thompson herself so ardently desired.

Mutuality, Marginality, Magnanimity

Like Thompson, Severn preoccupies Ferenczi throughout the *Clinical Diary*. But where he may be said to have failed with Thompson, he succeeded with Severn. In his opening entry, Ferenczi reports that in what can only be her case "the communication of the content of my own psyche developed into a form of mutual analysis, from which I, the analyst, derived much profit" (Dupont, 1985, p. 3), while in his closing entry he records not only Severn's hope that "what will *remain*" of their joint work "is a *reciprocal* 'honorable' recognition of mutual achievement," but also his own sense of accomplishment: "I released R.N. from her torments by repeating the sins of her father, which then I confessed and for which I received forgiveness" (p. 214).

Ferenczi's conviction that he "released R.N. from her torments" gains credence from Severn's interview with Eissler on December 20, 1952. Although Severn (1952) could not have known what Thompson had said to him, she calls into question the allegation that Ferenczi "dismissed" her from her analysis when she declares that, after a year of mutual analysis, neither she nor Ferenczi could stand it any longer, "and I was at the end of my strength and my money and everything else, and so I finally managed to get away from Budapest by sheer will force, a complete wreck" (p. 7). She reiterates, "it was the last year I was there that I did his analysis, and that was what helped me get on my feet, you see—to disconnect from him" (p. 13).

Beyond providing an alternative account of the end of her analysis, Severn exhibits a magnanimity toward Thompson that stands in stark contrast to Thompson's vituperativeness toward her. Concerning the fee arrangements for the mutual analysis, Severn explains that Ferenczi did not pay her anything but also stopped accepting money from her. In addition to disregarding a debt she had accumulated, Ferenczi had in analysis a wealthy American woman married to a Hungarian count. Ferenczi persuaded this woman, who had previously been Severn's patient, to lend or give her several hundred dollars, which Severn found "very humiliating" (p. 16), and he later told Severn that he was not charging this woman anything. "At the same time," Severn informs Eissler, "he was charging a young woman who was an analyst and earning her own living. I felt it was quite unfair. That the countess could pay, and it was hard for the other lady to pay. And he thought so, too, but he didn't do anything about it."

Thanks to Brennan (2015a), we know that the wealthy woman married to a Hungarian count is Harriot Sigray ("S.I.") and the financially struggling analyst is Thompson, although Severn tactfully refrains from identifying Thompson in this connection. Thompson must have been aware not only that Ferenczi was coming to Severn for analysis but also that he was not charging either her or Sigray, while she herself was expected to pay for her sessions. These inequities added insult to the injury of being excluded from mutual analysis and they undoubtedly fueled Thompson's grudge against Ferenczi as well as her hatred of Severn.

After Ferenczi's death, his wife assured Thompson (1952) that "he had often told her that I would be his best pupil" (p. 9). But this praise from beyond the grave did not outweigh her sense of not having been close to Ferenczi's heart. Paradoxically, therefore, whereas to all outward appearances Thompson was Ferenczi's "best pupil" in the United States, with Severn on the remotest margin, the truth as seen from inside is rather the reverse, with Severn being, as Ferenczi wrote to Groddeck on December 21, 1930, his "main patient, the 'Queen,'" to whom he devoted as much as "four, sometimes five hours daily" (Fortune, 2002, p. 96), and Thompson nursing an inferiority complex. Despite being, as her daughter Margaret recalled, "a one-woman show," with "no friends or colleagues, only patients" (Fortune, 1993, p. 105), and lacking an institutional base of any kind, Severn knew and understood Ferenczi more profoundly than anyone, including Michael Balint. Certainly, in her espousal in *The Discovery of the Self* (1933) of *"psychognosis"* (p. 148), she was more attuned than either Thompson or de Forest to his mystical tendencies or what Groddeck, in a letter to Gizella Ferenczi after Sándor's death, termed his "ascent to the stars" (Fortune, 2002, p. 114).

Severn on Psychoanalysis

By the time Severn began her eight-year odyssey with Ferenczi in 1925, she had published two books that engaged with Freud and his ideas and regarded herself as a practitioner of psychoanalysis. She had, moreover, as she informed Eissler, previously attempted analysis with Smith Ely Jelliffe, Joseph Asch, and Otto Rank. *The Discovery of the Self* (1933) is, therefore, the distillation not simply of her experience with Ferenczi but of her sustained immersion in psychoanalytic culture. The depth of her insight, her anticipation of later trends, and the cogency of her criticisms can all be gleaned from a handful of quotations. She pays tribute at the outset to Freud: "The truth is that there is a very large part of the mind, actively functioning, which is completely unknown to the conscious self. . . . The lifting of the invisible into visibility was a prodigious work and has entitled Freud to a distinguished place among the scientists and benefactors of mankind" (p. 24).

Although she acknowledges Freud as the indispensable starting point, Severn's emphasis on the permeability of the child's mind to environmental influences articulates a fundamental principle of relational thinking:

> It is little realized how sensitive the child's mind is, and especially how even in its "unconscious" years—that is generally until the third year—it is the constant recipient of the words, actions, and behavior (and I believe also the thoughts) of those in his environment.
>
> (p. 28)

Her comments on a boy who stole money and craved sweets cannot fail to remind contemporary readers of Winnicott on the antisocial tendency: "These too told that he did not receive enough love from his mother, and the angry outbursts were a positive symptom expressing his unconscious rage at the deprivation" (p. 101). Both Winnicott and Kohut would concur with Severn that the analyst ought "to provide the patient with just that psychic atmosphere which must have been absent in his early life, or he would not be compelled to seek the kind of help he is seeking now" (p. 68), while Kohut especially would applaud her recognition that the patient requires "endless understanding and 'Einfühlung,' as the Germans say it, a kind of 'feeling in' or identification with him and his problem, whatever it may be" (p. 53).

Beyond these prescient theoretical insights, Severn judiciously assesses "the *limitations* of psychoanalysis" (p. 51). Just as Ferenczi in the *Clinical Diary* faults Freud because he "introduced the 'educational' stage too soon" (Dupont, 1985, p. 62) into analysis, so, too, Severn (1933) stresses that the analytic "relationship should be anything but a pedagogic one" (p. 53). In her interview with Eissler, Severn (1952) states that during the second of her three meetings with Freud, in 1929, she expressed her conviction that his early students "had not been thoroughly analyzed" because "they had been analyzed in an intellectual manner" but "this limitation did not appear to Freud to be a limitation" (p. 3). Entirely in Ferenczi's spirit is Severn's (1933) espousal of the virtues of elasticity, tact, and humility: "The greatest objection to be made against psychoanalysis as such is, in my opinion, its *rigidity*. Being devised as a systematic and observational method, it lacks in flexibility and humanness in its personal application to sick people" (pp. 51–52). "The analyst has to be very tactful in this process," Severn adds, while the patient should have the right "to say when he thinks the analyst is wrong, since the person of the analyst represents an authority to him" (p. 52).

The Battle Lines

In a letter to Jones on May 29, 1933, one week after Ferenczi's death, Freud alleged that Ferenczi had fallen victim to "mental degeneration" that was manifested in his "technical innovations" and pointed his finger squarely at a "suspect American woman" with the most bizarre ideas:

> After she left, he believed that she influenced him through vibrations across the ocean, and said that she analyzed him and thereby saved him. (He thus played both roles, was mother and child.) She seems to have produced a *pseudologia phantastica*; he credited her with the oddest childhood traumas, which he then defended against us. In this confusion his once so brilliant intelligence was extinguished.
>
> (Paskauskas, 1993, p. 721)

Pseudologia phantastica. To Freud, Severn was a compulsive liar, while Ferenczi's willingness to credit her reports of the "oddest childhood traumas" was a symptom of the loss of his mind. Hence Freud's notorious condemnation of Severn as Ferenczi's "evil genius" (Jones, 1957, p. 407)—an epithet reserved for his choicest enemies he had previously used in *On the History of the Psycho-Analytic Movement* (1914a, p. 45) to denounce the German psychiatrist Alfred Hoche, who had attacked his followers as a sect, and that derives from Descartes' fear he was being seduced in his dreams, about which Freud (1929) would later comment in a letter to Maxime Leroy.

Ferenczi's rehabilitation of Freud's "seduction theory" is eloquently defended by Severn in *The Discovery of the Self* (1933):

> The importance of *trauma* as a specific and almost universal cause of neurosis was first impressed upon me by Ferenczi, who, probing deeply, had found it present in nearly all his cases. He thus resurrected and gave new value to an idea that had once, much earlier, been entertained by Freud, but which was discarded by him in favor of "fantasy." . . . Experience has convinced me, however, that the patient does not "invent," but *always tells the truth*, even though in a distorted form; and, further, that what he tells is mostly of a severe and specific injury, inflicted on him when he was young and helpless.
>
> (p. 91)

From this premise of the reality of traumatic experience, it follows that "emotional recollection and reproduction" is "the *sine qua non* of successful analysis." (p. 71). Severn continues:

> It is an important measure that was worked out between Ferenczi and myself in the course of my own long analysis with him—a development that enables the patient to relive, as though it were *now*, the traumatic events of the past, aided by the dramatic participation of the analyst.
>
> It is usually considered enough to recollect these events mentally, but the thing that made them harmful in the first place was, in every case, the *shock*, the psychic reaction to them. . . . The emotion created was of a nature or degree that made it incapable of assimilation by the person suffering it, and it is this feeling-quality that has to be

recovered and experienced again, in order to bring, first, conviction and, second, release through reconstruction.

(p. 72)

Or, in Severn's epigrammatic formulation: "'Hallucination,' they say—*Memory*, I say, a memory that had been kept alive in the unconscious and that was now, perhaps for the first time, projected outward into the objective world where we could see it" (p. 74).

The Case of Ferenczi

According to Fortune (1994), Severn "does not mention mutual analysis, and there are few references to Ferenczi" (p. 221) in *The Discovery of the Self*. Severn, however, told her daughter that Ferenczi had asked her not to divulge that they had engaged in mutual analysis, while in an addendum to her interview (1952) with Eissler she attested that *The Discovery of the Self* "replaced to some extent the plans Ferenczi and I had had for a more scientific mutual publication," and that "he saw the MSS. before I left and approved it" (p. 24). Thus, while respecting Ferenczi's wishes, Severn's book is not only about the experience of mutual analysis but is also a "mutual publication" insofar as it received his blessing before his death, and Ferenczi's spirit permeates every page.

The case history of Ferenczi appears in Chapter 5, "Nightmares Are Real," which forms the clinical heart of Severn's book. Severn (1933) introduces her patient as "a man of especially high moral and intellectual standing, with a very balanced outlook on life and marked serenity of manner. He suffered from various physical symptoms, which he ascribed mostly to bodily causes," and was "in a state of constant depression in regard to his health" (p. 96). Contending that the analysis disclosed not only a "definite psychological clinical picture quite sufficient to account for his state of physical deterioration" but also "a clearly outlined psychosis," Severn affirms, "the patient was not the balanced, well-adjusted person that he, and others, had imagined."

Ferenczi had been worried for decades about his health and by 1932 he was in a "state of physical deterioration," which he attributed in the *Clinical Diary* to the prospect of being "trampled under foot" by Freud's "indifferent power" (Dupont, 1985, p. 212)—a "definite psychological clinical picture." Severn's initial perception of her patient as "very balanced" and possessing a "marked serenity of manner" comports with Ferenczi's account of how he had been taught by Freud to exhibit a "calm, unemotional reserve" and "unruffled assurance that one knew better" (p. 185). In describing the "antipathy" and "apprehension" aroused in him by Severn, Ferenczi acknowledges, "I appear to have assumed, perhaps unconsciously, the attitude of superiority of my intrepid masculinity, which the patient took to be genuine, whereas this was a conscious professional pose, partly adopted as a defensive measure against anxiety" (p. 97). Although Severn's imputing of a "psychosis" to Ferenczi might seem extreme, it is corroborated by his avowal, "psychoanalytical insight into my own emotional emptiness, which was shrouded by overcompensation (repressed—unconscious—psychosis) led to a self-diagnosis of *schizophrenia*" (p. 160).[4]

Ferenczi's façade of "intrepid masculinity" crumbled during his analysis when, as Severn recounts, his "psychosis" was "involuntarily enacted":

> He spoke to me suddenly one day about Strindberg's play *The Father* and became himself almost immediately the insane son. He broke down and asked with tears in his eyes if I would sometimes think of him kindly after he had been put away in the asylum.
>
> (pp. 96–97)

Severn says that her patient "evidently expected to be thus sent away at that moment" and that he added "with terrible pathos, 'And we like, when the straitjacket must be put on us, that it shall be done by our mother.'" She elaborates, "I immediately saw by this that the patient was reexperiencing a severe trauma in which he expected his mother to send him away as insane."

In recounting Ferenczi's "emotional recollection and reproduction" of his "severe trauma" at the hands of his mother, "aided by the dramatic participation of the analyst," Severn fills in the contours of Ferenczi's description in the *Clinical Diary* of how, "to use R.N.'s mode of expression: in R.N. I find my mother again, namely the real one, who was hard and energetic and of whom I am afraid" (Dupont, 1985, p. 45). From Severn's (1933) perspective:

> We already knew something of this story, of his mother as an angry, hysterical woman, often scolding and threatening her child, and especially for a certain event that she had treated with such harshness and vituperation to make him feel completely crazy and branded as a felon.
>
> (p. 97)

As one can reconstruct from Ferenczi's self-analytic letter to Freud on December 26, 1912, while in the throes of his notorious triangle with his married mistress Gizella Pálos and her daughter Elma, with whom he had fallen in love after taking her into analysis, the "event" in question probably took place "at the age of about three" when he engaged in "mutual touching" with his sister Gisela, for which he was punished by his mother and the family cook and, indeed, "threatened with a kitchen knife" by the latter (Brabant, Falzeder, and Giampieri-Deutsch, 1993, p. 452).[5] But whereas Freud did not encourage Ferenczi to go beyond intellectual remembering of his childhood agonies to an emotional catharsis, with Severn (1933) "the unexpected reproduction in the analysis of a part of this painful scene" enabled him "to acknowledge this traumatically-caused insanity for the first time as a living fact in himself, which was the beginning of its dissolution" (p. 97).

After setting forth the primal trauma inflicted on Ferenczi, Severn proceeds to narrate "still another serious trauma, allied to that caused by the mother," namely "an unscrupulous attack by an adult person on the child's sensibilities, which was ruinous to his mental integrity and subsequent health" (p. 97). In this instance,

> he was a boy of six, his nurse the offender. She was a comely young woman of voluptuous type who, for the satisfaction of her own urgencies, seduced the child, i.e., used him forcibly as best she could in lieu of an adult partner.
>
> (p. 98)

Ferenczi, in the *Diary*, augments Severn's account by recalling his "reproduction of infantile experiences" in mutual analysis, specifically "passionate scenes" with a housemaid who "probably allowed me to play with her breasts, but then pressed my head between her legs, so that I became frightened and felt as if I was suffocating" (Dupont, 1985, p. 61). This trauma, Ferenczi proposes, is the source of his "hatred of females," leading him to feel not only murderous rage but also "exaggerated reactions of guilt at the slightest lapse."

Severn (1933) rounds out her case history by observing that the child was "horrified, frightened, and emotionally shocked by coming in contact with such emotional violence," but simultaneously

> he was in a real sense "seduced" in that he was made suddenly and unduly precocious, a *desire* was aroused in him that was beyond

his years and his capacity, but which remained, nevertheless, to act as a constant excitation, with an inclination to a repetition of the experience.

(p. 98)

Ferenczi, that is, became the prototype of the "wise baby," exhibiting the *"precocious maturity"* that, as he expounded theoretically in "Confusion of Tongues" (1933), results from *"introjection of the guilt feelings of the adult"* (pp. 165, 162) that is a large part of the price to be paid for being subjected to such an ordeal. As Severn (1933) puts it, the child is usually "too frightened to speak of it and too shocked to recognize the enormity of the sin *against him*," and consequently finds it easier "to feel himself the guilty one" (p. 98). Her patient, Severn concludes, "preserved his sanity" and reestablished "a seemingly normal relation to life after the trauma" by "what Ferenczi would call fragmentation" (p. 99). In other words, "he eliminated the entire affair . . . and his own fury" from his "psyche as a whole," although "the exploded bits continued to exist, spatially speaking, outside of him—where we had to 'catch' it, so to speak, before it could be restored."

By such a "remarkable compensatory mechanism" the child who became Severn's patient "grew to be a person of unusual intelligence, balance, and helpfulness," though "at what cost," Severn ruefully notes, "the reader can well imagine. He was deprived of both happiness and health for most of a lifetime, for it was fifty years after its occurrence that this trauma came under observation and treatment" (p. 99).

The Father as Son

The title of Strindberg's *The Father* (1887) is ironic, since the Captain, a military officer and freethinker who initially seems to dominate his household full of women with "intrepid masculinity," becomes obsessed with doubts that he is the father of his daughter, Bertha. The conflicts with his wife, Laura, lead to a regression in which she takes on a maternal role:

Weep then, my child, and you will have your mother with you again. Do you remember that it was as your mother I first came into your life? . . . You were a giant of a child and had either come into the world ahead of your time—or perhaps you were unwanted.

(p. 39)

The Captain confirms, "My father and mother did not want a child; and so I was born without a will of my own."

Strindberg here dramatizes the syndrome delineated by Ferenczi in "The Unwelcome Child and His Death Instinct" (1929) as well as the "precocious maturity" that is a concomitant of trauma. Laura's plan to have her husband declared insane and committed to an asylum is termed by her brother, the Pastor, "an innocent murder that cannot be reached by the law" (Strindberg, 1887, p. 45). As the straitjacket is placed on the unsuspecting Captain by his erstwhile nursemaid, Margaret, she reminds him, "Do you remember when you were my darling little child and I used to tuck you in at night and read 'God loves the little children dearly' to you?" (p. 51). Once pinioned, the Captain rages against every woman he has ever known as his "deadly enemy" (p. 53), but soon collapses on Margaret's breast:

> Let me put my head in your lap. There! It's so nice and warm! Lean over me so that I can feel your breast!—Oh, how wonderful to fall asleep at a mother's breast—whether mother or mistress . . . but most wonderful at a mother's!
>
> (p. 55; ellipses in original)

As the play ends, the Captain wails, "A man has no children, it is only women who bear children" (p. 55), before falling victim to a stroke. Feeling his pulse, the Doctor pronounces, "he may still come back to life: . . . but to what kind of awakening—that we cannot tell" (p. 56; ellipses in original).

In disclosing Ferenczi's identification with the character of Strindberg's Captain, Severn opens a window into his psyche. It is striking that she should write, "He spoke to me suddenly one day about Strindberg's play *The Father*, and became himself almost immediately the insane son," since the crux of the play is that the father *is* "the insane son" and psychically not a father at all. Ferenczi, of course, had only stepchildren, thus literalizing the Captain's plight. It is equally striking that Ferenczi should have said to Severn, "And we like, when the straitjacket must be put on us, that it shall be done by our mother," since in the play the straitjacket is put on the Captain not by his mother but by his nursemaid. But just as Margaret is conflated by the Captain with his mother, so, too, the childhood traumas relived by Ferenczi in his analysis with Severn were perpetrated not only by his mother but also by the cook and his nurse. As we read in the *Clinical*

Diary, when Ferenczi contemplated holding out against mutual analysis, he imagined Severn responding with a ferocity worthy of the Swedish dramatist:

> "And is it not one of your own peculiar analytic weaknesses of character that you are unable to keep any secrets to yourself, . . . that you have an uneasy conscience, as if you had done something wrong, and that you have to run to your mother or wife, like a small boy or submissive husband, to confess everything and obtain forgiveness!"
>
> (Dupont, 1985, p. 35)

Severn on Severn

A case history no less transparent than that of Ferenczi concludes "Nightmares Are Real." Introduced by Severn (1933) as "one on which I worked a long time," it concerns "a highly intelligent, mentally active woman of middle age" who concealed her "internal disintegration," but was nonetheless "a very sick woman, carrying on the necessary activities of her life by means of a superhuman will" (p. 107).

This is, of course, Severn herself, presenting her analysis with Ferenczi as though she were one of her own patients. "The analysis revealed, first, an astonishing story of almost complete amnesia prior to her twelfth year and, second, a history of incredible abuse that had filled her life during that time" (p. 107). The perpetrator was her "diabolically clever and secretly criminal father," aided by "a stupid enslaved mother who completely closed her eyes to all that took place." The father, it transpires, "had left the family after a final and violent crisis in connection with his daughter, evidently being satisfied that the culminating shock to which he subjected her had deprived her of all memory."

All these details concerning Severn's life are amplified and corroborated in the *Clinical Diary*. Ferenczi tells how R.N., "who was already split into three parts," was struck by "the last great shock . . . at the age of eleven and a half" (Dupont, 1985, p. 9). He specifies that "the most abominable cruelty" was that "she was forced to swallow the severed genitals of a repugnant black man who had just been killed" (p. 140), which led to her "extraordinary, incessant protestations that she is no murderer, though she admits to having fired the shots" (p. 17). Severn's analysis of the relationship between her "criminal" father and willfully blind mother is echoed when Ferenczi writes, "the most frightful of frights is when the threat from the father is coupled with simultaneous desertion by the mother" (p. 18). Severn (1933) highlights that "as part of the abuse heaped upon the child we found to have been the constant use of narcotic drugs" (p. 107), just as Ferenczi comments that R.N. "considers the effect of anesthetics a monstrous act of violence. . . . To be anesthetized is thus to be temporarily split off from one's own body: the operation is not carried out on me, but on a body to which I used to belong" (Dupont, 1985, p. 17).

Although Severn (1933) does not disclose that she had either committed or at least participated in a gruesome murder in which she was—almost unimaginably—"forced to swallow the severed genitals" of the castrated victim, the theme is conspicuous in her dream life.[6] She reports that her "patient" had "a dream entitled 'This is how it feels to be murdered'" (pp. 107–8), in which the scene of abuse by the father was repeatedly reenacted. "We went through the phase of considering it as a fantasy only," she observes, "but the amount and terrific intensity of the emotions that accompanied each and every manifestation finally convinced both of us beyond any question that it was a historical reality" (p. 108). Her account of what unfolded in her analysis with Ferenczi is complemented by his admonition that "patients cannot believe that an event really took place, or cannot fully believe it, if the analyst, as the sole witness of the events, persists in his . . . purely intellectual attitude," and one should therefore choose "actually to transport oneself with the patient into that period of the past (a practice Freud reproached me for, as being not permissible), with the result that we ourselves and the patient believe in its reality" (Dupont, 1985, p. 24).

Severn (1933) lets it be known that the patient who is really herself "had originally withstood the shock of repeated misuse" by means of "fragmentation," as a consequence of which "there gradually appeared at least three persons with distinctness and clarity" (p. 108). As we have seen, Ferenczi found that R.N. "was already split into three parts" when she received "the last great shock" in her twelfth year. Severn's fragmentation is depicted in a dream in which she performs or dances to music "played by another girl, her double, at a nearby piano," and though "both girls were thus active, they were also both *dead*, and the patient felt dead while dreaming it" (p. 108). In the course of the analysis, "the patient finally came to recognize herself as both these girls *at the same time*." Ferenczi writes of R.N. in the *Diary*: "frequently recurring form of dream: two, three, or even several persons represent, according to the completed dream-analysis, an equal number of component parts of her personality" (Dupont, 1985, p. 157).

In addition to her piano dream, Severn (1933) had another "double" dream, "'I attend my own funeral'" (p. 108). Against Freud's claim that "no one ever dreams of his own death," Severn counters that it is "perfectly possible for a person to be psychically 'killed,' or some part of him killed, while he still continues to live in the flesh" (pp. 108–9). Indeed, in her own case, "the patient was not so much looking back upon an earlier psychic catastrophe as she was expressing, exactly as it was registered in her mind, what had actually occurred at the time" (p. 109). According to this disguised autobiographical narrative of the origins of trauma theory she developed jointly with Ferenczi, which is simultaneously an account of how the mind becomes dissociated, what Severn relived in all her dreams "was nothing less than a recognition of the destruction or loss of an integral part of her being, while another part was sufficiently removed from the immediate psychic environment to look at what was occurring and suffer accordingly."

Severn concludes by drawing attention to "another illuminating type of dream" that showed "the remarkable resources of her psyche for preserving itself when thus attacked" (p. 109). She cites as an illustration a dream, "'The child's life is insured by magic.'" Here, the part of her fragmented psyche she termed her "Intelligence," which, as in Ferenczi's case,

> had developed to unusual proportions as a compensation for the damages done, came to her rescue like a ministering angel and took over the care of the child while she was physically and psychically exposed to the evils of her father.

"The Intelligence," Severn goes on, was "'magical,' had appeared very early in the child's life and continued to watch over her like a mother, giving her a kind of psychic sustenance by means of which she managed to withstand the cruelties both moral and physical that fate had placed upon her" (p. 109).

To learn the name of Severn's "Intelligence" we must turn to the *Clinical Diary*:

> Patient R.N. even imagines that at the time of the principal trauma, with the aid of an omnipotent Intelligence (Orpha), she so to speak

scoured the universe in search of help.... Thus her Orpha is supposed to have tracked me down, even at that time, as the only person in the world who owing to his special personal fate could and would make amends for the injury that had been done to her.

(Dupont, 1985, p. 121)

Recognizing that to many "it may seem as fantastic to believe in this kind of 'insurance' as in my proposal that all dreams are 'true' and but the ghosts of our past," Severn (1933) argues that this is "the same process that physiologists know so well in the bodily realm of compensation and adaptation," and, on a higher plane, "a manifestation of the intelligence of the unconscious, the trend toward 'good,' toward health, the healing tendency that is apparent throughout nature" (p. 109).

Soul Mates

In the *Clinical Diary*, Ferenczi reports a "dream fragment" of Severn's in which a female patient "forced her withered breast into R.N.'s mouth," adding that Severn saw this dream as "a combination of the unconscious contents of the psyches of the analysand and the analyst" (Dupont, 1985, p. 13), which could mean either of her patient and herself or of herself and Ferenczi. If Ferenczi initially appeared to Severn as a "balanced, well-adjusted person," she struck him as aloof and intimidating, but inside both shells were severely traumatized souls seeking healing and redemption. As children, both had experienced murder in a literal or symbolic form, as a result of which they were "psychically 'killed,'" though also endowed with preternatural gifts; and the "withered breast" of Severn's dream evokes the "severed genitals" of the murdered man that she was "forced to swallow." Ferenczi quotes Severn's summary of "the combined result of the two analyses": "'Your greatest trauma was the destruction of genitality. Mine was worse: I saw my life destroyed by an insane criminal'" (p. 14).

Ferenczi recapitulates how he and Severn found their way to mutual analysis. Initially, "the woman 'patient' was unable to put any trust in this man; it was not known why" (Dupont, 1985, p. 110). But when the man discovered that "his hatred of his mother in his childhood had almost led to matricide," the "'woman analyst'" then took the process further by helping him to see that "in order to save his mother the 'patient' has castrated himself." Only through being reenacted in his (counter)transference to Severn could Ferenczi unearth the roots of his "destruction of genitality":

> The entire libido of this man appears to have been transformed into hatred, the eradication of which, in actual fact, means self-annihilation. In his relationship to his friend the woman "analyst," the origin of guilt feelings and self-destructiveness could be recognized *in statu nascendi*.
>
> (p. 110)

In Ferenczi's conceptualization of the therapeutic process, which applies to his analysis by Severn as much as to his work with his own patients, although the analyst "may take kindness and relaxation as far as he possibly can, the time will come when he will have to repeat with his own hands the act of murder previously perpetrated against the patient" (p. 52).

Progress in Severn's analysis became possible only when Ferenczi allowed himself to be analyzed by her: "The first real advances toward the patient's gaining conviction occurred in conjunction with some genuinely emotionally colored fragments of the rather systematically conducted analysis of the analyst" (p. 26). Ferenczi responded to Severn's dream of the "withered breast" by associating to "an episode in his infancy" involving his nurse, even as she accessed "scenes of horrifying events at the ages of one and a half, three, five, and eleven and a half" (p. 13). Because of what each gave to the other, Ferenczi was "able, for the first time, to link *emotions* with the above primal event and thus endow that event with the feeling of a real experience," while Severn succeeded "in gaining insight, far more penetrating than before, into the reality of these events that have been repeated so often on an intellectual level" (pp. 13–14). Where both had once been sundered, "it is as though two halves had combined to form a whole soul" (p. 14).

The Last Word

"After she left, he believed that she influenced him through vibrations across the ocean, and said that she analyzed him and thereby saved him. (He thus played both roles, was mother and child.)"

Notes

1 I refer to the page numbers of my edition of Severn's book, rather than of the original, out-of-print edition of which Katy Meigs brought a photocopy to my office.
2 To specify only two of Rachman's errors, he gives the name of Severn's father as Charles Kenneth Heywood (p. 89), when it was actually Marcus M. Brown, and then correctly but confusingly identifies Heywood as Severn's husband on the following page; and he repeats a mistake of Masson's he takes it on himself to rectify by identifying the painting of Margaret Severn by Olga Dormandi as "Portrait of Mrs. Elizabeth Severn," even as he also labels it correctly immediately below (pp. 103–4).
3 The case history of her daughter Margaret, an internationally acclaimed dancer, is likewise presented in the guise of a "young actress" on pp. 103–6. I discuss the dynamics of the intergenerational transmission of trauma in Severn's family in my work-in-progress on mutual analysis and the origins of trauma theory in psychoanalysis.
4 These revelations from the inner workings of Ferenczi's analysis with Severn should not be misconstrued as lending credence to Jones's (1957) allegation that both Ferenczi and Rank "developed psychotic manifestations that revealed themselves in, among other ways, a turning away from Freud and his doctrines" (p. 45), discussed in Chapter 3.
5 I am indebted to Gianni Guasto for clarification of this point.
6 In a personal communication, Adrienne Harris has suggested that this "monstrous act of violence" against a black man in which the eleven-year-old Severn was both complicit and the second terrorized victim might have been a lynching.

Chapter 5

Trauma and Dissociation
Ferenczi between Freud and Severn

> "In nearly every case of deep analysis one becomes aware of separated parts of the person, as though each part had an existence of its own."
> —Elizabeth Severn, *The Discovery of the Self*

In their introduction to my recently republished edition of Elizabeth Severn's *The Discovery of the Self* (1933), Adrienne Harris and Lewis Aron (2017) quote from Christopher Fortune's groundbreaking paper on Severn in their 1993 volume, *The Legacy of Sándor Ferenczi*, which launched the Ferenczi renaissance a quarter-century ago. Quoting Harris and Aron quoting Fortune: "'Severn may have been the first sexually abused analysand whose actual childhood trauma was the focus of psychoanalytic treatment since Freud abandoned his seduction theory in the late 1890s'" (p. xii; see Fortune, 1993, p. 102).

Since the explosion of interest in Ferenczi's work, it has been almost universally acknowledged that the challenge he posed to Freud in the writings of the last four years of his tragically foreshortened life centered simultaneously on his return to a transformed version of Freud's pre-1897 euphemistically named "seduction" theory and on his modifications, if not outright rejection, of the classical conception of the analytic relationship, which is epitomized in the word "technique."[1] That these issues lay at the heart of Ferenczi's confrontation with Freud was clear even at the time, as can be seen, for instance, in Freud's letter to his daughter Anna, on September 3, 1932, in response to having heard Ferenczi read aloud, during what proved to be his last visit to Vienna, the paper he was about to deliver at the Wiesbaden Congress that we know today as "Confusion of Tongues between Adults and the Child" (1933), but which originally bore the title "The Passions of Adults and Their Influence on the Development of the Sexual Life and Character of Children." As Freud protested:

> He has made a complete regression to etiological views that I believed and renounced 35 years ago, that gross sexual traumas of childhood are the regular cause of neuroses . . . including therein remarks on the hostility of patients and the necessity to accept their criticism and to confess one's errors to them. . . . The whole thing is really stupid.
> (qtd. in Schröter, 2004, 2:829; first set of ellipses in original)[2]

From this standpoint, the effect of the metamorphosis of Severn from her identity as R.N., the star patient in the *Clinical Diary*, into a subject, psychoanalyst, and author in her own right, who inscribed her own version of the experience of mutual analysis in *The Discovery of the Self*, is to elevate her into a full partner in these enduring accomplishments of Ferenczi's final period.

As it dawned on me only after I had completed my edition of Severn's book and the initial version of my manuscript, *Mutual Analysis: Ferenczi, Severn, and the Origins of Trauma Theory*, however, the crucial missing piece in this account is that trauma theory has as its corollary a model of the mind based not on repression but on dissociation. I think it is fair to say that this omission is a limitation not simply of my own previous work, but of the cornucopia of otherwise excellent scholarship on Ferenczi (Hainer, 2016). There is, conversely, a vast literature on dissociation, including landmark contributions by Jody Messler Davies and Mary Gail Frawley (1994), Donnel Stern (1997, 2010, 2015), Philip Bromberg (1998, 2006, 2011), and Elizabeth Howell (2005; Howell and Itzkowitz, 2016), which, for its part, engages only tangentially with Ferenczi. What is now needed, accordingly, is a confluence of these two streams of psychoanalytic thought and writing, so that Ferenczi—and Severn—can be given their due as progenitors of the revival not merely of trauma but also of dissociation theory.

Once this awareness has been assimilated, a great many things fall into place. First of all, since Freud, in his "Preliminary Communication" with Breuer, adhered to the view, derived from Janet, that a "splitting of consciousness . . . is present to a rudimentary degree in every hysteria, and that a tendency to such a dissociation, and with it the emergence of abnormal states of consciousness . . . is the basic phenomenon of this neurosis" (Breuer and Freud, 1893–1895, p. 12), but even before the publication of

Studies on Hysteria had come to repudiate this framework, it can be said that before he abandoned the seduction theory Freud had already abandoned the dissociation theory (Van der Hart, 2016), and both these seeming advances have in reality been profound losses for psychoanalysis. We are therefore able to appreciate anew the truth of Ferenczi's words in "The Principle of Relaxation and Neocatharsis" (1930) that

> the sudden emergence in modern psycho-analysis of portions of earlier technique and theory should not dismay us; it merely reminds us . . . that we must constantly be prepared to find new veins of gold in temporarily abandoned workings.
>
> (p. 120)

In addition, since Severn, like Anna O., suffered from what would today be called a Dissociative Identity Disorder (Brenner, 2016), just as she shared with Emma Eckstein a history of gross sexual abuse (Bonomi, 2015), we can amend Fortune's statement to say that Severn was not only the first patient "whose actual childhood trauma was the focus of psychoanalytic treatment since Freud abandoned his seduction theory in the late 1890s" but also the first patient whose experience of trauma-induced dissociation was the focus of her analysis since Freud abandoned the dissociation theory a few years earlier in that same formative decade.

Bringing Ferenczi together with the tradition of writing on dissociation also impacts our understanding of psychoanalytic history. In brief, we can trace the outlines of a configuration that begins with Janet and runs through Breuer, Ferenczi, Fairbairn, and Sullivan to the leading representatives of the interpersonal-relational school in our own day.[3] As Bromberg (1998) has observed, "Sullivan's theory of interpersonal analysis, reduced to its essentials, is . . . a theory of the dissociative organization of personality in response to trauma" (p. 215), so Sullivan certainly belongs on this list. Fairbairn, too, comes to seem astonishingly prescient when we read his declaration (1949) that "a theory of the personality based upon the conception of the splitting of the ego would appear to be more fundamental than one based upon Freud's conception of the repression of impulses by an unsplit ego" (p. 159). Fairbairn continues:

> The theory which I now envisage is, of course, obviously adapted to explain such extreme manifestations as are found in cases of

multiple personality; but as Janet has pointed out, these extreme manifestations are only exaggerated examples of the dissociation phenomena characteristic of hysteria. Thus, if we implement the slogan "Back to hysteria," we find ourselves confronted with the very phenomenon of splitting upon which my theory of repression is based.

(p. 159)

Fairbairn deserves immense credit not only for recognizing the continuity of dissociative phenomena, from the ordinary panoply of self-states at one end of the spectrum to full-blown multiple personalities at the other, but, perhaps even more, for acknowledging that his object relations theory has its roots in Janet.[4]

If we come now to Ferenczi and his partnership with Severn, and ask why it has taken so long to integrate his work with the tradition of literature on dissociation, I think that part of the answer lies in the inadequacy of the currently available edition of Ferenczi's writings in English, in which Janet's name does not appear in the index. Notwithstanding this defect, Gabriele Cassullo (2018, 2019) has documented that there are in fact a handful of references to Janet scattered throughout the three volumes of *Contributions to Psychoanalysis*, whereas the Italian edition of Ferenczi's *Opere* published by Cortina, despite being translated at second hand from the French edition from Payot, gives a much more accurate picture inasmuch as it contains as many as twenty-five references to the French psychologist.[5] In his tribute to his deceased mentor and father-figure Miksa Schächter, Ferenczi (1917) recalls that his early experiments in automatic writing, which led to the publication in 1899 of his "first medical paper," "Spiritism," in Schächter's journal *Gyógyászat* (*Healing Arts*), found a justification in the fact that "Janet had already published interesting observations on this phenomenon" (p. 430), so it is incontrovertible that Ferenczi had read Janet as a young physician, a decade before his first meeting with Freud in 1908.

Despite the frequency with which Ferenczi alludes to Janet in his writings, however, the crucial point is that he does so only between 1912 and 1924—that is, during his period of unwavering fealty to Freud—and when Ferenczi invokes Janet, as he does in "Exploring the Unconscious" (1912a), he depicts him, together with Charcot and Möbius, as having failed to draw the "general conclusions from the phenomena of hysteria" that it was left to Freud to uncover:

> they continued to believe that divisibility and disintegration of consciousness is to be found only in a pathologically affected mind, which is perhaps congenitally too weak for the necessary synthesis, for integrating the forces of the mind. They did not notice that hysteria only shows in an exaggerated and distorted form what occurs in every human being, although not in such a conspicuous way.
>
> (p. 309)

Ferenczi goes on to say that ever since Freud heard and understood the importance of Breuer's report concerning the case of Anna O., which was "the first time that anyone had succeeded with a predetermined method in recognizing the content of ideas hidden in unconsciousness," the "exploration of the underworld of the mind has been connected solely with the name of Freud" (p. 311).

Ironically, the corollary of Ferenczi's glorification of Freud is that, just when one would have expected Janet to become truly indispensable to him, during the years from 1925 to 1933 when Ferenczi undertook his treatment of Severn and moved haltingly but inexorably toward intellectual independence, he drops out of the picture altogether. Thus, it is not simply the deficiencies of the English edition but, above all, Ferenczi's own apparent obliviousness to Janet's importance as a kindred spirit and precursor to his ideas about trauma and fragmentation that accounts for the paucity of scholarship on Ferenczi's place in the family tree of writing on dissociation of which Janet is the taproot. When, in his most revealing reference to Breuer in the *Clinical Diary*, Ferenczi contrasts him with Freud, he does so not with respect to Breuer's theory of hypnoid states or "splitting of consciousness," which would have aligned Breuer with Janet, but solely to bolster the revival of trauma theory and his disagreements with Freud over issues of technique: "Return to trauma (Breuer). In opposition to Freud I developed to an exceptional degree a capacity for humility and for appreciating the clearsightedness of the uncorrupted child (patient)" (Dupont, 1985, p. 160). Unlike Fairbairn, with his slogan "Back to hysteria," when Ferenczi says "Return to trauma," he does not make the link to dissociation, which has made it very difficult for those analysts who march under his banner to see how indispensable this missing piece is to the entire argument.

If, as Bromberg (1998) has memorably put it, "it is not hard to imagine the restless ghost of Pierre Janet, banished from the castle by Sigmund Freud a century ago, returning for an overdue haunting of Freud's current descendants" (p. 189), then Ferenczi cannot be said to have opened the door to the psychoanalytic castle to Janet more than a crack. Despite remaining somewhat underemphasized, however, Ferenczi does in his late work grasp the connection between trauma and dissociation, and it is clear that he owes his breakthrough on this score above all to Severn. Not only do the themes of "shock" and "fragmentation" form a leitmotif in the *Diary*, particularly in his commentary on the case of R.N., but in "The Principle of Relaxation and Neocatharsis" (1930), his magnificent lecture at the 1929 Oxford Congress that forms a bookend with "Confusion of Tongues," Ferenczi expressly credits "discoveries made by our colleague, Elizabeth Severn, which she personally communicated to me," when he affirms:

> The first reaction to a shock seems to be always a transitory psychosis, i.e. a turning away from reality. . . . In every case of neurotic amnesia, and possibly also in the ordinary childhood-amnesia, it seems likely that a psychotic splitting off of a part of the personality occurs under the influence of shock. The dissociated part, however, lives on hidden, ceaselessly endeavouring to make itself felt, without finding any outlet except in neurotic symptoms.
>
> (p. 121)

Here we can hear the rattling chains of Janet's ghost, just as we have a foreshadowing of Sullivan's "theory of the dissociative organization of personality in response to trauma" as well as of Fairbairn's "theory of the personality based upon the conception of the splitting of the ego."

When Ferenczi cites personal communications from Severn, he may in part have in mind what he has learned from her as his patient in the first four years of her analysis. But it should not be overlooked that she almost certainly also taught him about dissociation in a more formal fashion. Already in her first book, *Psycho-therapy* (1913), Severn had invoked Morton Prince's "famous case of Sally Beauchamp" as an illustration of dissociation that "leads in extreme cases to a complete anaesthesia of certain parts or faculties, or to such phenomena as double personality" (p. 63), while she expatiates in her sequel, *The Psychology of Behavior* (1917): "the greatest danger to the personality is that of dissociation," which, "in its extreme form," results in "multiple or alternating personality, where one phase emerges with such strength and vividness as to temporarily, or perhaps for a long period of time, eclipse the others," while "disintegration is the logical outcome of dissociation and other negative disturbances of the personality," and "in its most serious and final form it results in insanity or suicide" (pp. 335–37). By virtue of her familiarity in the American tradition with Prince's classic *The Dissociation of a Personality* (1906), Severn would have been able to supply Ferenczi with some of the intellectual ballast of which he had been deprived by following Freud in consigning Janet to psychoanalytic oblivion, and thus to aid him in articulating a theory of dissociation as the inevitable consequence of, and counterpart to, trauma.

It would not be farfetched to surmise that Severn's interest in dissociation arose out of an attempt to make sense of her own experience, which brought her to the verge of "insanity or suicide." That this is so is confirmed by the fact that when she returns to the subject for a final time in *The Discovery of the Self* (1933), she does so in the paragraph immediately before she launches into what we now know to be a disguised version of her own case history, as she had gleaned it through her eight years of analysis with Ferenczi, presented as though she were one of her own patients. Severn prefaces her gripping account of "incredible abuse" perpetrated by "a diabolically clever and secretly criminal father" and abetted by "a stupid enslaved mother who completely closed her eyes to all that took place" with the following reflections:

> In nearly every case of deep analysis one becomes aware of separated parts of the person, as though each part had an existence of its own. In severe cases of "double" or split personality each of these portions is like a separate entity, well organized, sometimes with a name of its own, and capable of independent action. The whole subject of split personality needs a further examination and study than has as yet been given to it. No outstanding work on the subject yet exists, except the comparatively slight contribution made by Morton Prince some twenty years ago in America.
>
> (pp. 106–7)

Having returned from her own descent into the underworld, Severn is now able to dismiss Prince's book as a "comparatively slight contribution," in which "neither the explanation nor the therapy in this case was . . . very convincing" (p. 106), implicitly leaving it up to herself and to Ferenczi to fill the gap in the psychological literature she has pinpointed.

As Rachman (2018) has reminded us, we know from Jones (1957) that Freud referred to Severn as "'Ferenczi's evil genius'" (p. 457). Although intended as a rebuke, this epithet ironically ascribes to Severn a great, albeit malevolent, influence, as if Freud could not help recognizing the hold she exerted over Ferenczi's soul, over which the two of them were battling like good and bad angels. What if we were now to take the theoretical model of trauma and dissociation that I have delineated here and use it as a searchlight to illuminate the intersubjective field created by this triad of mighty ancestral spirits?

In invoking the notion of a psychoanalytic "field," I am particularly indebted to the work of Donnel Stern (1997), who has written:

> A fully interpersonal conception of treatment is a field theory. . . . It is the field that determines what will be dissociated and what will be articulated, when imagination will be possible and when the participants will be locked into stereotypic descriptions of their mutual experience. . . . The field is the only relevant context.[6]
>
> (p. 110)

To this I would add that the field is not solely a two-person phenomenon, but is open to potentially limitless expansion and constituted ultimately by the boundaries one wishes to draw for the purposes of a given piece of description and analysis. In this instance, although the dyadic relationships between Freud and Ferenczi and between Ferenczi and Severn each forms a "relevant context" and thereby a field, a larger context is formed by the fields of force circulating among the three of them. Even larger contexts are formed by the group of patients who were in "polygamous analysis" (Berman, 2015) with Ferenczi in Budapest, as well as by the connections between Ferenczi's patients in Budapest and Freud's patients in Vienna—as when Edith Jackson relayed to Freud what she had heard about Ferenczi's "kissing technique" from Clara Thompson (Brennan, 2015b), which prompted Freud to wrote a letter of rebuke to Ferenczi, who then responded in the *Clinical Diary*—and by the ambivalent bonds of love and hate among Freud and his disciples, including Jones and Ferenczi, and so on ad infinitum.

What I would propose, in brief, is that in his attack on Severn Freud was projectively lashing out not merely at the "bad" but at the dissociated parts of himself—what Sullivan (1953) terms the "not-me"—just as in his relationship with Severn Ferenczi was unconsciously seeking an antidote to his toxic relationship with Freud, which, after an initial burst of optimism, he had not been able to obtain from Groddeck. The repudiated aspects of himself that Freud could not abide in Severn—and which also estranged him from Ferenczi—were, first, his feminine or maternal side and, second, his vulnerability and identity as a patient. The first is summed up in Freud's comment recorded by H.D. (1956) during her analysis with him in 1933, "'I do not like to be the mother in the transference.... I feel so very masculine'" (pp. 146–47), while the second is encapsulated in the missile Jung fired at Freud in his letter of December 3, 1912, after Freud had acknowledged that a "bit of neurosis" had precipitated his recent fainting attack in Munich. "As for this bit of neurosis," Jung inveighed, "may I draw your attention to the fact that you open *The Interpretation of Dreams* with the mournful admission of your own neurosis—the dream of Irma's injection—identification with the neurotic in need of treatment. Very significant" (McGuire, 1974, p. 526).

The reason that Freud felt compelled to dissociate both his maternal qualities and his identity as a patient is that, unlike Ferenczi and Severn, he was never able to acknowledge that he himself had been severely traumatized in his childhood, just as he never paid more than lip service to trauma as a concept after his retrograde turn of 1897. As Robert Pyles (2018) has observed, the "projective demonization of Ferenczi" by Freud and Jones constituted "a dramatic 'enactment' of exactly the issue that Ferenczi was trying to describe" in "Confusion of Tongues"—namely, how often it happens that a "narcissistic parent fails to listen carefully to his own child, in order to discover the true nature of that child," but instead "attributes his own thoughts and feelings to the child, undermines the child's confidence in his or her own perceptions, and tries to convince the child that the thoughts and feelings of the parent are really the child's own"—and, Pyles adds, this scapegoating of Ferenczi "was very likely a reenactment of Freud's experience with his own very narcissistic mother."

Pyles's use of the term "enactment" is particularly apt in this context in light of Stern's (2010) definition of enactment as the "interpersonalization of dissociation," which functions as "the last-ditch unconscious defensive effort to avoid being the person one must not be, accomplished by trying to force onto the other what defines the intolerable identity" (pp. 14, 16). Seen from this perspective, Freud's entire relationship with Ferenczi forms one giant enactment, in which Ferenczi participated for some two decades until he began to fathom how thoroughly he had been manipulated and to resist Freud's combination of browbeating and blandishments. A signal illustration of Ferenczi's cooperation in the enactment with Freud, is furnished by his letter of December 26, 1912—the same one in which he conveys his disavowed knowledge of Freud's affair with Minna Bernays—where he lambastes Jung for a sputtering attempt at what he himself would do full throttle twenty years later:

> Mutual analysis is nonsense, also an impossibility. Everyone must be able to tolerate an authority over himself from whom he accepts analytic correction. . . . I, too, went through a period of rebellion against your "treatment." Now I have become insightful and realize that you were right in everything.
> (Brabant, Falzeder, and Giampieri-Deutsch, 1993, p. 449)

But when Ferenczi began to stand up for himself, as he did in his letter of January 17, 1930, by mildly taking Freud to task for having failed to "comprehend and bring to abreaction in the analysis the partly only transferred, negative feelings and fantasies" (Falzeder and Brabant, 2000, p. 382), Freud could not hear what Ferenczi was saying and, even after Ferenczi's death, repeatedly insisted that he bore no responsibility for what he viewed as Ferenczi's neurotically motivated antagonism, which, as he alleged in "Analysis Terminable and Interminable" (1937), sprang up "for no assignable external reason" (p. 221). In the final phase of their relationship, therefore, the situation had shifted fundamentally inasmuch as Ferenczi was able genuinely to hear and understand Freud without becoming defensive, whereas Freud remained locked in his one-sided narrative in which everything was Ferenczi's fault and he himself was blameless. Thus, on Ferenczi's side, the relationship had evolved to the point that it became, in Stern's (2010) language, an enactment but no longer a "mutual enactment." As Stern explains:

this kind of enactment is what takes place when, in the face of one person's enactment, the other person in the interaction manages to respond in a way that recognizes the dissociation without responding from within a dissociation of his own. The analyst who is not caught in a reciprocal enactment is instead able to mentalize his own experience.

(pp. 15–16)

Freud, on the other hand, still quoting Stern, serves as a prototype of

what happens when the analyst has no idea that he is selecting an inadequate context for what he is trying to understand. That is, the analyst does not understand but believes he does. . . . What may appear to the analyst to be an interchange is no more than the unwitting and unilateral imposition of an interpretive frame on the patient's experience, monologue disguised as dialogue. . . . The analyst does not see that he is looking for evidence of what he already knows and, as a consequence, is liable to feel (however guiltily) that the patient is recalcitrant.

(pp. 47–48)

An antithetical situation obtains in Ferenczi's relationship with Severn. Not only did they come to agree, as she wrote in *The Discovery of the Self* (1933), that the patient must be brought "to relive, as though it were now, the traumatic events of his past, aided by the dramatic participation of the analyst" (p. 72), but the decisive breakthrough in their work occurred when, as Ferenczi recorded in the *Clinical Diary*, Severn "maintained that she sensed feelings of hatred in me, and began saying that her analysis would not make any progress unless I allowed her to analyze those hidden feeling in me" (Dupont, 1985, p. 99). After holding out "for approximately a year," Ferenczi "decided to make this sacrifice," and to his "enormous surprise" he "had to concede that the patient was right in many respects." By allowing himself to be analyzed by Severn, he faced the realization that, in his words, "I have retained from my childhood a specific anxiety with regard to strong female figures of her kind." The "exaggerated friendliness" he had displayed was merely a mask and was "identical with the feelings of the same kind I had for my mother," so that "in actual fact and inwardly . . . I did hate the patient, in spite of all the friendliness I displayed; this is what she was aware of" (p. 99).

In the end, therefore, it was not merely Severn who relived "the traumatic events of her past," aided by the "dramatic participation" of Ferenczi as her analyst, but Ferenczi who did the same with the roles reversed. Exactly how this happened is spellbindingly recounted by Severn in her disguised case history of Ferenczi in *The Discovery of the Self* (1933):

> He spoke to me suddenly one day about Strindberg's play *The Father* and became himself almost immediately the insane son. He broke down and asked with tears in his eyes if I would sometimes think of him kindly after he had been put away in the asylum. He evidently expected to be thus sent away at that moment, adding as his last word, with terrible pathos, "And we like, when the straitjacket must be put on, that it shall be done by our mother." I immediately saw by this that the patient was reexperiencing a severe trauma in which he had expected his mother to send him away as insane. . . . He had already gained much insight in regard to himself, and the unexpected reproduction in the analysis of a part of this painful scene enabled him to acknowledge this traumatically-caused insanity for the first time as a living fact in himself, which was the beginning of its dissolution.
> (pp. 96–97)

To elucidate Ferenczi's mutually transformative encounter with Severn, I again turn to the hermeneutically informed reflections of Stern (2010), who notes that "to work with an enactment, the analyst must actually give himself over to the nonrational, affect-laden parts of the experience, and sometimes for fairly lengthy periods" (p. 88). As exemplified by Ferenczi, in stark contrast to Freud, "the analyst's role is not defined by invulnerability . . . but by a special (though inconsistent) willingness, and a practiced (though imperfect) capability, to accept and deal forthrightly with her vulnerability" (p. 89). Indeed, Stern adds that "the analyst's desire to cure the patient allows the analyst to accept the patient's desire to cure her" (p. 99).

Once we see Ferenczi's willingness to take the risk of opening himself as fully as he did to Severn in its true light we will also immediately discern how misguided is Bromberg's (1998) reference to "Ferenczi's failure with 'mutual analysis' as a technique" (p. 262). What Ferenczi undertook with Severn was the furthest thing imaginable from a "technique"; it was, instead, the fullest expression of what Bromberg himself hails as the distinctive feature of the interpersonal tradition, namely, "its fundamental commitment to the process being shaped by who the specific individual is as a human being rather than by its theoretical assumptions, making it an approach rather than a technique" (p. 154).[7]

It is commonplace to celebrate the Ferenczi relationship with Freud as a "dialogue," as André Haynal and Ernst Falzeder (1991) do when they proclaim, "It was a dialogue, it was friendship; more, it was 'an intimate community of life, feelings, and interest'" (p. 4). The quoted phrase is taken from Freud's penultimate letter to Ferenczi, dated January 11, 1933. Freud, however, conspicuously refers to this "intimate community" in the past tense, as something that "was" and that he can only "conjure . . . up from memory today." He proceeds to console himself with "the certainty" that he has "contributed especially little to this change," which he ascribes exclusively to "some psychological misfortune or other" in Ferenczi (Falzeder and Brabant, 2000, p. 446). Far from being evidence of a dialogue, therefore, Freud's nostalgic tribute actually perpetuates his unilateral enactment, a dissociation that Ferenczi had for several years been able to recognize "without responding from within a dissociation of his own."

The counterpart to the widespread veneration of Ferenczi's relationship with Freud as a "dialogue" is the condemnation of his mutual analysis with Severn as the worst sort of enactment, or, as Glen Gabbard (1997) has written, a "boundary violation" that constitutes "a direct exploitation of the patient, in that the patient's needs are completely subordinated to the analyst's need for help" (pp. 571–72). But, as we have seen, it is because Severn insisted that "*her* analysis would not make any progress" unless Ferenczi permitted her to analyze the unconscious roots of his misogyny that "he decided to make this sacrifice." To be sure, Ferenczi, too, was in still in search of the healing he had not received from Freud or even Groddeck, but far from being an "exploitation" of Severn, in temporarily ceding his role as her analyst, Ferenczi was placing her needs above his own. If, as Stern (2010) has argued, "enactment can be defined as the interruption of true conversation" (p. xvi), then the conventional wisdom must be reversed. It is the supposed "dialogue" between Freud and Ferenczi that was, in reality, an enactment, and the supposed enactment with Severn that proved to be an authentic dialogue.

To describe "the kind of productive clinical process" that "becomes impossible in the presence of dissociation and enactment," but "takes place once again when dissociation and enactment are resolved" (p. xvii), Stern (2010) employs the term "witnessing." And since, as he elaborates, "dissociated experience is unformulated experience," which "cannot be represented, consciously or unconsciously," it follows that "mutual enactments are our only route of access to these parts of our patients' minds"; and, "as enactments end, the experience can finally be formulated" (p. 179). As Severn and Ferenczi became each other's witnesses by reliving their past traumas, so, too, in the *Clinical Diary* and *The Discovery of the Self*, they each succeeded in formulating what had hitherto been not only their own dissociated experience but also that of Freud, and thereby accomplished together what the Master was never able to do for himself.

Notes

1 Exceptions include Peter Hoffer (2010), who argues that Freud's "negative reaction" to the work of Ferenczi's final period "was not in response to its assertion of the reality of infantile trauma, or the prevalence of sexual abuse of children by adults, but rather to the technical measures that Ferenczi employed in the pursuit of that reality" (p. 102), and Miguel Gutiérrez Peláez (2009), who likewise denies that "Freud's anger with Ferenczi was due to the latter's having revived his early trauma theory" (p. 1226); but the totality of the evidence leaves no doubt that these are one-sided views and that both theory and technique were at stake in their conflict.
2 The English edition of the correspondence between Sigmund Freud and Anna Freud (Meyer-Palmedo, 2014), translated by Nick Somers, makes a hash of the passage by confusing the words *Traumen* and *Träumen*, and thus rendering it as "sexual dreams in childhood" instead of "sexual traumas of childhood" (p. 386).
3 A partial outline of this tradition is sketched by Emanuel Berman (1981) in his first psychoanalytic paper, written in the "dark ages" before the Ferenczi renaissance.
4 On Janet and Fairbairn, see the excellent paper by Davies (1998), who notes that Fairbairn "chose to write his 1929 doctoral [actually, M.D.] thesis on the differences between dissociation and repression" (p. 54). Quoting Fairbairn's declaration therein that "'it is upon the work of these two men'"—Charcot's pupils, Janet and Freud—"'that the whole structure of modern psychopathology is founded,'" Davies goes on to argue that "Fairbairn's work involved him in lifelong dialogues—one manifest, the other latent," with Freud and Janet, respectively (p. 54; see Fairbairn, 1929, p. 16).
5 I am grateful to Cassullo for sharing the fruits of his research with me, and what I am able to say here about Ferenczi and Janet relies on his work. See also the first (2014) in Cassullo's series of seminal papers, which stresses the contribution of Ian Suttie to the paradigm shift effected by Fairbairn. The four-volume German edition of the *Bausteine zur Psychoanalyse* lacks a name index, which makes it nearly impossible to track down Ferenczi's mentions of Janet even in this otherwise authoritative text.

6 Stern uses this passage from his first book as the jumping-off point for his third (2015).
7 See also Parsons (2014), who defends Ferenczi against the criticism that "he did not have any kind of theory of clinical technique," and sees him as forerunner of the belief of analysts in the British Independent tradition that what is of paramount importance in clinical work is "the quality of the patient's experience of the analytic relationship" (pp. 188–89).

Chapter 6

Groddeck's Lessons

> "Where am I to begin? Where to end? My childhood wakes up, and something within me is weeping."
>
> —Groddeck, *The Book of the It*

In seeking to pay tribute to Georg Groddeck on the 150th anniversary of his birth on October 13, 1866, I imagine that he would indeed feel "more regal than any monarch, and blissfully happy" to know that there are still those for whom he is the "lord of the earth" (1925, pp. 18, 13) at least for this one day and that his memory has endured into the twenty-first century. In keeping with Groddeck's (1923) own reminder that, "since everything has two sides, so we can always consider it from two points of view" (p. 229; Letter 31), however, as well as with Wolfgang Martynkewicz's (1997) observation that "every birthday is also for Groddeck a retrospective fantasy of a past, lost paradise" (p. 32), I think this jubilee must be tinged with a sense of melancholy and graced with the tears that not only Groddeck but everyone whose visionary gleam has fled may feel moved to shed whenever our childhood awakens within us.

According to Count Hermann Keyserling, Groddeck was "the greatest magician among the psychoanalysts and without doubt the most important human personality of them all," though Keyserling does not fail to add that he, like all analysts, was "an unresolved analytical case" (qtd. in Schacht, 1977, p. 21). In returning to Groddeck for the first time since the publication of my book *Reading Psychoanalysis* (Rudnytsky, 2002a), I wish simultaneously to echo Keyserling's praise by affirming the inspiration I continue to derive from his work, especially *The Book of the It* (1923), my first encounter with which—as happened to Groddeck himself when he discovered the power of symbols—produced an "intoxication such as I have never experienced before or since" (p. 225; Letter 31), but also to offer some reflections on what I regard as his limitations, which I will link to his status as "an unresolved analytical case." I propose, therefore, to speak first of "Groddeck's teaching" in the laudatory sense of what I believe to be the incontestable value of his contributions—even as I recognize, in Martynkewicz's (1997) words, the paradox that Groddeck seeks to avoid anything that one might "call a system or a teaching, which has a communicable content" (p. 304)—before turning to "Groddeck's lessons" in the cautionary sense of what we may learn from studying the blind spots that weaken his enormously compelling vision of psychoanalysis and indeed of life itself.

In his initial letter to Freud on May 27, 1917, recounting what he calls "the history of my conversion" to psychoanalysis, Groddeck confesses that his reading of *On the History of the Psycho-Analytic Movement* has led him to "become doubtful whether I may number myself among the psychoanalysts by your definition" (Giefer, 2008, p. 48). After voicing the hope that Freud would agree that, beyond its concern with the neuroses, the true domain of psychoanalysis is "the whole of human life," from which it follows that "in themselves there do not exist any essential differences that could compel us to make an attempt at psychoanalysis here and not there," Groddeck again acknowledges, "Here now is the point where I doubt whether I have the right to give myself out in public as a psychoanalyst or not" (pp. 49–50). In response to this appeal, Freud, on June 5, 1917, remarks that he would evidently be doing Groddeck "a great service" were he to banish him to the place "where Adler and Jung, among others, are standing" but that he "cannot do it." On the contrary, Freud continues in a justly famous passage:

> I must stake a claim on you, must affirm that you are a splendid analyst who has unalterably grasped the essence of the matter [*Sache*]. Whoever recognizes that "transference and resistance are the hubs of treatment" belongs once and for all irrevocably to the wild army. Whether he also calls the "unconscious" the "It" makes no difference.
>
> (p. 59)

From the very beginning, accordingly, the question of who is a psychoanalyst lies at the center of Groddeck's relationship with Freud. Ironically, whereas Freud broke with Adler and Jung because he refused to tolerate their theoretical differences, he insisted that Groddeck was a "splendid analyst" despite Groddeck's misgivings as to whether he was entitled to call himself by this name. Although Freud must have been reassured to read Groddeck's declaration that the It "stands in a secret connection with sexuality, with Eros or whatever else one wants to call it" (pp. 49–50), since it was Freud's insistence on the primacy of his libido theory that precipitated his ruptures with the dissidents, by singling out transference and resistance as the "hubs of treatment" Freud offers his most expansive definition of what makes a psychoanalyst, according to which not only Groddeck but also Adler and Jung would continue to qualify since they never challenged these concepts. In praising Groddeck for having "grasped the essence of the matter," moreover, Freud revises his customary use of the word "*Sache*" to refer to the psychoanalytic movement in the sense of a "cause" and deploys it instead to mean the core tenets of psychoanalysis, just as his designation of his followers as "the wild army" inverts his usual disparagement of "'wild' analysis" (Freud, 1910) in order to elevate "wildness" into an integral attribute of the psychoanalytic spirit.

Through his contact with Groddeck, therefore, Freud was moved to reaffirm the radical nature of his discovery of a dynamic unconscious and to liberate himself at least temporarily from his obsession with doctrinal orthodoxy and political loyalty by which he betrayed the noblest ideals of psychoanalysis itself. In view of this encouragement by the master, it is not surprising that Groddeck, in his first public appearance before the psychoanalytic world at the 1920 Congress in the Hague, should have introduced himself with the words, "I am a wild analyst," before launching into a free-associative monologue that irritated the conservatives while it delighted the progressives, including Ferenczi, Rank, Ernst Simmel, and Karen Horney (Grossman and Grossman, 1965, pp. 96–97). Simmel, in his encomium of Groddeck on his sixtieth birthday, followed suit by hailing him as a wild analyst, among other reasons, because he "owes his training to no one except himself" and because his "passionate nature" made him "a fanatic in the cause of healing" (Schacht, 1977, pp. 7–8), while Carl and Sylva Grossman fittingly titled their still extremely valuable biography of Groddeck *The Wild Analyst*. Embracing his role as the unruly It of psychoanalysis, Groddeck compared himself in a letter to Freud on August 6, 1921, to "a little pepper that is not at all to be despised" (Giefer, 2008, p. 152; see Poster, Hristeva, and Giefer, 2016); and, as Martynkewicz (1997) has remarked, "he sought to turn the spear" against his detractors when he wrote in 1925, "'As far as I know, not one of the leading psychoanalysts has been trained in such a fashion that he can purport to do anything other than analyze wildly'" (p. 311).

Groddeck's unsurpassed ability to convey the revolutionary power of Freud's ideas, and hence of psychoanalysis as a whole, gives his writings their perennial freshness. Concerning the intertwined concepts of transference and resistance, for example, Groddeck (1926a) observes in his paper on bowel function that

> in the image which he makes for himself of the doctor, the patient seeks and finds points of vantage which make it possible for him, under cover of real or fancied resemblances and analogies, to lay on the shoulders of the doctor that burden of guilt which is so actively exercising himself and making his disease necessary to him.
> (p. 106)

Since "resistance itself is included . . . in the transference," he elaborates, whenever "a new symptom emerges, I am accustomed to put two questions to the patient: 'What do you think I have done wrong?' and 'What have you done wrong against me?'" (pp. 107–8). As Groddeck repeatedly demonstrates, *everything* that passes through the mind—dates, numbers, words, names—becomes a signifier irradiated with meaning and can be interpreted by tracing what Christopher Bollas (2007) calls the "logic of sequence" that emerges through the process of free association. At his best, as again in his paper on bowel function, Groddeck (1926a) is capable not only of lightning flashes of brilliance but also of subtle discriminations: "The unconscious is indeed the source of much conscious lying, but never does it lie itself; it merely hides, but when it speaks, it speaks the truth on every occasion and under every condition" (p. 108).

Nowhere is Groddeck's genius displayed more fully than in *The Book of the It*. So passionately does he expound Freud's shibboleths of the Oedipus and castration complexes and pursue his own unremitting quest for sexual symbols that, even though I have embraced the "relational turn" in psychoanalysis and would ordinarily be skeptical of these classical formulations, I cannot help falling under their spell once again. By casting his masterpiece in the form of letters to a "lady friend," moreover, Groddeck (1923) through his persona of Patrik Troll is able not merely to expound but to *enact* his teachings. A notable instance occurs in Letter 6 when he interprets his correspondent's loss of a ring given to her by her deceased sister. Troll notes that whereas he had spoken in his previous letter about transference, resistance, and symbolism, she had mentioned only the first two topics in her reply but bypassed symbolism, which he had illustrated by equating the ring with "the woman's sex organ" (p. 53). He infers in his ensuing missive that "instead of naming the symbol in your letter, you actually lost it in the form of your topaz ring," a parapraxis he attributes to the likelihood that this sister had initiated his charming lady into "the ring play, with learning to masturbate" (p. 64).

The reply of the lady friend to which Patrik Troll refers is purely imaginary, but by bringing his interlocutor to life in this way Groddeck makes his text truly a *dialogue* between the author and reader, just as every psychoanalytic treatment is an encounter between two human subjectivities. Whereas in his interpretation of the ring as a symbol and of the significance of the lady's loss of her ring Groddeck appears in his capacity as the seemingly omniscient analyst who unmasks the hidden truths of the unconscious, on a deeper level *The Book of the It* is a work of self-analysis in which Groddeck is the patient who remains eternally a mystery unto himself. By giving himself the pseudonym Patrik Troll, Groddeck has fused Pat, his own nickname as a child, with Troll, his pet name for Emmy von Voigt, the Swedish widow who became his second wife in 1923 and who—together with Freud and Groddeck's earlier correspondent and likely also romantic interest, Hanneliese Schumann—must be considered one of the models in real life for the lady friend whom he fantasized himself to be addressing in his letters.[1] "Patrik Troll" is thus simultaneously Groddeck and Emmy, analyst and patient, and in this conflation of roles Groddeck exemplifies the dialectical reversal he underwent with his patient Miss G., whom he credits with setting him on the path to becoming a psychoanalyst. Not only was she "a seriously ill woman" in 1909 when he began her treatment, but he describes himself as having been psychically "bankrupt" and subsequently told by one of his critics that he was "hysterical" (p. 221) at the time. In the course of his work with Miss G., as he reports in Letter 30, he

> was confronted with the strange fact that I was not treating the patient, but that the patient was treating me; or, to translate it into my own language, the It of this fellow-being tried so to transform my It, did in fact so transform it, that it became useful for its purpose.
>
> (p. 223)

In accepting the retrospective diagnosis of himself as hysterical, Groddeck states that he did so "with all the more certainty because it was made without any personal knowledge of me, simply from the impression given by my writings" (p. 221), thereby lending his imprimatur to the enterprise that Fromm (1992b) would later denominate "literary psychoanalysis" (p. 22). Consulting the Grossmans' biography (1965) as a Baedeker, we may note that his life was shaped by the following events: the absence of a wet nurse for several days after his birth in 1866 as the youngest of five children (p. 17); his only sister and next-oldest sibling Lina's privileged position in the family due to her illnesses (p. 18); his mother's depression following the death of her father, the eminent pedagogue August Koberstein, in whose memory she wore a black dress for the rest of her days (p. 20); his mother's disdain for his father, which his father's family reciprocated by believing that he had married beneath him (p. 22); being dressed in girls' clothes and sent to a girls' school until the age of nine (p. 22); being torn from his family at twelve and dispatched to Pforta, the elite boarding school (also attended by Nietzsche) where his grandfather had been headmaster and where young Georg was a "chronic bedwetter" (p. 24) and repeatedly thrashed until his graduation (p. 26); his family's financial ruin and move from the spa town of Bad Kösen to Berlin when he was fifteen (p. 27); contracting scarlet fever at sixteen (p. 28); his father's agonizing death at eighteen (p. 33); being conscripted into the army for eight years as recompense for his medical education (p. 39); his mother's death in 1892 when he was twenty-six (p. 40); and the death of Lina in 1903 (p. 51) followed by that of his three older brothers Wolf in 1906 (p. 51), Karl in 1909 (p. 52), and Hans in 1914 (p. 63), leaving him, as he wrote to Freud on August 6, 1921, "the lone surviving member of my family" (Giefer, 2008, p. 135).

This list of misfortunes does not purport to be exhaustive, but I think it suffices to establish that Groddeck was a severely traumatized individual. When he alludes in Letter 10 of *The Book of the It* (1923) to "the inconsolable loneliness of my schooldays" and claims that he remembers "as good as nothing of those years between twelve and seventeen, except that I had to pass them away from my mother" (pp. 83–84), this alleged amnesia is no ordinary forgetting but is rather due to his need to repress or dissociate the memories of exceedingly painful experiences. Perhaps the most dramatic proof of the impact of Groddeck's traumas is provided in Letter 25 where he analyzes his habit of expressing his displeasure by saying,

"'I've already told you that 26,783 times'" (p. 183). Groddeck notes first that he was twenty-six when his mother died, then that his parents were twenty-six when they married and that his father was born in 1826, which explains the twenty-six, but also makes it significant that the last three numbers—seven, eight, and three—add up to eighteen. If one multiplies the initial two by the ensuing six plus seven, one again gets twenty-six, just as happens if one adds the same two to the final eight times three. Groddeck himself, moreover, was born on 13/10/66, and if one adds thirteen to one plus zero to six plus six, lo and behold, one again arrives at the magical twenty-six.

But this is only the beginning of Groddeck's numerotechnics. Having separated out the initial two in his previous operations, he now sets it aside and pairs the remaining numbers to make sixty-seven, seventy-eight, and eighty-three, which he interprets as follows: "Sixty-seven was the age of my mother at the time of her death. Seventy-eight is the date I had to leave my parents' house in order to move into the dormitory of the school. In '83 my old home was lost to me forever, for in that year my parents left the town where I was born, to settle in Berlin" (p. 184). Also in 1883, Groddeck was told by a fellow-student at Pforta, "'If you go on masturbating like this any longer, you will soon go crazy; as it is you are half-mad'" (p. 184). Soon after being thus publicly humiliated, Groddeck "fell ill with scarlet fever, as a result of which I contracted nephritis," setbacks that made the year eighty-three, corresponding "to its prominent position as the end figures of the mystery number 26,783," impose itself "as especially important in its influence upon my external existence" (p. 185).

Since these are Groddeck's own associations, I in no way wish to cast doubt on their validity or to question the psychic determinism that governs his alighting on the number 26,783. My point is rather the twofold one that Groddeck through his numerology has unfurled a red thread to his traumatic history, and that he has done so without realizing it. Thus, in underscoring the truth of Keyserling's observation that Groddeck is himself "an unresolved analytical case," this extremely impressive piece of self-analysis brings me to a consideration of the blind spots that restrict his vision.

In assessing Groddeck's limitations, I begin by setting aside any possible indictment of his racism and anti-Semitism, as I see no evidence of these moral failings in his psychoanalytic writings, or of his sexism, which is no worse than that which is so pronounced in Freud. The more salient issues center on what Martynkewicz (1997) has characterized as Groddeck's "deep-seated antimodernism" (p. 147) that "separates him from the Enlightenment aspiration of psychoanalysis" (p. 10). This cast of mind is manifested by Groddeck's lack of any theory of trauma, such as Ferenczi (spurred on by Severn) espoused in his final period. For if there is one theme that Groddeck never tires of reiterating it is, as he says in Letter 31 of *The Book of the It* (1923), that although "we shall find, if we take the trouble, that for every event of life there is both an external and an internal cause," he himself has "been led more and more to seek out the internal cause" to the point where his "Troll arrogance" leads him to discern not only within himself but also within other people "an It, a God, whom I could make responsible for everything," so that he maintains: "'Illness does not come from without; a man creates it for himself, uses the outer world merely as an instrument with which to make himself ill'" (p. 229).

The allegation that Groddeck denies external causes seems to require qualification in light of a series of statements concerning the mother-child relationship. "If anything goes wrong with a baby," he writes in "The Body's Middleman" (1933), "the first question ought to be, 'What is wrong with the mother?'" (p. 74). He adds in "Bowel Function" (1926a):

> Whoever wants to doctor children would be well advised . . . to look very carefully into the conditions of the child's environment. . . . Above all, it is worth while to deal with the mother's mental attitudes, since nearly all infantile complaints are acts of revenge against the mother.
> (p. 87)

Both these splendid passages could have been written by Winnicott, as could his declaration later in the same paper, "I have made a practice of studying the mother's unconscious whenever a baby's health is disturbed" (p. 91).

The Groddeck who comes to the fore here is a brilliant object relations theorist, just as his prescient recognition of the bidirectional nature of the analytic relationship makes him a relational or intersubjective therapist. The problem, however, is that these insights are not integrated into the larger framework of Groddeck's thought, which revolves around his denial of external causes and even of external reality altogether, along with his desire to make the It "responsible for everything." As he comments in a paper (1927) on Goethe's *Faust*, "never is the external truly real. . . . It is the unconscious which is real" (p. 196), and again in "The It in Science, Art and Industry" (1926b), "Man is in no way the creation of his environment; on the contrary, he creates his own world for himself; whatever lies outside his personality has no existence" (p. 153). Not only do such assertions contradict his statements concerning the mother-child relationship but they overlook the fundamental point, which is no less integral to Fromm's concept of the social character than it is to the outlooks of Winnicott and Ferenczi, that what takes root in the unconscious is not purely endogenous and instinctual but is rather molded from the outset by environmental influences, from the interactions between mother (or other primary caretaker) and baby to the symbolic orders of wealth and power that undergird all societies and have brought the planet as a whole to the brink of catastrophe, whether in the form of a nuclear Armageddon or a mass extinction of species through the destruction of our natural world.[2]

In large measure, therefore, what is missing from Groddeck's system is a proper appreciation of the role of trauma in the etiology of mental illness, notwithstanding the extent to which he was traumatized in his own life. This turning away from external reality is a more extreme version of what we find in Freud after his abandonment of the "seduction" and dissociation theories in 1897. It is entirely in Freud's spirit that Groddeck should write, "Sex neuroses are due, not to traumas in childhood, but to the conflict set up by the conscious lying of the child, who is aware that he has invited the trauma" (1951, p. 124). Groddeck denies that neuroses are caused by traumas and instead chooses to blame the child for being abused by a presumably adult perpetrator. In the same vein, Groddeck claims in *The Book of the It* (1923) that it is "quite impossible for a man to take possession of a woman if she is not, in some way or other, consenting" (p. 36; Letter 4), thereby condoning the abolition of rape as a criminal offense, and likewise insists that "the child wants to be punished, he yearns for it, he pants for a beating, as my father used to say" (p. 96; Letter 12), as he himself was beaten for his transgressions at Pforta and, it would appear, also by his father at home.

Not only does Groddeck focus exclusively on internal causes and refuse to give due weight to environmental factors despite having been repeatedly traumatized in his own life, but this blind spot in his vision can—as is also true of Freud—be understood analytically as being the *result* of his inability to acknowledge and work through these very traumas. As is well known, it is common for victims of abuse to engage in what Ferenczi (1933) termed "introjection of the aggressor" (p. 162), so that the child internalizes the guilt feelings of the adult and—like the fallen Adam and Eve in *Paradise Lost*—mistakenly judges himself or herself to be, in Groddeck's phrase, "responsible for everything." Seen from this perspective, Groddeck's theory of the godlike omnipotence of the It comes into focus as a compensatory formation that enables him to disavow the painful reality of his traumas and instead to convince himself that he must have "panted" for his beatings and "yearned" to be sent to boarding school, longed for his scarlet fever and the death of every member of his family, and so forth. In similar fashion, when Groddeck describes in Letter 26 of *The Book of the It* (1923) how he requires "this subtle type of loving, this remoteness, because I am centered upon myself, because I love myself immeasurably, because I am what the learned call a narcissist," the grandiosity that causes him to say, "'I come first of all, and then come I again, then nothing comes for ever so long, and then come other people'" (p. 194), likewise masks an underlying lack of a genuine sense of self-worth due to not having been loved unconditionally or been allowed to form sufficiently secure attachments to his parents during childhood.

Groddeck speaks of himself with astonishing frankness, revealing what for many people would be shameful secrets concerning his adolescent bedwetting and notoriety as a masturbator, for instance, without apparent inhibitions. But Groddeck does not regard these behaviors as neurotic symptoms or try to explain their meaning in light of his own experiences, just as he does not recognize that his associations to the number 26,783 lead to traumatic memories. A further revealing fact, highlighted by Grossman and Grossman (1965), is that Groddeck, beginning at eighteen with the abrupt loss of his father, "did not respond to death with grief" (p. 34). As he seeks to persuade the reader in *The Book of the It* (1923):

> Did you ever see a little child mourn for the dead? . . . But why, then, do people mourn for a whole year? Partly to vaunt themselves before other people, but more than all, before themselves, in the manner of the Pharisees, to deceive themselves.
>
> (p. 145; Letter 18)

From the standpoint of attachment theory it possible to see Groddeck's "absence of grief" (Deutsch, 1937) and mockery of mourning as yet another symptom of his inability to come to terms with his repeated experiences of abandonment and bereavement.

The absence of grief is not the only conspicuous omission in Groddeck's life and work. Nowhere in his published writings to my knowledge does he mention his divorce in 1914 from his first wife, Else von der Goltz, who suffered from depression, which meant also being separated from her children Joachim and the extremely disturbed Ursula, to whom he was a devoted stepfather. Nor does he acknowledge the tragic story of Barbara, his only biological child, who likewise ceased to live with him after the divorce from Else and was never able to sustain an independent existence, being so paralyzed with anxiety, as the Grossmans (1965) report, that even when "fully grown she dared not walk down a flight of stairs without clinging to her mother's hand" (p. 43).[3] And while Groddeck rhapsodizes about being the youngest of five children, only in Martynkewicz's biography (1997) do we learn that he was actually the *sixth* Groddeck since there was a firstborn daughter who died after only one month, following which "the mother recovered only after a few months from an illness" (p. 26). The theme of replacement, given consummate expression in the postcard Freud wrote to Groddeck, and cosigned by all six members of the Secret Committee, on September 23, 1921, after the first of Ferenczi's annual pilgrimages to Baden-Baden, "Hope you were in agreement with the substitute-man" (Giefer, 2008, p. 156), thus hangs over Groddeck from before his birth, while the wounds left by his disappointments with his first wife and especially with his daughter must have been too painful for him to be prepared to expose them to the gaze of the reading public.

These, then, are the principal lessons that I think we may glean from Groddeck in contemplating the one-sidedness in his world-view. The critique that could be offered of his rejection of science and medical diagnosis—the notion, as he says in *The Book of the It* (1923), that "every kind of treatment is the right one for the sick man, that he is always and under all circumstances rightly treated, whether according to the method of science or the method of the old wife" (p. 220; Letter 30)—follows from the slighting of external reality on the plane of theory that is paradoxically a consequence of the traumas that he experienced in his life. Since, as Groddeck recognized, "truth is always ambivalent, both sides are true" (1951, p. 261), what is required is a genuinely dialectical perspective that synthesizes Groddeck's romantic vision with Freud's allegiance to the legacy of the Enlightenment. Just as Groddeck revered Freud, "who with four lines of writing could bring a whole world into being, and then, in three more, laugh at his own words with such god-like irony" (1926c, p. 120), so, too, do I continue to love Groddeck for his greatness as a man and the enduring value of his contributions to psychoanalysis. The perfect balance was struck by Ferenczi when he wrote in Groddeck's guest book as his first visit to Baden-Baden drew to a close: "Came to teach, and was instructed; left wholly smitten, half-converted" (qtd. in Martynkewicz, 1997, p. 284).[4]

Notes

1 Martynkewicz (1997) seeks to cast doubt on Emmy von Voigt's identity as "the real model" (p. 293) for the lady friend on the grounds that she was translating Freud's *Psychopathology of Everyday Life* into Swedish and was already familiar with psychoanalytic concepts, but this hardly makes it less likely that Groddeck would have had her, as well as Freud, at the forefront of his mind as the addressee of his letters.
2 Despite the divergences in their outlooks, Fromm wrote of Groddeck in a 1957 letter to Sylva Grossman, "Even if I was never his student in any technical sense, his teaching influenced me more than that of other teachers I had" (qtd. in Funk, 1999a, p. 62).
3 According to Martynkewicz (1997), "At the age of forty-eight Barbara Groddeck came as an invalid to a municipal nursing home in Baden-Baden, where she died on August 7, 1957" (p. 160).
4 *Kam zu lehren und wurde belehrt; schied ganz begeistert, halb bekehrt.*

Part 3

Basic Faults

Chapter 7

Othello and *Macbeth*
Complementary Borderline Pathologies at the Basic Fault

> "Shakespeare dramatizes what psychoanalysis theorizes."
> —David Willbern, *Poetic Will*

In her intervention in the critical debate triggered by Jacques Lacan's "Seminar" (1956) on Poe's short story "The Purloined Letter," Shoshana Felman (1980) has called for dispensing with the traditional notion of "applied" psychoanalysis since "the concept of 'application' implies a relation of *exteriority* between the applied science and the field it is supposed, unilaterally, to inform" (p. 152). Instead, she argues, once we recognize that "there is no longer a clear-cut opposition or a well-defined border between literature and psychoanalysis," and that psychoanalysis inhabits literature just as literature inhabits psychoanalysis, what is required is a methodology that proceeds on the basis not "of the *application* of psychoanalysis *to* literature, but rather, of their *interimplication in* each other" (p. 153).

Although I do not share Felman's conviction that only the postmodernist version of psychoanalysis espoused by Lacan furnishes a model for such an approach, I agree that there is much to be gained from trying to go beyond "applied" analysis to a mode of clinical as well as critical practice that sees the realms of literature and psychoanalysis as reciprocally intertwined. It makes little difference whether we call this hybrid discipline "implied psychoanalysis" or, with Fromm (1992b), "literary psychoanalysis."

By way of illustration of this braiding, I begin with a seemingly casual reference to Shakespeare in Caroline Polmear's paper, "The Basic Fault and the Borderline Psychotic Transference," which I came across while foraging for sustenance and inspiration in the volume *Independent*

Psychoanalysis Today (Williams, Keene, and Derman, 2012). What particularly captivated me in Polmear's elaboration of Michael Balint's ideas in *The Basic Fault* (1968) was her observation (2012) that Balint's use of the term "'harmonious interpenetrating mix-up'" "to describe the relationship between fetus and environment before the interruption of birth" could be expanded so that birth is viewed instead as "a metaphor which captures graphically the borderline patient's experience of being 'untimely ripped' from a desired state of oneness," whether that rupture occurs "as a traumatic failure of maternal attunement" during early childhood or in the transference through "the analyst's failure to understand and contain the patient's feeling in the consulting room" (pp. 362–63).[1]

The phrase "untimely ripped," of course, is taken from the end of *Macbeth*, in which Macduff shatters the false sense of invulnerability Macbeth had derived from the apparition conjured by the three Witches of a bloody child who had told him that "none of woman born / Shall harm Macbeth" (4.1.79–80).[2] In a climactic instance of the theme of "equivocation" that pervades the play, Macduff heralds Macbeth's doom by revealing that he "was from his mother's womb / Untimely ripped" (5.8.15–16)—that is, brought into the world by caesarean section, thereby answering the riddle of how it is possible for there to be a man who was not "of woman born."

If Polmear finds in Shakespeare's phrase an insight relevant to her work with patients at the level of the basic fault, then the question spontaneously arises whether her paper can, reciprocally, deepen our reading of Shakespeare's tragedy. As Janet Adelman (1992) has argued, *Macbeth* "represents in very powerful form both the fantasy of a virtually absolute and indestructible maternal power and the fantasy of absolute escape from this power" (p. 131). Whereas in the opening battle scene the traitor Macdonwald is betrayed by the "whore" Fortune and "unseamed . . . from the nave to th' chops" by "brave Macbeth," who here represents the epitome of masculine "Valour" (1.2.15–22), in the concluding battle scene the roles are reversed so that it is Macbeth who is now tainted by his associated with femininity, which renders him helpless before the purely masculine Macduff.

Although pertaining literally to the circumstances of Macduff's birth, the phrase "untimely ripped" is charged with enigmatic meanings throughout the play. Macbeth, who "carved out his passage" (1.2.19) to face Macdonwald, performs what David Willbern (1997) aptly terms a "grotesque parody" (p. 104) of a caesarean section both on the rebel soldiers and on the body of his enemy double. And in perhaps the most haunting passage of this ghost-ridden play, Lady Macbeth goads Macbeth into suppressing his qualms concerning the murder of Duncan by evoking the image of a traumatic rupture not at birth but at the oral stage:

> I have given suck, and know
> How tender 'tis to love the babe that milks me:
> I would, while it was smiling in my face,
> Have plucked the nipple from his boneless gums,
> And dashed the brains out, had I so sworn,
> As you have done to this.
>
> (1.7.54–59)

Because the play hinges on the fact that the Macbeths' marriage is childless, this baby that Lady Macbeth claims to have suckled and murdered in horrific fashion is best understood neither as a pure hallucination nor as a realistic reference to a child from a previous marriage known to history but otherwise unmentioned in the play, but rather—like Macbeth's "fatal vision" (2.1.43) of the daggers before he murders Duncan—as an ontologically indeterminate phantasm that haunts her mind no less than it does the imagination of the audience. The key point is that her speech exemplifies the lethal attacks on the mother-infant bond that are a hallmark of the play. In this instance, it is the mother who destroys her toothless child, who is expressly said to be a male (although "his" in Shakespeare can also bear the impersonal meaning of "its"), while in the birth imagery it is the infant who destroys the mother, especially since, as Willbern (1997) has noted, "Caesarean section in early seventeenth-century England was literally a matricidal procedure, performed only on mothers already dead or certain to die" (p. 101). In whichever direction the arrow may fly, however, we have in the phrases "untimely ripped" and "plucked the nipple," not to mention the description of the gruesomely murdered baby, the twin elements of prematurity and violent separation, both of which are characteristic features of psychic trauma.

In employing the idea of the basic fault as a metaphor for borderline experience, Polmear (2012) makes the point that what Balint calls "ocnophilia" and "philobatism" are "rigid defensive organizations against the terror of annihilation" that arises "when birth or early experience such as a lack of attunement ruptures the desired state of harmony before the subject is developmentally prepared" (p. 363) to cope with the feeling of separation from the mother. Although Balint's terminology may seem arcane, his essential distinction is not difficult to grasp.[3] In ocnophilia, from the Greek *oknein* ("to hesitate") plus *philia* ("love"), as Polmear explains, the baby "clings in anxiety to emerging objects (the other) and fears the spaces between them," whereas in philobatism (modeled on "acrobat"), "he clings to the objectless expanses as safe and friendly spaces between objects, while the objects are felt to be treacherous hazards" (p. 363).

Having established that the ocnophil "clings to objects" whereas the philobat "clings to spaces," Polmear then crucially adds that these character structures are in fact "not opposites, although they often sound like it in Balint's descriptions. Instead, they are two different attitudes branching from the same stem" (p. 363). Because both organizations "are responses to the abrupt discovery of the 'otherness' of the object" (p. 364), a traumatic experience that can be avoided when the mother affords her baby a calibrated experience of disillusionment, their outward polarity conceals the degree to which they are both "defensive attempts to recreate the state of primary love and harmonious mix-up" of which these individuals were deprived at the beginning of life, a catastrophic environmental failure that causes patients in analysis on the borderline between neurosis and psychosis to "try to bring us into line by any means they can when separateness emerges" in the analysis (p. 364).

Polmear further delineates the defining qualities of these complementary orientations, which can be exhibited by the same person either simultaneously or in oscillation:

> The ocnophil clings to the object, overcathecting the relationship, turning the object into a mighty and vital person who *must* respond to his clinging with complete care, while the philobat overcathects his own ego function, developing skills in this way in order to maintain himself alone or with very little help from his objects.
>
> (p. 364)

She continues:

> Philobatic people seem to me to be deeply traumatized, suffering an irretrievable and unprocessed loss, who have developed autistic defenses or shells which have extended from defensive modes of survival to personalities. Ocnophilic people, perhaps the more classical

impulse-driven borderline people, are those whose survival depends on tyrannical control of their object, forcing the object to provide (and fail to provide) the harmonious environment that they require to defend themselves against their lack of internal containment and the terrible unprocessed loss of separation.

(p. 365)

Especially since Polmear herself uses the phrase "untimely ripped," I am unable to hear these descriptions of philobatic and ocnophilic characters, the former of whom "have developed autistic defenses or shells" whereas survival of the latter "depends on tyrannical control of their object," without being struck by how snugly they fit Macbeth and Othello, respectively. In Macbeth's two soliloquies in Act 5, first when he says,

> my way of life
> Is fall'n into the sere, the yellow leaf,
> And that which should accompany old age,
> As honour, obedience, love, troops of friends,
> I must not look to have;
>
> (5.3.22–26)

and, still more famously, in his "Tomorrow, and tomorrow, and tomorrow" (5.5.18) speech following the news of the death of his wife, in which he sums up life as "a tale / Told by an idiot, full of sound and fury / Signifying nothing" (25–27), the Scottish king exemplifies the schizoid philobat who sees with utter lucidity what it would be like to have led a fulfilled and meaningful life even though he is incapable of experiencing it as an emotional reality. Othello, conversely, is the "impulse-driven borderline" whose very being depends on an attempt to exert "tyrannical control" over *his* wife, and whose "lack of internal containment" and "terrible unprocessed loss of separation" become palpable when he raves in response to hearing Iago's concocted report that Cassio admitted to having slept with Desdemona: "Pish! Noses, ears, and lips! Is't possible? Confess! handkerchief! O devil" (4.1.42–43). In diametric contrast to Macbeth, Othello is a welter of unmetabolized feelings with no capacity for reflective functioning, and he concludes this outpouring of agony by falling into a psychogenic trance.

Drawing on the ideas of Margaret Mahler (1974), who writes of "man's eternal struggle against fusion on the one hand and isolation on the other"

(p. 305), Richard P. Wheeler (1981) divides Shakespeare's major tragedies and late romances into two broad groups, which he terms the "*trust/merger* group and the *autonomy/isolation* group." In each of the two sets of paired terms, the first—trust and autonomy—refers to the positive version of these dialectically opposed human strivings, while the second—merger and isolation—refers to the "characteristic danger that accompanies it" (p. 201). Wheeler aligns Othello with Lear and Antony (from *Antony and Cleopatra*) as representatives of the "trust/merger group" whose protagonists typically die "in a union with a beloved other," whereas Macbeth, like Timon and Coriolanus, belongs to the "autonomy/isolation group," whose heroes end their lives "desperately and defiantly alone," whether consumed by an "impotent rage" or "hacked to death by enemies" (p. 202).

Wheeler's contrast between Shakespeare's "trust/merger" plays and "autonomy/isolation" plays corresponds to Polmear's deployment of Balint's antithesis between ocnophilic and philobatic orientations. Shakespeare's artistic genius not only brings these character-types to life but also allows us to see, much as one might in an analysis, how the structures originate and take hold in infantile experience. In *Macbeth*, the leitmotifs of traumatic birth and weaning provide the backcloth for Shakespeare's tracing of philobatism to its primitive roots. In *Othello*, the Moor apologizes to the Venetian nobles for his unrefined language in explaining how he has wooed and won Desdemona by recalling:

> For since these arms of mine had seven years' pith
> Till now some nine moons wasted, they have used
> Their dearest action in the tented field.
>
> (1.3.84–86)

As Jeffrey Stern (2016) has highlighted in an essay on Othello's narcissistic rage, by having him specify that he has been a soldier since the age of seven "Shakespeare must think it important that we know that Othello—to paraphrase Macduff—was from his mother's arms (if not her womb) untimely ripped and consider its possible effects" (p. 14).

In the present context, Stern's borrowing of the same phrase from *Macbeth*, "untimely ripped," to describe Othello's separation from his mother is uncannily apt and points to the far-reaching affinities between the two plays. For, as Polmear has stressed, what is at stake in the notion of being "untimely ripped" from the womb is not the literal experience of birth so much as it is the loss of a "desired state of oneness" with the mother, for which Macduff's caesarian section serves as a metaphor. Othello's reference to becoming a soldier at the age of seven, moreover, evokes the early modern cultural practice known as "breeching," a rite of passage in which upper-class boys were taken from their mothers or nursemaids and dressed in knee-length trousers instead of in the petticoats that had hitherto rendered them indistinguishable from girls. In *The Winter's Tale*, Leontes muses as he gazes on the face of his son Mamillius, who is evidently seven years of age, "methoughts I did recoil / Twenty-three years, and saw myself *unbreeched* / In my green velvet coat" (1.2.154–156; italics added).[4] Othello's premature loss of "the desired state of harmony" with the mother thus reflects a social as well as a personal trauma, and he closes the synopsis of his military career by saying that it has been "some nine moons" since he left the "tented field."[5] Nine months is, of course, the duration of a human pregnancy, while the moon is a feminine symbol, so Othello, upon commencing his courtship of Desdemona, reenters the maternal realm where he had experienced a rupture as a child. As with the oblique allusion to breeching, this image cluster recurs in In *The Winter's Tale*, where Polixenes announces his intention to depart from Sicily for Bohemia by remarking that it has been "Nine changes of the watery star" (1.2.1) since he occupied his throne, which triggers in Leontes the jealous delusion that his wife Hermione's pregnancy is due to her having cuckolded him with his brother king.[6]

That Othello's desperate clinging to Desdemona, which drives him to attempt to exert "tyrannical control" over her, results from his unconsciously identifying her with his mother is established through the role of the handkerchief as the fulcrum of the plot in the play. Once Iago informs Othello that he has seen Cassio wipe his beard with Desdemona's handkerchief—a slander concocted after his wife Emilia had found it on the ground where it had fallen when Desdemona had attempted to bind Othello's head with it—Othello demands that Desdemona produce the lost article as proof of her love for him. When she is unable to do so, he admonishes her by reciting a tale of the origin and history of the handkerchief that, whatever its historical truth may be, expresses a psychic reality in articulating the supreme value he places on this talismanic object:

> That handkerchief
> Did an Egyptian to my mother give,
> She was a charmer and could almost read
> The thoughts of people. She told her, while she kept it

> 'Twould make her amiable and subdue my father
> Entirely to her love; but if she lost it
> Or made a gift of it, my father's eye
> Should hold her loathed and his spirits should hunt
> After new fancies. She, dying, gave it me
> And bid me, when my fate would have me wive,
> To give it her. I did so, and—take heed on't!
> Make it a darling, like your precious eye!—
> To lose't or give't away were such perdition
> As nothing else could match.
>
> (3.4.57–70)

That the handkerchief was allegedly given to Othello's mother by an "Egyptian charmer" with nearly telepathic powers transports him into a realm of magical thinking in which fantasies are indistinguishable from actions. By assigning the handkerchief a symbolic importance as the guarantor not only of his own marriage but also of his father's fidelity to his mother, as Arthur Kirsch (1978) observes, Othello evokes "the primitive world of a child's merger with his mother," and in the prospect of parental adultery lie "the seeds of his own primal betrayal" (p. 736). But whereas this places the handkerchief in a context of triangular relationships, the preoedipal dimension is augmented by the fact that Othello says he received the handkerchief as a gift from his mother at her death, presumably during his boyhood. As Adelman (1992) remarks, "Othello's mother enters the play only by allusion to the moment of her death," in the same way that "the handkerchief becomes imaginatively present to Othello only in its absence, and only after he believes Desdemona lost to him" (p. 68). Thus, when Othello concludes his speech by cautioning Desdemona that to lose or give away the handkerchief—which, moreover, he must have kept from the time he received it from his mother until he bestowed it on Desdemona—"were such perdition / As nothing else could match," he is displacing onto the handkerchief the sense of abandonment he believes he has just experienced by her treachery. This experience of rejection revives what Polmear has called the "terror of annihilation" due to a fracture in "the desired state of harmony" in the mother/infant dyad against which his ocnophilia is a precarious bulwark.

To describe the handkerchief in these terms—which is also to say that Othello is unable to love Desdemona unless she has it in her possession—is to recognize that it functions in his psychic economy as a *fetish*. On an oedipal level, as I argued decades ago in "The Purloined Handkerchief in *Othello*" (Rudnytsky, 1985), the handkerchief—like the letter in Poe's story—lends itself to a Lacanian interpretation as a representation of the phallus as a "transcendental signifier," as well as to interpretation along classical Freudian lines as the fantasied maternal penis that male fetishists require female partners to have on their persons to ward off their own castration anxiety. However, as Arnold Cooper (1986) has sagaciously commented, what appears on the surface to be castration anxiety is frequently better understood as a "façade" or "a desperate attempt to 'escape forward,' as it were, to more advanced levels of representation, escaping from the more primitive and frightening versions of narcissistic threat" (p. 155). And so it is with Othello, "untimely ripped" from the mother whom he knows only through the anguish of her loss, a perspective that allows us to view the handkerchief as a fetish not merely in the phallic sense but also as one that develops out of its failure to serve as a transitional object that would have buffered him as a child against an overly abrupt expulsion from "the state of primary love and harmonious mix-up" that is a precondition for healthy mental functioning in later life.

Indeed, in putting forward the idea that "the transitional object may eventually develop into a fetish object and so persist as a characteristic of the adult sexual life," Winnicott (1953, p. 9) cites Mosche Wulff's paper, "Fetishism and Object Choice in Early Childhood" (1946), which adduces a series of clinical examples in order to arrive at "the conclusion that in the young child the fetish, through its odor, its pleasant warmth, and the particular tactile sensations which it produces, takes the place of and is the substitute for the mother's breast and the mother's body" (p. 462). Among Wulff's vignettes is that of a four-year-old boy with enuresis who, after being given a *handkerchief* by his mother to take with him to bed at night, "demanded this handkerchief again and again, smelled of it, and refused to be parted from it," going so far as to stuff it into his pajamas and press it against his genitals, "saying that in this way it could not get lost" (p. 457).[7]

That castration anxiety functions as a "façade" for "more primitive and frightening versions of narcissistic threat" also in *Macbeth* can be seen in the Porter scene, which serves as a fulcrum of the philobatic tragedy in much the same way that the handkerchief does in its ocnophilic counterpart. Occurring in the interval between the commission of the murder of Duncan—an act that dooms its perpetrators to spiritual damnation—and its discovery, the scene depicts the drunken Porter of Macbeth's castle, roused by the persistent knocking of Macduff and Lenox, imagining himself as the porter of Hell Gate admitting a series of damned souls to his infernal regions. The scene brings to the fore the theme of "equivocation," or telling the technical truth under oath with an intention to deceive, which had been central to the trial of the Jesuit priest Henry Garnet, who was executed on May 3, 1606, for his role in the Gunpowder Plot of the previous year. In answer to a question from Macduff concerning the consequences of drinking, the Porter explains that whereas it leads directly to "nose-painting, sleep, and urine," its effect on male sexuality is more ambiguous:

> Lechery, sir, it provokes, and unprovokes: it provokes the desire, but it takes away the performance. Therefore, much drink may be said to be an equivocator with lechery: it makes him, and it mars him; . . . makes him stand to, and not stand to; in conclusion, equivocates him in a sleep and, giving him the lie, leaves him.
>
> (2.3.27–35)

The phallic imagery in the Porter's speech is patent. Alcohol "provokes the desire, but it takes the away the performance," it causes the penis to "stand to" only to make it "not stand to," and in finally inducing the inebriated sot to fall asleep, it "gives him the lie"—a threefold pun meaning at once to render him prostrate, to befoul himself with his own "lye" or urine, and to fob him off him with an erotic dream in place of the sexual act that he is incapable of performing in reality.

In its comic riffing on the subjects of masculinity and impotence, the Porter's speech, as is invariably the case with Shakespeare's fools, sounds the chords that reverberate most profoundly in *Macbeth*. But the phallic jokes are, as it were, only the tip of the iceberg of what Willbern (1997) calls "the core assault from both sides of the mother-infant bond" (p. 101) that is mounted through Lady Macbeth's fantasy of "dashing out" the brains of her nursing baby and the motif of birth by caesarian section that holds the key to the Witches' riddles. Indeed, the Porter's harping on equivocation and lying in all its senses foreshadows Macbeth's stunned acknowledgment in Act 5 that he has been deceived by the "juggling fiends" that "keep the word of promise to our ear, / And break it to our hope" (5.8.19–22), as he learns from Macduff how it is possible for there to be a man who has not been contaminated by femininity by passing through the birth canal. By placing the Porter's rumination on male sexual anxiety and the duplicity of language immediately following the offstage murder of Duncan, Shakespeare makes this interlude a substitute for the regicide that he leaves to the imagination of the audience, just as in *Othello* the handkerchief functions for the jealous Moor as the displacement of the fantasized "primal scene" of his wife having sex with Cassio, and for the audience as the surrogate for our analogous desire to solve the mystery of whether the marriage of Othello and Desdemona was ever consummated.

Among the conundrums of *Macbeth* is the fact that Macduff, as Adelman (1992) puts it, "has inexplicably abandoned his family" and thereby leaves his wife and children "vulnerable to destruction when he goes off to offer his services to Malcolm" (pp. 143–44) in the war against Macbeth. Lady Macduff declares to a Scottish thane at the outset of Act 4, Scene 2, before her son and then she and the other innocents are slaughtered by Macbeth's henchmen, "His flight was madness" (3), adding, "He loves us not; / He wants the natural touch" (8–9). Struggling to account for this "inexplicable abandonment," Adelman concedes that it "severely qualifies Macduff's force as the play's central exemplar of a healthy manhood that can include the possibility of a healthy relationship to women" (p. 144). The usually impeccable Adelman falters here, as she also does in interpreting his delivery by caesarian section as "affirming that Macduff has indeed had a mother" and thereby serving to counter "the fantasy of male self-generation" (p. 144). Rather than being an "exemplar of healthy manhood" and someone who "had a mother," Macduff outdoes Macbeth in being a philobat who absconds from his primary objects and takes refuge in "the objectless expanses as safe and friendly spaces," to invoke Polmear's locution. It would be more accurate to say that Macduff never had a mother since he killed her in the process of being torn from her womb, "an irretrievable and unprocessed loss," to quote Polmear again, which he recreates when, in Adelman's words, "we discover dramatically that Macduff has a family only when we hear that he has abandoned it" (p. 144), thus making him indirectly responsible for the deaths of those nearest and dearest to him at the hands of Macbeth's assassins.

No less bewildering is the ensuing scene of Act 4, in which Macduff, having fled to England, has his loyalty tested by Malcolm, Duncan's eldest son, who professes himself guilty of all manner of execrable vices until Macduff overcomes the heir apparent's doubts by vowing to desert his cause and turn his back on Scotland altogether. Only when Macduff has done so does Malcolm reveal that it was all a charade and assure the noble soldier, "My first false speaking / Was this upon myself" (4.3.130–31). In his classic essay "How Many Children Had Lady Macbeth?" (1933), which anticlimactically never attempts to address the question posed by the title but simply takes it as a starting point for inveighing against the critical tradition of analyzing Shakespeare's characters as though they were real people, L. C. Knights comments that "the conversation between Macduff and Malcolm has never been adequately explained" (p. 42).[8] He proffers his own attempt at an answer by noting that Malcolm "has ceased to be a person" and that his self-accusations "repeat and magnify the evils that have already been attributed to Macbeth, acting as a mirror wherein the ills of Scotland are reflected" (p. 43).

It is not necessary to accede to Knights's dismissal of character analysis, as though this were incompatible with attentiveness to Shakespeare's language, to recognize that the wooden quality of the dialogue between Macduff and Malcolm demands an explanation if it is not to be deemed a blemish on the play. Although Knights takes a step in the right direction by portraying the fictitious misdeeds confessed by Malcolm as a distorted "mirror" of the crimes of Macbeth, what is required to account for the scene is not a retreat from psychology but a more daring and radical mode of psychoanalytic reading. Polmear (2012), it will be recalled, describes both ocnophilia and philobatism as "rigid defensive organizations" that arise when "birth or early experience such as a lack of attunement ruptures the desired state of harmony before the subject is developmentally prepared" to tolerate separation from the mother. Utilizing a Kleinian framework, she proposes that "ordinary splitting into good and bad breasts has failed" with borderline patients, "and the task of integration has become impossible as a result" (p. 363). Whether the clinging is to "emerging objects" or to "objectless expanses," she continues, the pathology at the level of the basic fault "is aimed at keeping the idealized good relationship in place against the fearful bad one."

To grasp that these complementary pathologies are "rigid defensive organizations" enables us to elucidate the exchange between Malcolm and Macduff. Its artificiality and seeming implausibility come into focus as manifestations of the philobatic structure of *Macbeth* as a whole, analogous to the ocnophilic structure of *Othello*. Shakespeare, that is, explores the effects of early trauma not only in his creation of an incomparable gallery of characters but also in the language and artistic form of his plays. As in the first part of his dialogue with Macduff, in which Malcolm finally reveals himself to be "Unknown to woman" (4.3.126)—and thus exhibits the same complete repudiation of femininity that allows Macduff to defeat Macbeth—when Malcolm goes on to describe how the English King Edward has gone forth to lay his hands on "a crew of wretched souls" (141) and thereby miraculously cures them of "the Evil" (146) of scrofula, this glimpse of idealized kingship represents the antithesis to Macbeth, the Scottish tyrant who wreaks havoc on his land under the supernatural sway of the Weird Sisters. This is splitting, to be sure, but not "ordinary splitting" that serves as a prelude to the "task of integration" in Klein's depressive position. Both *Othello* and *Macbeth* are nightmares of what it means to be stuck in the paranoid-schizoid position, whether this takes the form of "black-and-white" thinking applied to both race and gender, and the overpowering anguish in the face of the loss of the loved object, on the one hand, or the impossibility of distinguishing between truth and lies or between what is male and female in the prophecies of bearded women, and the equally overpowering fear of engulfment, on the other.

What if, instead of regarding *Macbeth* and *Othello* as two distinct works, we were to read them as constituting, in Willbern's (1997) phrase, a single "irrational dreamscape" (p. 97)? As we have seen, both the Porter scene and the handkerchief function as surrogates for the unrepresented acts that are the mainsprings of their respective plays. Both tragedies are portraits of a marriage. In one, a husband murders his wife and then commits suicide over her body; in the other, the wife commits suicide and the solitary husband is slain by his enemies. Shakespeare's unearthing of the roots of male sexual anxiety extends to the tendrils of language in both plays. When Macbeth describes the daggers he planted on the pillows of Duncan's retainers as "Unmannerly breeched with gore" (2.3.117), he figuratively equates the blood on the blades with the breeches that mark the rite of passage for boys implied by Othello's allusion to becoming a soldier at the age of seven, although "unmannerly" also punningly connotes Macbeth's failure ever truly to become a man. After Othello stabs himself with a dagger he had concealed on his person, the Venetian noblemen, Lodovico and Gratiano, exclaim, "O bloody period!" and "All that's spoke is marred" (5.2.355). As Willbern (1997) brilliantly explicates, since "period" in rhetoric means a complex sentence, these commentaries ask us to view Othello's deed as "a final and fatal punctuation to an excellent discourse" (p. 5). But to call Othello's suicide a "bloody period," Willbern elaborates, is "not only a metaphor of a written sign. It designates a blood spot, and is hence a mark of female sexuality: of virginity (bridal sheets), murder (deathbed sheets), and menstruation ('napkin' also bears this significance)."

As "a mark of female sexuality," the "bloody period" that signals Othello's end, when he inflicts on himself the wound that is a symbolic castration, thus returns us to the handkerchief, which, in one of Shakespeare's inimitable touches, is described by Iago as "Spotted with strawberries" (3.3.438), whereas in the novella by Geraldi Cinthio (1566) that is Shakespeare's source it is simply "embroidered most delicately in the Moorish fashion" (p. 246). Through the word "spotted," the strawberries on the handkerchief are associated with the "lust's blood" by which Othello envisions Desdemona's bed will be "spotted" (5.1.36) when he exacts retribution for her supposed adultery, as well as with the wedding sheets that, in a popular custom of early modern culture, were publicly displayed to prove that the bride had been a virgin at the time of her marriage.[9] When Desdemona initially attempts to bind Othello's head with the handkerchief, he brushes it aside with the words, "Your napkin is too little" (3.3.291). If the handkerchief can be interpreted as a phallus in the sense of a "transcendental signifier" as well as the missing maternal penis in one of its functions as a fetish for Othello, it is simultaneously a "feminine napkin" inscribed with the blood of menstruation, of defloration, and of death. In a final irony, however, Othello ultimately resolves he will "not shed her blood" (5.2.3) and instead kills Desdemona by strangulation, thereby either restoring her virginity in his fantasy or else preserving it intact.

What Willbern terms the "blood spot" that stains Desdemona's "napkin" with the "period" that brings *Othello* to a close seeps into and soaks the imagery of *Macbeth*. It can be found on the daggers, "unmannerly breeched with gore," as well as in Macbeth's realization that "all great Neptune's ocean" cannot cleanse his hand of Duncan's blood, which "will rather / The multitudinous seas incarnadine, / Making the green one red" (2.2.61–64).[10] It also clings to the apparition of "blood-boltered Banquo" (4.1.122) during Macbeth's final encounter with the Witches, pervades Lady Macbeth's dissociated recollection of Duncan's murder during the sleepwalking scene, "Yet who would have thought the old man to have had so much blood in him?" (5.1.39–40), and, with eerie precision, return in her cry as she obsessively seems to wash her hands, "Out, damned spot" (35).

Just as in *Othello*, moreover, the "damned spot" that cannot be eradicated from *Macbeth* is, in one of its covert but crucial aspects, the blood of menstruation. As Alice Fox (1979) was the first to point out, when, prior to the assassination, Lady Macbeth implores the demonic spirits to "unsex me here" and "make thick my blood" so that "no compunctious visitings of nature / Shake my fell purpose" (1.5.41–46), the phrase "visitings of nature" is in the medical literature of the Renaissance "a common euphemism for menstruation," and her wish for "blocked menses" is, therefore, a "metaphor for blocked conscience" (p. 129). In the same soliloquy, Lady Macbeth invites the "murdering ministers" to "Come to my woman's breasts, / And take my milk for gall" (1.5.47–48)—that is, to bewitch her breast milk and turn it indigestible bitterness—showing once again how both plays return us to the female body and lay bare the lethal consequences of the sundering of the primal bond between mother and baby for the men these babies grow up to become and the women they marry in later life.

Having been inspired by Polmear's appropriation of the phrase "untimely ripped" to describe the experience of borderline patients, and by her demonstration that the character-types of ocnophilia and philobatism are "not opposites" but rather "two different attitudes branching from the same stem," I have used her exposition of Balint's theory of the basic fault as the springboard for a reading of *Othello* and *Macbeth* as paired plays. But if I have succeeded in showing that clinical psychoanalysis enhances our reading of Shakespeare, it remains for me to demonstrate how our reading of Shakespeare through the lens of Balint's concepts can reciprocally illuminate our clinical work. Accordingly, I propose to conclude by sketching the cases of two patients, one bearing the lineaments of Othello and the other of Macbeth, both of whom experienced "a traumatic failure of maternal attunement" during their formative years that adversely impacted their ability to form stable romantic relationships with women in adulthood.

Mr. A. came to me in crisis through a referral from his mother. A man in his mid-twenties, he was nearly suicidal because of his ex-girlfriend. When they first met five years earlier, she was coming off of a breakup with someone to whom she was still emotionally attached, which made the patient feel insecure, but over time she became "like part of me" and "part of my identity." She would say that sex with him was perfect and she could never imagine having sex with another guy, but even in paying him this compliment the thought of being with other men was still present (in the form of a negation) in her mind. Over time, the relationship became toxic and Mr. A. convinced her that they needed to take a break, even though he still loved her. After their separation, he became depressed and put on a lot of weight, but slowly got back on track with his diet and exercise and began feeling better. They texted intermittently and saw each other for lunch once in a while. Four months after their breakup, she told the patient she had met someone new. He was initially angered and couldn't believe she had moved on so quickly. He again became depressed but resolved to get on with his own life and had been doing well until the crisis that brought him into treatment.

The previous weekend, his ex-girlfriend had asked to see him because she was distraught at having run into the man she was now dating at a club with another woman. It had almost led to a fight between the women. When they met up, she talked about this other man the whole time. She and Mr. A. had shared so much history together, but now she was obsessed by someone she barely knew, and he couldn't stop thinking about her with this other guy. Just when he was starting to get over her, she had dragged him back into her life and made him want to rekindle their romance. He fired off a series of angry and desperate text messages, following which she blocked him on social media. This was the final push that nearly sent him over the edge.

In our few sessions together, which managed to get Mr. A. out of the emergency room, so to speak, although circumstances did not permit us to embark on long-term therapy, we came to understand why he felt that "the whole world had collapsed under his feet," or, in Othello's words, "Chaos is come again" (3.3.92) when he lost her love. His current experience was a repetition not only of what had happened at the beginning of his relationship with his ex-girlfriend but also of a pattern formed in his childhood. His father had been an entertainer and his older brother had been a star athlete. Despite being divorced, his mother would say that Mr. A. was not as handsome as her ex-husband. Up to the age of eight, all he had wanted to do was impress her, but she would get wrapped up in her boyfriends until they broke up with her. Feeling abandoned by his mother, he took an overdose at thirteen but, at least outwardly, stopped caring about her promiscuity by the time he turned sixteen. Thus, the desolation that overtook him at having but not having his girlfriend, at hoping he might regain her only to be cut off from her forever, revived his anguish at losing his mother not simply to his father but to a series of other men, just as Othello's jealousy of Desdemona is superimposed on the memory of having been torn from his mother at the age of seven, on the scenarios of betrayal inscribed in the history of the handkerchief, and on the irrevocable loss of his mother to death.

Like Mr. A., Mr. B. suffers from what Germaine Guex (1950) has dubbed an "abandonment neurosis," albeit of the philobatic rather than the ocnophilic variety.[11] Twice married and, as it happens, also a younger brother, his case is not from my practice but is rather a famous one in the annals of psychoanalysis. Although his analyst, writing in the 1960s, affirmed that "his main problem was his castration anxiety vis-à-vis a phallic mother figure" (Kleinschmidt, 1967, p. 124), it is clear in hindsight that what might once have appeared to be castration issues should instead be conceptualized, in Cooper's formulation, as a "façade" behind which loom "more primitive and frightening versions of narcissistic threat." In one memorable episode disclosed by the analyst and confirmed independently by Mr. B.:

> He was six when he threatened to leave home because of his displeasure with his mother's discipline. He remembers that, at one point, his mother packed a little bag for him, told him to go ahead and leave the house, as he had said he would, but then he suddenly found himself outside the locked door, while trying in vain to get back inside by hammering at the door and crying to be permitted to come back.
>
> (p. 124)

It would be difficult to invent a more compelling example of "a traumatic failure of maternal attunement" that is bound indelibly to scar the child " 'untimely ripped' from a desired state of oneness" with the "harmonious interpenetrating mix-up" that should have been provided as the matrix for his budding sense of self.

Drawing on Guex's work, Frantz Fanon encapsulates the essential dynamic of the philobatic form of abandonment neurosis in his masterpiece of psychoanalytically informed postcolonial theory, *Black Skin, White Masks* (1952). Fanon writes:

> I do not want to be loved. Why? Because one day, a very long time ago, I attempted an object relation and I was *abandoned*. I have never

forgiven my mother. Since I was abandoned, I shall make the other suffer, and abandoning the other will be the direct expression of my need for revenge.

(p. 56)

How this dynamic manifested itself in Mr. B.'s love life is movingly documented by his second wife. Even though she had been forewarned by his disastrous first marriage about his "need to escape from a woman at the moment when he realizes his affection makes him vulnerable to her" (Bloom, 1996, p. 169), she humiliated herself by signing a prenuptial agreement that her divorce lawyer subsequently described as "the most brutal document of its kind he had ever encountered" (p. 222); and, in the end, the man who had initially presented himself as "the warm and protective father" she had longed for as a girl, and as the gallant knight who would rescue her from her previous malevolent enchanters, showed his true colors and metamorphosed into "the fleeting shadow of the one who disappeared" (p. 236).

As astute readers will already have divined, the second wife in this vignette is Claire Bloom, the analyst is Hans Kleinschmidt, and the famous patient is Philip Roth. The corroboration that it was indeed Roth whose mother locked him out when he was a boy is supplied by Roth himself in *Portnoy's Complaint* (1969), where the same memory is recalled by Alexander Portnoy in the course of his psychoanalysis.[12] Like Macduff, who was abandoned by his mother when she died in giving birth to him, Roth was abandoned by his mother when she made him hammer at the door and beg to be allowed back into the home; and, like Macduff, Roth acted out his "need for revenge" by deserting his wife so as to deny having any chinks in his armor of masculinity and to forestall being abandoned again.

Like that of Mr. A., the case of Mr. B. comes originally from real life, though our only access to it now is mediated through a series of texts. Should we therefore exalt the first report as "clinical," while relegating the second to the suburbs of "applied" psychoanalysis? Or do they not conjointly exemplify the "interimplication" of psychoanalysis and literature? If the case histories of both these avatars of Othello and Macbeth, with their complementary borderline pathologies at the level of the basic fault, are weighed in the balance, I think they testify with equal eloquence not only to how psychoanalysis can enhance our appreciation of Shakespeare but also—as Dorothy and Jerome Grunes (2014) have put it in the title of their book—to what Shakespeare teaches us about psychoanalysis.

Notes

1. I have Americanized Polmear's British spellings and silently corrected her grammar in my quotations from her paper throughout this chapter.
2. All quotations from *Macbeth, Othello,* and *The Winter's Tale* in this chapter are taken from the latest Arden editions of the plays.
3. In a fascinating study, Raluca Soreanu (2019) has shown how Balint arrived at his final choice of terms through a prolonged epistolary exchange with the classical scholar David Eichholz.
4. As John Pitcher points out in his excellent notes on the ages of the characters in *The Winter's Tale*, the pairing of the ages of seven and thirty is also found in *Hamlet*, since Hamlet, whose age at the time of the play is established by the First Gravedigger in Act 5 to be thirty, recalls playing with the jester Yorick, who has been buried for twenty-three years, which means that Hamlet must have been seven at the time of Yorick's death.
5. A direct descendant of the collective trauma of breeching may be found in what Simon Partridge, in a paper (2011) on Charles Rycroft, has termed "British Upper-Class Complex Trauma Syndrome" stemming from the practice of removing socially privileged boys from their homes at the age of eight in order to send them boarding schools, where beatings were common. Compare Groddeck's recollections of being beaten (and enuresis) at Pforta and Orwell's harrowing narrative of his uncannily similar experience during his boarding-school years in "'Such, Such, Were the Joys . . .'" (1952). Not coincidentally, the same passage from *Macbeth* about Macduff being "untimely ripped" from the womb is taken by Partridge as an epigraph to his earlier autobiographical paper on the same subject, "Trauma at the Threshold: An Eight-Year-Old Goes to Boarding School" (2007).
6. In a reprise of the link between premature birth and disrupted weaning in *Macbeth*, Hermione, who appears to have died upon being falsely accused and imprisoned, "is, somewhat before her time, delivered" (2.2.24) of Perdita, while her firstborn Mamillius, whose name signals his connection to the breast, perishes simultaneously by osmosis.
7. Also pertinent to *Othello* is Winnicott's (1953) observation that, although illusion "is inherent in art and religion," it "becomes the hallmark of madness when an adult puts too powerful a claim on the credulity of others, forcing them to acknowledge a sharing of illusion that is not their own" (p. 3).
8. The bookends of this tradition of character analysis for Knights are Maurice Morgann's "Essay on the Dramatic Character of Sir John Falstaff" (1777) and A. C. Bradley's *Shakespearean Tragedy* (1904), while other landmarks include the reflections of Goethe (1795) and Freud (1900) on Hamlet, as well as the work of Harold Bloom (1998) in our own day. Despite being taken to task by Knights, Bradley (1904) no less disappointingly opines that "we cannot say" anything meaningful concerning the existence of Lady Macbeth's child, "and it does not concern the play" (p. 462).
9. On the symbolic ramifications of the handkerchief, see Boose (1975). The strawberries that signify blood also carry an antithetical meaning of purity, since, as Ross (1960) has shown, they were considered in the Renaissance to be emblematic of the Virgin Mary as well as of both true and deceitful goodness.
10. I have removed the comma inserted by the Arden editor after "green." The Folio text of the play has a comma after "one," which makes it clear that the

line should be construed as "making the green ocean red," rather than "making that which is green one red thing."

11 In a parallel to Balint's antithesis between oconophilia and philobatism, Guex distinguishes between two categories of abandonment neurosis, the "positive-attractive" and the "negative-repulsive," to the first of which belongs "the patient who, above all, must find love," while the second "is the subject who is inconsolably stricken by resentment for not having been loved" (p. 17). As Guex stresses in her introduction, "the syndrome of anxiety attached to abandonment," like the basic fault, originates at a "much earlier stage of the individual's development" than the Oedipus complex, and the analyst who remains "confined exclusively to the path of classic interpretation" will inevitably end up "concealing the patient's neurosis" (pp. xxiv–xxv).

12 For comprehensive documentation of the correspondences between Kleinschmidt's case history and Roth's autobiographical confessions in both *Portnoy's Complaint* and *My Life as a Man* (1975), which prove that Roth had been Kleinschmidt's patient, see Jeffrey Berman's chapter on Roth by in *The Talking Cure* (1987), as well as Berman's (2007) account of his own tragicomic encounter with Kleinschmidt. As Berman details, what first put him on the scent was Roth's description in *My Life as a Man*, in the guise of his persona Peter Tarnopol, of how his analyst had left the journal with the incriminating article in his waiting room where Tarnopol could not help but see it, which led to a major blow-up in the analysis. There can be no doubt that Kleinschmidt's countertransferential enactment must have caused Roth serious damage and compounded the effects of his childhood traumas, rather than helping him to recover from them.

Chapter 8

"I Am Not What I Am"
Iago and Negative Transcendence

"Thus, the ultimate choice for man, inasmuch as he is driven to transcend himself, is to create or to destroy, to love or to hate."
—Erich Fromm, *The Sane Society*

I

Together with Hamlet and what, at least since the nineteenth century, has seemed to readers his puzzling delay in carrying out his revenge on Claudius for the murder of his father, no character in Shakespeare's plays has aroused more controversy and bewilderment among critics than has Iago, whose soliloquy at the end of Act 1, Scene 3, Coleridge (1822–1827) indelibly described as "the motive-hunting of motiveless malignity" (p. 190). The problem is not that Iago lacks motivation for his all-consuming hatred but that, both here and in his ensuing soliloquy in Act 2, Scene 1, he furnishes too many reasons for it. Not only has Cassio been promoted by Othello over Iago to the position of his lieutenant, but Iago voices fleeting and implausible suspicions that both Othello and Cassio may have cuckolded him with his wife Emilia, not to mention the claim that he himself does "love" (2.1.289) Desdemona, though this is in part simply to get even with Othello for what he has supposedly done to him with Emilia.[1]

Perhaps the most convincing psychological reading of Iago is Harold Bloom's (1998) insistence that his "only true motive" is his "evidently sickening loss of being at rejection" by Othello, against whom he rebels out of what Satan, his literary epigone in *Paradise Lost*, calls "a Sense of Injured Merit" (pp. 434–35).[2] To be sure, a psychic injury of this magnitude, where Iago is traumatized by Othello's elevation of Cassio as Satan is by God's anointing of the Son as the ruler of Heaven, does go some way toward rendering comprehensible the havoc he wreaks, and Kohut's (1972) concept of "narcissistic rage" is therefore not without value in trying to make sense of Iago's words and actions.

The insurmountable stumbling block to all such readings, however, is that they fail to take into consideration the lack of any sense of inwardness that would be necessary to account for Iago's character in realistic terms. In diametric opposition to Hamlet, who has "that within which passes show" (1.2.85), Iago's one-dimensionality stands in contrast not only to Othello but also to Desdemona, Cassio, and even subordinate characters such as Roderigo, Brabantio, Emilia, and Bianca, all of whom seem to feel recognizably human emotions. Coleridge is therefore fundamentally correct in ascribing to Iago a "motiveless malignity," and all attempts to refute this view, from A. C. Bradley's at the dawn of the twentieth century to Bloom's at its close, are conversely misguided. According to Bradley in *Shakespearean Tragedy* (1904), "there is no mystery in the psychology of Iago," whose "longing to satisfy the sense of power is . . . the strongest of the forces that drive him on" (p. 214). In countering Coleridge, Bradley maintains that to imagine an Iago who is animated by "a disinterested delight in the pain of others" is, "if not a psychological impossibility, at any rate not a *human* being," and "in a purely human drama like *Othello*" such a character "would be a ruinous blunder" (p. 197). Hence, Bradley resolves to "look more closely into Iago's inner man" (p. 204) and finds it inconceivable that he could be impelled by the "love of evil simply as evil" to take "pleasure in the pain of others simply as others," rather than inflicting pain as a way of achieving some ulterior purpose such as harming a competitor or satisfying a "thwarted sense of superiority" (pp. 212–13).

From Augustine's recounting of his theft of the pears as an adolescent in his *Confessions* to Raskolnikov's murder of the pawnbroker in *Crime and Punishment*, however, the orthodox Christian understanding of evil is that it is in its essence a *gratuitous* act, something done purely for its own sake, rather than springing from a motive that, however base, renders the deed comprehensible and thereby less horrifying. For Bradley to assert that "there is no mystery in the psychology of Iago," consequently, could not be more mistaken since, if he is the incarnation of evil, then it follows that he must be an unfathomable mystery. The same goes for Bradley's assumption that it is possible to "look . . . into Iago's inner man," since that illusion of interiority is just what Shakespeare deprives us of in Iago's character. Finally, Bradley's belief that "a disinterested delight in the pain of others" is a "psychological impossibility" is contradicted by the gallery of sociopaths adorning the museum of human history, who attest that the possibility of repudiating all fellow feeling is an existential virus that has always lurked in the heart of man.

On a more mundane level, in arguing that a thoroughly evil Iago would not be "a *human* being" and that such an aberration would ruin "a purely human drama like *Othello*," Bradley discounts the extent to which Shakespeare's tragedy, as Bernard Spivack (1958) has shown in a classic study, is indebted to the morality-play tradition going back to *Everyman* and *Mankind*, and Iago the descendant of the Vice figure dominating many of these fifteenth-century spectacles for whom evil is "solely an organic function and an artistic pleasure" and whose "total euphoria leaves . . . no room for conscience" (p. 45). Indeed, Spivack classifies *Othello* as a "hybrid" drama in which modern psychological realism fleshes out the allegorical skeleton that Shakespeare inherited from his medieval forebears. Because of this lineage, Iago is not, in fact, a completely "*human* being," and *Othello* mesmerizes audiences in no small measure because it is *not* "a purely human drama." Bradley (1904) is on much more solid ground when he observes that a "fit companion" for Iago is to be found not in Milton's poignantly humanized "archangel ruined" but rather in that spirit of pure negation, Goethe's Mephistopheles, who exhibits "something of the same deadly coldness, the same gaiety in destruction" (pp. 195–96) of which Shakespeare distills the essence in Iago. Bradley's animadversions on Iago's "deadly coldness" and "gaiety in destruction" likewise underscore the justice of W. H. Auden's (1962) comparison of Iago to a practical joker who is "without motive" in any positive sense but is "certainly driven" by the negative "fear of lacking a concrete self, of being nobody," and whose malice takes the form of a "projection of his self-hatred onto others, and in the ultimate case of the absolute practical joker, this is projected onto all created things" (p. 257).

2

If Iago, as both Coleridge and Auden have concluded, is "without motive" that would render his character comprehensible in ordinary human terms, then all attempts at grasping his psychology as an individual are bound to founder. Neither his indiscriminate sexual jealousy, nor his supposed "love" for Desdemona—the passion that propels the Ensign in the 1566 novella by Giraldi Cinthio that is Shakespeare's source for *Othello*, but of which Iago makes only the barest mention—nor even his thwarted ambition suffices to account for his cascading sequence of evil deeds. Were Iago driven by the desire for promotion, he would have no reason to wreak further vengeance once he has displaced Cassio and been made Othello's lieutenant at the end of Act 3, Scene 3, but this belated triumph does not appease him, so it cannot constitute an adequate explanation of his actions. And if Iago's smorgasbord of avowed motives must be deemed unsatisfactory, still more is this true of the more speculative interpretations habitually favored by psychoanalytic readers, such as that Iago's paranoia follows Freud's script and can be attributed to his unconscious homosexual love for Othello.

It is not that this last hypothesis is implausible or that no evidence can be found to support it. As part of his scheme to arouse Othello's jealousy, Iago, in Act 3, Scene 3, recounts an incident—whether real or fabricated is immaterial—in which he shared a bed with Cassio, who, while calling out in a dream that he loved Desdemona, pressed kisses on Iago's mouth and "lay his leg o'er my thigh" (426). Similarly, when Iago cites as one of his grounds for enmity against Othello the suspicion that "the lusty Moor / Hath leapt into my seat" (2.1.293–94), the phrase "leapt into my seat," in addition to insinuating that Othello has copulated with his wife Emilia, conjures up the image that Othello has anally penetrated Iago himself. Homoerotic motifs are, accordingly, incontestably present in the play, but they give us only one more straw at which to clutch in seeking to unravel the enigma of Iago.

In view of the dead end at which we arrive in trying to analyze Shakespeare's archvillain using the tools of a purely individual psychology, I propose that we take a different tack and consider Iago instead with the aid of the ideas of Erich Fromm, beginning with his seminal concept of the "social character," which Fromm (1947) defines as "the core of a character structure common to most people of a given culture" (p. 60) or social class. If we do so, many otherwise puzzling features of Iago's character—both in the sense of his distinctive qualities and of his function in the play—fall into place. More specifically, since Shakespeare not only writes the play in the early years of the seventeenth century but takes over from Cinthio its mercantile Venetian setting, let us examine what Fromm has to say, in *The*

Sane Society (1955b), about the defining features of early modern capitalism. "Briefly," Fromm writes, "these common features are":

> 1—the existence of politically and legally free men; 2—the fact that free men (workers and employees) sell their labor to the owner of capital on the labor market, by contract; 3—the existence of the commodity market as a mechanism by which prices are determined and the exchange of the social product is regulated; 4—the principle that each individual acts with the aim of seeking a profit for himself.
> (p. 83)

At the same time, Fromm cautions, in this incipient phase of capitalism, unlike its full-blown form in the nineteenth and twentieth centuries, "the practices and ideas of medieval culture still had a considerable influence on the economic practices of this period" (p. 84).

With these statements in mind, Iago comes into focus as a paradigm of capitalist man driven by the profit motive. What is his incessantly repeated advice to Roderigo, "Put money in thy purse" (1.3.340), but a pithy summation of the ethos of capitalism? When Iago commends those in subordinate positions who throw "but shows of service on their lords" in order to "well thrive by them" and "Do themselves homage" (1.1.51–53), he reiterates the principle that all behavior should be guided by this narrow conception of self-interest. Similarly, when he tells Roderigo, concerning his qualifications to be Othello's lieutenant, "I know my price, I am worth no worse a place" (10), he takes for granted "the existence of the commodity market as a mechanism by which prices are determined and the exchange of the social product is regulated." At the same time, Iago still lives in a partially feudal world, since he complains that "Preferment" no longer goes "by old gradation, where each second / Stood heir to th' first," but rather "by letter and affection" (35–37)—that is, by favoritism—although he admits to Roderigo with characteristic inconsistency that he himself had dispatched "Three great ones of the city" (7) to plead his case for promotion to Othello.

Despite having the profit motive as its engine, Fromm (1955b) emphasizes that the attitudes inculcated by the capitalist system, including the privileging of "quantification and abstractification," transcend "the realm of economic production, and spread to the attitude of man to things, to people, and to himself" (p. 113). Iago's proclivity to engage in "quantification and abstractification" is everywhere apparent in his discourse. When Roderigo contemplates drowning himself over his unrequited love for Desdemona, Iago chastises him: "I have looked on the world for four times seven years, and since I could distinguish betwixt a benefit and an injury I never found a man that knew how to love himself" (1.3.312–15). A footnote in the latest Arden edition of *Othello* asks in puzzlement: "Why does Shakespeare make such a point of Iago's precise age?" But Fromm has already supplied the answer. Iago gives his age using the multiplication table because, as the embodiment of capitalist man, this is simply how he thinks. When Iago extols knowing the difference between a "benefit" and an "injury" and exhorts Roderigo to "love himself," he again subscribes to the principle enunciated by Fromm that, in a market-based society, "each individual acts with the aim of seeking a profit for himself" and, as "politically and legally free men," they owe loyalty to none but themselves.

The anal imagery in the play to which I have already alluded in connection with the conventional psychoanalytic interpretation of Iago's paranoia as stemming from repressed homosexual love for Othello likewise takes on additional meaning in light of Fromm's ideas. As Fromm argues first in *Man for Himself* (1947) and again in *The Sane Society* (1955b), the character-types that Freud developed in the context of his drive theory can be reformulated in interpersonal terms so that they are understood as manifestations not of "various types of libido organization" but rather of "specific kinds of a person's relatedness to the world" (1947, p. 58). Fromm distinguishes between "productive" and "nonproductive" orientations, the latter of which he breaks down into the "receptive," "hoarding," "exploitative," and "marketing" orientations.

Most directly relevant to Iago is the hoarding orientation, which Fromm (1955b, p. 91) equates with Freud's "anal character" and for which "fill thy purse with money" (1.3.348) serves as the perfect slogan. But insofar as capitalism is based on the principle of "the use of man by man" (Fromm, 1955b, p. 94), Iago is equally a representation of the exploitative orientation, which implies "a sadistic kind of relationship" (Fromm, 1947, p. 111), such as Iago displays most blatantly with Roderigo and Othello but in actuality governs all his dealings with others; and, as Fromm (1955b) notes, the hoarding is "blended with the exploitative orientation" (p. 136) when capitalism reaches its full bloom in the nineteenth century. Finally, insofar as the marketing orientation is characterized by the absence of a "specific and permanent kind of relatedness" apart from a "changeability of attitudes" in response to whatever may be demanded by the immediate situation, a byproduct of which is an essential "emptiness" and "loneliness of man" (pp. 75, 77), it is surely justified to see in the chameleon Iago also the traits of the marketing orientation—and thus of at least three of Fromm's four nonproductive orientations.

Underlying Fromm's typology of orientations is the dichotomy between humanistic and authoritarian ethics he introduces in *Man for Himself*, as well as the *"normative humanism"* he further expounds in *The Sane Society* (1955b, p. 12). A key ingredient of Fromm's conceptual armamentarium is what he designates as the *"pathology of normalcy,"* which is not an "individual pathology" (p. 6) but is rather the consequence of the realization that "the very person who is considered healthy in the categories of an alienated world, from the humanistic standpoint appears as the sickest one— although not in terms of individual sickness, but of the socially patterned defect" (p. 203). Could there be a better description of "honest" Iago, who is seen by everyone in the play as the paragon of reliability and helpfulness and who gives the crudest expression to the racism and misogyny that are the ideological underpinnings of the Venetian state, than that he is the exemplar of the "pathology of normalcy," that is, the one who is "considered healthy" by this "alienated world" but is in reality "the sickest" because he is the most virulent carrier of its "socially patterned defect"?

3

As early as *The Sane Society* (1955b), Fromm posits a desire for transcendence as one of the cornerstones of a humanistic psychoanalysis. If a person, confronted with "the passivity and accidentalness" of his existence as a created being, is incapable of love, and therefore of living with a sense of "purposefulness and freedom," he writes:

> There is another answer to this need for transcendence: if I cannot create life, I can destroy it. To destroy life makes me also transcend it. Indeed, that man can destroy life is just as miraculous a feat as that he can create it, for life is the miracle, the inexplicable.
>
> (p. 37)

This argument, which hearkens back to the antithesis between positive and negative responses to the dilemmas of modernity brilliantly explicated by Fromm in *Escape from Freedom* (1941), in turn looks ahead to the overtly metaphysical concerns of his later works from *The Heart of Man* (1964a) to *The Anatomy of Human Destructiveness* (1973). Although I owe the phrase "negative transcendence" not to Fromm himself but to the commentary of Daniel Burston (1991, p. 70), it captures the essence of Fromm's idea and opens new vistas for our analysis of Iago as a "social character" who comprises an amalgam of the "unproductive orientations" spawned by early modern capitalism.

If, as Fromm (1955b) maintains, "man, being torn away from nature, being endowed with reason and imagination, needs to form a concept of himself, needs to say and to feel 'I am I'" (p. 60), then the choice between creation and destruction faced by every human being is likewise one between achieving a "sense of identity" by "developing the unique and particular entity which is 'he' to a point where he can truly sense 'I am I'" and, conversely, an alienation that "tries to solve the problem" of how to relate to the world "in a different way, namely by conforming" (p. 197). The alienated man, therefore, is "estranged from himself" (p. 120); and in modern society, Fromm adds, such alienation "is almost total; it pervades the relationship of man to his work, to the things he consumes, to the state, to his fellow man, and to himself" (p. 124). It follows that the most thoroughly alienated man suffers from the "pathology of normalcy," and "since he experiences himself as a thing, an investment, to be manipulated by himself and by others, he is lacking a sense of self." This condition "creates deep anxiety" and can lead a person not only up to but beyond the "border of madness" because, when confronted with the "vision of nothingness," he or she "cannot say 'I' any more" (p. 204).

Here I think we are as close as it is possible to come to plucking out the heart of Iago's mystery. While preaching his gospel of selfishness in his opening exchange with Roderigo, Iago engages in head-spinning double-talk:

> It is as sure as you are Roderigo,
> Were I the Moor, I would not be Iago:
> In following him I follow but myself.
> (1.1.55–57)

Then, after vowing never to wear his heart on his sleeve, Iago concludes: "I am not what I am" (64). In both instances, the Arden editor is again at a loss. He arbitrarily changes the final period of the former passage, found in both the Quarto and Folio texts of the play, to a colon in order to "make the lines slightly less baffling," while he opines that "I am not what I am" "appears to mean 'I am not what I seem,'" although he rightly notes the allusion to God's declaration to Moses in Exodus, "I am what I am" (3:14), echoed by St. Paul in 1 Corinthians, "By the grace of God, I am what I am" (15:10). But to reduce Iago's metaphysical paradoxes to platitudes—appearance may not correspond to reality, and were he in Othello's position, he would not let a servant get away with what he himself is now doing—is to show oneself incapable of grasping Shakespeare's language. Not only is it true, as Fromm observes in *Man for Himself* (1947), that "the selfish person does not love himself too much but too little," and "in fact he hates himself" (p. 131), but Iago, the radically alienated man, is unable to even to *say* "I am I." Consequently, he can solve the problem of existence only by inverting God's "I am," an annihilation of personal identity that is bound to result in an orgy of destruction.

As with the hypothesis that we approach Iago as a "social character," many more things become comprehensible once we have recourse to Fromm's concept of "negative transcendence." Whether or not we agree with Bloom (1998) that Iago's "only true motive" is his rejection by Othello, Bloom ends up in the right place when he speaks of Iago's "loss of being," for this is precisely what Fromm, in *The Anatomy of Human Destructiveness* (1973), means by the "*existential failure*" of "man the destroyer," who has "failed to become what he could be according to the possibilities of his existence" (p. 296). When Bloom disparages Auden's interpretation of Iago as "the apotheosis of the practical joker" as an attempt to "restrict Iago's genius" because he "is a great artist and no joker" (p. 435), he misses the ontological dimension of Auden's argument, and thus the degree to which it anticipates his own. Indeed, when Auden discerns in Iago the "fear of lacking a concrete self, of being nobody," and explains his behavior as a "projection of his self-hatred . . . onto all created things," he not only spells out what it means to experience the "loss of being" but also gives a Frommian reading of Iago's character, although Auden himself nowhere acknowledges his affinity with Fromm.[3]

To speak of Iago as a "great artist" is not incompatible with seeing him as an embodiment of what Fromm (1973) calls "destructiveness and cruelty" in their purest form, which results from "the only true perversion" of "*life turning against itself in the striving to make sense of it*" (p. 31). When Iago concludes his first soliloquy by exulting, "I have't, it is engendered! Hell and night / Must bring this monstrous birth to the world's light" (1.3.402–3), he employs metaphors of conception and pregnancy to describe his newly hatched plot, since only by perverting the language of life can he capture what it feels like to destroy life. As Fromm recognizes, sadism possesses a "'devotional'" quality because it has "no practical aim," but is essentially *"the transformation of impotence into the experience of omnipotence,"* or, in other words, "the religion of psychical cripples" (p. 323). Fromm's analysis of sadism shows once again why Bradley is mistaken in doubting that Iago could be driven by the "love of evil simply as evil" to take "pleasure in the pain of others simply as others" and likewise fails to comprehend that the absence of any positive motivation makes it impossible for readers to "look more closely into Iago's inner man."

That the "loss of being" propelling Iago's sadism is a form of "impotence" that makes him a "psychical cripple" can be seen most clearly in his aggressive banter with Desdemona in Act 2, Scene 1, after they have both landed in Cyprus and are awaiting the arrival of Othello. When Desdemona seeks to pass the time by asking Iago how he might praise her, he prefaces his mock encomium in rhymed couplets with an apology for the slowness of his wit:

> my invention
> Comes from my pate as birdlime does from frieze.
> It plucks out brains and all; but my muse labours
> And thus she is delivered.
>
> (125–28)

Here, too, as his use of the words "labours" and "delivered" indicates, Iago resorts to the language of pregnancy as a tactic to deflate his listeners' expectations concerning his poetic gifts. But though such expressions of humility are a literary convention, there is nothing commonplace about how Iago describes what emerges from his head. As Janet Adelman (1997) has explicated in her scintillating Kleinian reading of the play, "birdlime" is a "soiling agent" that cannot be peeled off without also removing the nap of the coarse woolen cloth to which it adheres, so what he produces is a "dangerous evacuation" that amounts to a "vindictive fantasy of a fecal pregnancy . . . that can project Iago's inner monstrosity and darkness into the world" (p. 141).

Thus, the anal imagery that suffuses the play, which I have linked to Iago's "hoarding orientation," surfaces once again to infect and besmirch the idea of childbirth. As his exchange with Desdemona continues, Iago runs through the permutations of four categories of women—fair and wise, foul and wise, fair and foolish, foul and foolish—the upshot of which is that they are all sluts.[4] When Desdemona then asks what Iago would say about a truly virtuous woman, after a lengthy preamble in verse, he declares that she would be good for nothing save mindless domesticity—"To suckle fools, and chronicle small beer"—to which Desdemona responds, "O, most lame and impotent conclusion!" (2.1.160–61). Beneath the banter, Iago vents his misogynistic stereotypes of women as either whores or drudges, while Desdemona strikes back by diagnosing him as at once "lame"—that is, a "psychical cripple"—and "impotent."

Desdemona's language converges uncannily with Fromm's, and by pairing "lame" with "impotent" in her rebuke of Iago she lends credence to Fromm's (1973) contention that "sexual impotence is only a small part" of the condition that he calls "complete vital impotence," which a man "will do almost anything to overcome," including in extreme instances "cruelty and murder" (p. 266). Contemporaneously with Kohut, Fromm notes that when a narcissistic person is wounded by an injury to his self-esteem he "usually reacts with intense anger or rage" (p. 228), and it draws Fromm's thought closer to Bloom's if we apply to Iago what he says in *The Heart of Man* (1964a), namely that "revengeful violence" frequently has its origin in a *"shattering of faith"* (p. 28) that can cause "the deeply deceived and disappointed person" to "begin to hate life" (p. 30). This hatred of life leads to the desire to destroy it, which brings us back to negative transcendence because "to destroy life also means to transcend it and to escape the unbearable suffering of complete passivity" (p. 31).

Although it would be pointless to dispute that Iago suffers from a narcissistic pathology ignited by his "shattering of faith" in Othello, my concern is not to reconstruct the etiology of Iago's rage or with pursuing the will-o'-the-wisp of his motives. It is rather to demonstrate that his malignity is, as Fromm (1973) writes of aggression, but one component of a *"syndrome"* that includes such features as "strict hierarchy, dominance, class division, etc.," and is thus "to be understood as part of the *social character*, not as an isolated behavior trait" (p. 193). Building on his opposition between productive and the various unproductive orientations, Fromm (1964a) in his later works contrasts the "syndrome of growth" with the "syndrome of decay," or what he also calls "biophilia" with "necrophilia." The latter is fueled by a "malignant narcissism" that *"prompts men to destroy for the sake of destruction"* (p. 23) and constitutes "the most morbid and the most dangerous among the orientations to life of which man is capable" (p. 45). Just Fromm had earlier reformulated Freud's theory of character-types in interpersonal terms, so too, in his final period he offers a humanistic counterpart to Freud's mythic duality of Eros and the death drive by postulating that "there is no more fundamental distinction between men, psychologically and morally, than the one between those who love death and those who love life" (p. 38).

Fromm's recasting of anality as a manifestation of the hoarding orientation evolves into the proposition that necrophilia is *"the malignant form of the character structure of which Freud's 'anal character' is the benign form,"* and that such psychically crippled individuals "have a deep interest in and affinity to feces as part of their general affinity to all that is not alive" (1964a, pp. 54–55). Our insight into Shakespeare's characterization of Iago unfolds in tandem with Fromm's ideas. The "fantasy of a fecal pregnancy" that Adelman has discerned in Iago's repartee with Desdemona becomes more fully intelligible in light of Fromm's analogy (1973, p. 407n36) that necrophilia is to anality as biophilia is to genitality, as well as his observation that "just as sexuality can create life, force can destroy it" (1964a, p. 40). Iago is driven to destroy both Othello and Desdemona, as well as everyone else who crosses his path, because their incandescent love represents the positive transcendence that he can never hope to experience, and thus his only recourse is to the use of force, which, quoting Simone Weil, Fromm defines as "the capacity to transform a man into a corpse" (p. 40).

Immediately after Desdemona humiliates Iago by mocking his "lame and impotent conclusion," she converses with Cassio, who takes her by the hand and, in a courteous gesture, kisses his fingers. In an aside, Iago murmurs, "would they were clyster-pipes for your sake!" (2.1.176). Again Adelman's (1997) commentary is masterful. By transforming Cassio's fingers into enema tubes, she submits, the latest iteration of Iago's fantasy "violently brings together not only lips and feces, mouth, vagina, and anus, but also digital, phallic, and emetic penetration of a body . . . imagined only as a container for feces" (p. 132). The common denominator is Iago's necrophilia, or his obsession with feces as "part of his general affinity to all that is not alive."

"I Am Not What I Am" 199

One of the most puzzling features of *Othello* is the Clown, whose character is so feebly drawn—by comparison with such scene-stealers as the Gravedigger in *Hamlet*, Lear's Fool, and the Porter in *Macbeth*—that he is frequently bypassed altogether by critics. But when he approaches the musicians who have been hired by Cassio to serenade Othello and Desdemona, the following dialogue ensues:

CLOWN Why, masters, have your instruments been in Naples, that they speak i'th' nose thus?
I MUSICIAN How, sir? How?
CLOWN Are these, I pray you, wind instruments?
I MUSICIAN Ay marry are they, sir.
CLOWN O, thereby hangs a tail.
I MUSICIAN Whereby hangs a tail, sir?
CLOWN Marry, sir, by many a wind instrument that I know. But, masters, here's money for you, and the general so likes your music that he desires you, for love's sake, to make no more noise with it.
(3.1.3–13)

The reference to Naples is due to the association of the city with syphilis, one of the most grotesque symptoms of which is damage to the nose, which the Clown uses to mock the "nasal" sound of the musicians' instruments. His interlocutor's inability to follow his witty logic leads the Clown to ask if they are playing "wind instruments," following which he puns on the phrase "hangs a tale" by saying that tails hang "by many a wind instrument" that he knows, a joke about farting. "Tail," moreover, is slang for "penis" while also alluding to the tails of animals, so the passage that begins with an image of phallic disease then collapses genitality into anality, a microcosm of the larger movement of the play in which Iago's necrophilia destroys the biophilia represented by the sexual passion of Othello and Desdemona.

Since this seemingly irrelevant scene between the Clown and the Musician thematically reflects Iago's dominance of the world of this tragedy, it becomes significant that money is exchanged, and the repetition of the word "instruments" can be interpreted as a symptom of Iago's personification not only of *"the malignant form of the anal character"* but also of the "marketing character," the modern type of capitalist man for whom, as Fromm (1973) writes, "everything is transformed into a commodity—not only things, but the person himself, . . . and whose principle it is to make a profit by favorable exchange" (pp. 387–88). Whereas both Iago's hoarding and marketing orientations are epitomized by the maxim "Put money in thy purse," his instantiation of the even more alienated being whom Fromm labels "cybernetic man" is encapsulated in his avowal to Desdemona before launching into his diatribe against women, "I am nothing if not critical" (2.1.119). As Fromm elaborates, cybernetic man could also be called "*monocerebral man*" because his "approach to the whole world around him—and to himself—is cerebral"; and "this cerebral-intellectual approach goes together with the absence of an affective response" (p. 391), a combination evinced in Iago. No less pertinent is Fromm's observation that "monocerebral man" is also characterized by "a special kind of narcissism that has as its object himself—his body and his skill—in brief, himself as an *instrument* of success" (p. 391; italics added). Iago's gloating is seen in such exclamations as "I have't, it is engendered!" or the resolution to "plume up my will / In double knavery" (1.3.392–93), and in boasting of how he uses his "will" as an "instrument of success" Iago may be said to compose the score for the "wind instrument" to which the Clown jocularly adverts in his banter with the Musician.

Iago's most fulsome paean to the will occurs as he berates Roderigo for his thoughts of suicide over his hopeless infatuation with Desdemona. When Roderigo laments that it is not in his "virtue to amend" his feelings of despair, Iago responds:

> Virtue? a fig! 'tis in ourselves that we are thus, or thus. Our bodies are gardens, to the which our wills are gardeners. . . . If the balance of our lives had not one scale of reason to poise another of sensuality, the blood and baseness of our natures would conduct us to most preposterous conclusions. But we have reason to cool our raging motions, our carnal stings, our unbitted lusts; whereof I take this, that you call love, to be a sect or scion.
>
> (1.3.319–33)

According to Iago, it is solely up to the will to choose what to plant in the "gardens" of our bodies, and it is incumbent on reason to restrain "the blood and baseness of our natures." But all the energy of his language goes into spelling out what lies on the irrational side of the scale, and his claim that what is popularly known as love is nothing but a "sect or scion" of lust brings his view of human nature into conjunction with that of Freud, for whom love is likewise merely an illusory sublimation of sexual desire.

In pondering "the connection between the anal-hoarding character and necrophilia," Fromm (1973) delineates a continuum that goes from the "normal anal character" at one end, through the "sadistic character" in the middle, to the full-blown "necrophilous character" on the other. The severity of the pathology "is determined by the increase of narcissism, unrelatedness, and destructiveness" (p. 387) as one moves along the spectrum. Although sadism is for Fromm "a perverse kind of relatedness," he points out that "sadists are still *with* others; they want to control, but not to destroy them," whereas the aim of necrophiles "is to transform all that is alive into dead matter; they want to destroy everything and everybody, often even themselves; their enemy is life itself" (p. 387).

If we apply Fromm's schema to the play, the Clown may be said to represent the "normal" anal character, which resembles the oral and genital characters in that it "belongs to a period before total alienation has fully developed" and is possible only "as long as there is real sensuous experience of one's body, its functions, and its products" (p. 388). Iago, by contrast, despite his use of corporeal metaphors in "clyster-pipes," "leapt into my seat," "monstrous birth," and the like—not to mention his obsession with Othello and Desdemona "making the beast with two backs" (1.1.114–15)—is, in fact, totally alienated from his body, which "he experiences . . . only as an *instrument* for success" (p. 388). And while he might appear to engage in that "perverse kind of relatedness" that "wants to control, but not destroy" others—as when Iago professes to Roderigo to be "knit to thy deserving with cables of perdurable toughness" (1.3.338–39)—even this pretense of advancing the interests of his victim as a means of exploiting him financially is merely a façade that screens the complete lack of relatedness that makes Iago the "inhuman dog" (5.1.62) that Roderigo discovers him to be only in the moment when his purported benefactor plunges the knife into his chest. Iago sums up the sociopath's creed in the last line of his second soliloquy, "Knavery's plain face is never seen, till used" (2.1.310).

In Iago, Shakespeare illustrates Fromm's (1964a) definition of evil as *"man's loss of himself in the tragic attempt to escape the burden of his humanity"* (p. 148). Iago's rage for negative transcendence combines an insatiable will to power with an absolute loss of being and, with it, a sense of self. Always improvising while endlessly repeating his "no" to life, Iago lacks the inner core of personality that is for Fromm (1947) "the reality behind the word 'I' and on which our conviction of our own identity is based" (p. 206). It is for this reason that he is likewise devoid of the "primary imagination" that Coleridge, in Chapter 13 of *Biographia Literaria* (1817), holds to be "a representation in the finite mind of the eternal act of creation in the infinite I AM" (p. 167), and can only utter in its place, "I am not what I am."

4

It is an abiding paradox of Fromm's thought that the originator of the concept of "social character" also espoused a *"normative humanism"* that unapologetically sought, as he wrote in *The Sane Society* (1955b), to "arrive at a correct description of what deserves to be called human nature," and "is based on the assumption that, as in any other problems, there are right and wrong, satisfactory and unsatisfactory solutions to the problem of human existence" (pp. 13–14). Although originally founded on a philosophical anthropology in the tradition of Spinoza and the early Marx, Fromm in his later writings increasingly made his case also on the grounds of natural science and evolutionary psychology. Fromm's critique of Freud for claiming that his theories were universal truths without recognizing the degree to which they were extrapolated from culturally bound assumptions is, as we have seen in Chapter 2, the obverse of his own lifelong undertaking to mount a genuinely compelling and credible version of the same psychoanalytic project.

In this analysis of Iago through the lenses of Fromm's binocular vision, I have striven to forge a synthesis between an exegesis of Iago as a "social character" in what Marjorie Garber (2004) has described as Shakespeare's supreme tragedy of "race, class, and gender" (p. 588) and Bloom's (1998) homage to Iago as a "negative ontotheologian, a diabolical prophet who has a vocation for destruction" (p. 464). Like Shakespeare himself, Iago is—to vary Ben Jonson's tribute in the First Folio—both of his age *and* for all time. He is at once the apotheosis of early modern capitalist man and the archetype of all those, from Caligula to Hitler, and now also Trump, for whom, as Fromm (1973) has written, "madness is a way of life . . . because it serves the illusion of omnipotence, of transcending the frontiers of human existence" (p. 323). Indeed, when Fromm remarks that "what is special in Hitler's case is the disproportionality between the destruction he ordered and the realistic reasons for it" (p. 446), he could equally well have been describing Iago, whose "motiveless malignity" forever eludes our comprehension not because there are too few reasons for it but because there are too many.

In the final scene of the play, after he has murdered Desdemona, Othello confronts Iago overwhelmed by the horror of the deed his treacherous confidant had induced him to perpetrate: "I look down towards his feet, but that's a fable. / If that thou be'st a devil, I cannot kill thee" (5.2.283–84). He thereupon surprises the onlookers by attacking his pinioned adversary with a sword, to which Iago retorts, "I bleed, sir, but not killed" (285). The absence of a cloven foot means that Iago does not possess the Devil's telltale mythical feature, yet Othello succeeds only in wounding but not killing him. As Fromm (1973) appositely observes, *"it is man's humanity that makes him so inhuman"* (p. 149). *"Hence, as long as one believes that the evil man wears horns, one will not discover an evil man"* (p. 480).

After begging Cassio's pardon for his unjust suspicions, Othello implores his cashiered and now also maimed lieutenant to "demand that demi-devil / Why he hath thus ensnared my soul and body?" (5.2.298–99). Iago again responds with defiance: "Demand me nothing. What you know, you know. / From this time forth I never will speak word" (300–1). Shakespeare here coins the word "demi-devil" in the English language to confirm Iago status as the hybrid descendant of the Vice figure who bestrode the medieval stage while also sealing the oxymoron of his inhuman humanity. The eternal adversary cannot be killed, which means he is a devil; but he bleeds and his feet are intact, so he must be a man. Like the outwardly nondescript gambler Stephen Paddock, who, on October 1, 2017, carried out from his Las Vegas hotel room the largest mass shooting in modern American history, Iago leaves us with nothing to attenuate the mystery of his iniquity. And since Iago's character rivals only Hamlet's as a conundrum for critics, it is fitting that his closing vow of muteness mirrors that of the Danish prince: "the rest is silence" (5.2.365). But whereas flights of angels and the soldier's music accompany Hamlet to the undiscovered country, Iago is surely destined for the other place.

Notes

1 All quotations from *Othello* in this chapter are to the latest Arden edition of the play, by E. A. J. Honigmann, while my lone quotation from *Hamlet* is from the earlier Arden edition by Harold Jenkins.

2 In his recent monograph on Iago, Bloom (2018) merely restates his earlier view that Iago, like Satan, suffers from "a Sense of Injured Merit" and that being passed over for promotion has "devastated his sense of being" (p. 4). Stanley Edgar Hyman (1970), in the final book of his distinguished career, rejects "any single critical method" in favor of a "pluralist criticism" in which all approaches to the question of Iago's motivation "are equal, cooperating partners in a critical symposium," though he acknowledges his own predilection for a "theological reading" in which "the figuration of Satan . . . is Iago's richest and most resonant meaning" (pp. 139–40).
3 As Rollo May points out in *The Age of Anxiety* (1950), "there is a remarkable similarity between the picture of our culture" given by Auden and Fromm, inasmuch as they are "both impressed by the same characteristics of . . . automaton conformity, the alienation of man from himself and his fellows, and the destruction of individuality and originality resulting from the apotheosis of commercial values" (p. 173n59).
4 To cite only one instance, Iago says of the ugly but intelligent woman, "If she be black, and thereto have a wit, / She'll find a white that shall her blackness fit" (2.1.132–33), where "white," in the sense of "fair-complexioned man," echoes "wit" and puns on "wight" or "creature," while "blackness" means not only "foulness" but also the woman's genitals, which the penis of the man will "fit" (or, in the Quarto version, "hit"). The wordplay on blackness and whiteness in the lines evokes the theme of interracial sexual union in *Othello*.

Chapter 9

Did Freud Masturbate?
The Folly of Élisabeth Roudinesco

> "Confronted by a human being who impresses us as great, should we not be moved rather than chilled by the knowledge that he might have attained his greatness only through his frailties?"
>
> —Lou Andreas-Salomé, *Freud Journal*

It is useful to think of Freud biographies as falling into three main categories. The first may be called the hagiographical. It starts with Ernest Jones's three monumental volumes (1953, 1955, 1957) and is refurbished in Peter Gay's *Freud: A Life for Our Time* (1988). While purporting to take a "warts and all" approach, and despite minor differences of emphasis, writers in this camp are unequivocally "pro-Freud" and espouse a fundamentally classical version of psychoanalytic theory. At the opposite extreme are the "Freud-bashers," who, while not denying his outsized cultural influence, see Freud as having been wrong about almost everything and reject psychoanalysis *in toto* as both a theory and a therapy. The godfather of this debunking tradition is Emil Ludwig in *Doctor Freud: An Analysis and a Warning* (1947), and it reaches its apotheosis in Frederick Crews's *Freud: The Making of an Illusion* (2017). In the middle are the revisionists, beginning with Helen Walker Puner in *Freud: His Life and His Mind*—also published in 1947—with other notable milestones being Erich Fromm's *Sigmund Freud's Mission* (1959b), Paul Roazen's *Freud and His Followers* (1975), and Louis Breger's *Freud: Darkness in the Midst of Vision* (2000).[1] The revisionists see Freud as unquestionably a genius but also as a tragically flawed and traumatized human being, and they propound a conception of psychoanalysis that has more in common with Ferenczi or Fromm than with that of Freud himself.

From my standpoint as a scion of the revisionist tradition, the insuperable problem with Élisabeth Roudinesco's fast-paced and expertly conducted narrative, *Freud in His Time and Ours* (2014), is not that it falls squarely into the Freud-worshiping camp but that she fails to recognize that what she herself has to say is inevitably shaped by her perspective and not the presentation of an objective truth about Freud. Both the tone of apodeictic certainty and the lack of any sense of nuance that afflict her biography are on display beginning in her introduction. In alluding to the "several dozen biographies" that have been written about Freud, "from the one published during his lifetime (1934) by his disciple Fritz Wittels, who had become an American, to Peter Gay's" (p. 2), Roudinesco leaves out of account the works by Puner, Fromm, and Breger, as though their important contributions simply did not exist, as indeed they do not for her, while she disparages Roazen in the epilogue as the spearhead of "dissident historiography" that ought to have set the stage "for the imposition of an authentic school of Freudianism" (p. 423). From beginning to end, she lambastes "the many practitioners of radical anti-Freudianism (Freud-bashing)," who, in her view, have given us "the organizer of a clinical gulag, the demoniacal, incestuous, lying, counterfeiting, fascist Freud" (p. 2) and, heaping Pelion on Ossa, "made Freud out to be a swindler, a rapist, and incestuous" (p. 423).

No authentic dialogue about whether Freud might, for instance, have been less than fully truthful on some occasions, or behaved like a cad in his financial dealings with his future brother-in-law, Eli Bernays, as well as with his patient Horace Frink, or displayed authoritarian tendencies, is possible in the face of such a barrage, which turns any attempt to see Freud critically into an instance of "Freud-bashing," which can then be dismissed out of hand. This reductive approach leads Roudinesco to aver that

> after multiple returns to his texts punctuating the history of the second half of the twentieth century, we have great difficulty knowing who Freud really was, so thoroughly have the commentaries, fantasies, legends, and rumors masked the reality of this thinker, in his time and ours.
> (p. 2)

The clear implication, of course, is that, in Roudinesco's book, we will finally learn "who Freud really was," freed of all the distortions that, in the hands of others, have "masked the reality of this thinker" that Roudinesco alone—as the doyenne of "the authentic school of Freudianism"—has the power to lay bare.

The epistemological naïveté—and presumption—inherent in Roudinesco's denial of her own subjectivity is compounded by the countless factual errors that mar her text. Her mention of Wittels, for starters, contains but one but two mistakes, since his biography of Freud was published not in 1934 but in 1923, and thus not after but nine years *before* he "had become an American." Roudinesco asserts in the opening paragraph of the introduction that "even if [Freud] once destroyed some working documents and letters so as to complicate the task of his future biographers ... what was lost hardly matters in the face of what has been preserved" (p. 1). This is not only unpsychoanalytic, since "what is lost" through a deliberate act of suppression does not therefore become irrelevant to understanding the person who sought to cover his tracks in this fashion, but it is also misleading since Freud is known to have destroyed his personal records not only in 1885—the occasion when he expressly defied his future biographers—but also in 1877 and again in 1907.

So it goes throughout this highly acclaimed book, recipient of the Prix Décembre, one of France's most prestigious literary awards. Roudinesco's errors (in the English translation I read) range from the trivial, to the mildly compromising, to the downright inexcusable and disqualifying. Her peccadilloes include writing "1884" instead of "1844" (p. 11), "Wandbek" instead of "Wandsbek" (p. 37), "*Lebenserinnerunguer*" instead of "*Lebenserinnerungen*" (p. 208; p. 467n89), "Stepanski" instead of "Stepansky" (p. 499n86), and referring to the "Count of Essex" (p. 274; p. 283), the "Count of Oxford" (p. 284), and the "Count of Southampton" (p. 483n64) when all three of these Elizabethan noblemen were actually Earls. It qualifies as at least a venial sin that Roudinesco should say that Sophocles devoted a "trilogy" to "the Labdacid family" (p. 79) when his three Theban plays were actually written decades apart, or that it was "Jung himself who had drawn [Freud's] attention" (p. 133) to Jensen's *Gradiva*, when it was actually Wilhelm Stekel, or describe *Nasamecu*, published in 1913, as Groddeck's "first book" written under the influence of "Ernest Scheninger" (p, 208), when the doubly misspelled name of Bismarck's physician was actually Ernst Schweninger, while *Nasamecu* was preceded by both *A Woman Problem* (1902) and *Toward God-Nature* (1909).

Among Roudinesco's truly unpardonable lapses are the claim that Freud "showed considerable enthusiasm" for cocaine "between 1884 and 1887" (p. 39), but then "stopped definitively in 1892" (p. 436*n*18), since Freud admitted to Fliess that he was still using cocaine at the time of his father's death in 1896, as well as her perpetuation of the misconception (originating with Walter Boehlich in the introduction to his edition of Freud's letters to Silberstein) that it was Gisela Fluss, "sister of his comrade Emil Fluss," to whom he gave "the name 'Ichthyosaurus'" (p. 20), when Freud's letter to Eduard Silberstein on August 17, 1872, in which he reports that he had asked Fluss "if he still hankered after Ichth." (Boehlich, 1989, p. 11), shows it to be out of the question that the unknown girl upon whom Freud bestowed this code name of a prehistoric creature—which should properly have the feminine form "Ichthyosaura"—could be Fluss's sister. Nor was it Max Schur, as is generally believed and Roudinesco (2014) takes for granted (p. 413), who assisted Freud in his suicide, but rather—as Roy B. Lacoursiere (2008) has shown—Josephine Stross who was present at his death.[2] And surely any graduate of a lycée, let alone Roudinesco (2014), the Head of Research in History at the University of Paris Diderot, should know better than to compare the relationship between analyst and patient to "Vergil guided by Dante in the *Divine Comedy*" (p. 259), when it was Dante who was guided through much of the poem by Vergil![3]

Roudinesco goes no less badly astray in her treatment of Freud's disciples and dissidents. Of Ferenczi and his love triangle with Gizella and Elma Pálos, she proclaims, "Believing that he loved the daughter, he actually loved the mother" (p. 124), thus presuming to know what is Ferenczi's heart, notwithstanding his protest in his Christmas-day 1921 letter to Groddeck (Fortune, 2002, p. 9) that he should have married Elma but for Freud's objections; and Roudinesco (2014) writes of Ferenczi's activities during World War I that he "was also trying to solve his problems with his wife, Gizella, during this period" (p. 173), undeterred by the fact that Ferenczi and Gizella did not marry until 1919, after the war had ended. With respect to Jung, Roudinesco twice declares that it was during his "first meeting with Freud" (p. 129) and his "first visit to 19 Berggasse" (p. 230) that he and Freud heard a noise coming from Freud's bookcase, which Jung accurately predicted would be repeated. Had Roudinesco consulted the Freud/Jung correspondence, however, which does not appear in her bibliography, or paid closer attention to Jung's autobiography, *Memories, Dreams, Reflections*, she would have learned that this incident occurred not during Jung's first visit to Vienna, in 1907, but during his second, in 1909. Since Roudinesco praises Deirdre Bair's biography of Jung as "the best source for the story of Jung's personal life" (p. 452n33), and Bair (2003, p. 116) makes the same mistake in her book, it seems highly likely that Roudinesco took a shortcut and based her account on this secondary source instead of on her own reading of the original documents.

Things go from bad to worse when Roudinesco turns to the 1909 expedition by Freud, Jung, and Ferenczi to America. According to Roudinesco (2014), it was "during the crossing" (p. 151) on the outbound journey that Jung had his dream of the two skulls. Although in *Memories, Dreams, Reflections* Jung does not specify exactly when he had the dream, in his 1925 Zurich seminar, published by William McGuire (1989) under the title *Analytical Psychology*—again not cited by Roudinesco—he discloses (p. 22) that it occurred on the return voyage, so she is mistaken about this. Roudinesco (2014) likewise states that Jung explained that "the skulls were those of Freud's wife and his sister-in-law," but "Freud didn't believe it" (p. 152). This is a howler of epic proportions. For in his autobiography, Jung (1963) writes that he told Freud the skulls were those of "'My wife and my sister-in-law'"—that is to say, *his own* relatives and *not* Freud's— and that Freud, far from not believing him, was "greatly relieved" by his reply (pp. 159–60). So eager is Roudinesco (2014) to discredit Jung and exonerate Freud that she literally cannot read the words on the page. The humiliation that Freud endured when he urinated down his trousers on Riverside Drive in New York in front of Jung and Ferenczi is airbrushed into merely a "urinary weakness," while Jung's belief that Freud had "engaged in sexual relations with his sister-in-law" is dismissed as a projection of "his own polygamy," and the most momentous confrontation in the history of psychoanalysis is, in Roudinesco's estimation, nothing more than a series of "senseless jousts" (p. 153).

It is, above all, on the crucial question of Freud's sexuality that Roudinesco shows her true colors. As she points out, Freud "is not known to have had any significant liaisons before his marriage" (p. 24) in 1886, when he was thirty of age, and the "sex life of the greatest modern theoretician of sexuality" with his wife Martha effectively ended after the birth of their sixth and last child, Anna, in 1895, and "thus presumably lasted nine years" (p. 50). Surely there is an enigma here worth pondering, but Roudinesco refuses to open the door to any serious inquiry into Freud's intimate life. In one of her litanies that conflates any psychoanalytic revisionism with out-and-out Freud-bashing, Roudinesco protests that Freud has been "accused on a number of occasions of being a libidinous bourgeois, of practicing clandestine abortions, frequenting whorehouses, masturbating, and unhesitatingly concealing his sexual relations with his sister-in-law" (p. 50). What is most peculiar about this list is Roudinesco's inclusion of masturbation among the activities of which Freud has been "accused," since this must mean that Roudinesco believes not only that Freud never indulged himself in this way but also that it would have been shameful had he done so, whereas it should be obvious to anyone with a pulse that a man with Freud's impoverished sexual history would have masturbated both before and after he married, and that it would be a cause for alarm had he *not* done so.

The explosive issue, of course, is not a "masturbating" but rather (to go back to her all-consuming obsession) an "incestuous" Freud. Derisive snorts about "certain commentators" who "imagine a dark story about a clandestine abortion" (p. 236) and "have supposed that there was a liaison, undiscoverable in the archives, between Sigmund and his sister-in-law" (p. 38) are sprinkled throughout the book. The indefensibility of Roudinesco's position on this topic, however, is exposed by the following pronouncement, contained in a footnote: "Dozens of novels, articles, and essays have been devoted to this 'liaison,' which *doubtless never happened* and which has become, in any case, one of the commonplaces of the late-twentieth-century anti-Freud movement" (p. 473*n*9; italics added). Whether Freud had an affair with his sister-in-law, Minna Bernays, as Peter J. Swales (1982) argued in a landmark paper, but which Roudinesco does not deign to cite in her bibliography, is a purely historical question that should have nothing to do with whether one is "pro-Freud" or "anti-Freud." For her to say this "doubtless never happened" is the height of hubris, based solely on her own preconceived opinion, which she mistakenly equates with "knowing who Freud really was."

Once again, Roudinesco (2014) compounds her readiness to make *ex cathedra* pronouncements with factual errors that expose her lack of genuine familiarity with the subject. In addition to the paper by Swales, the other indispensable source concerning Freud's relationship with Minna Bernays is an article by John M. Billinsky (1969) containing the transcript of a conversation he had with Jung in 1957, in which Jung confided that when he first visited Freud in Vienna in 1907, Minna herself had told him about her affair with Freud. Even Kurt R. Eissler, Jung's most vociferous detractor, was forced to admit in *Three Instances of Injustice* (1994, p. 111) that Billinsky's report of Jung's testimony was accurate since it was independently confirmed by Jung's closest associate, Carl A. Meier. Yet Roudinesco (2014) allows herself to be driven into the ditch for a second time by Bair, to whom she appeals in a vain effort to cast doubt on Billinsky: "Deirdre Bair asserts that Billinsky attributes to Jung statements that he had not made" (p. 473*n*7). Had Roudinesco done her homework, she would have known that Bair's assertion is false, but—just as with her mistake about the date of the noise-in-the-bookcase incident—she is content to base herself on an unreliable secondary source that appears to support her prejudiced ideas.

Roudinesco further compromises herself in an earlier footnote where she insists that "no serious historian has ever offered the slightest proof of the existence of this 'liaison' that gave rise to a large number of articles and several books" (p. 457*n*10). This is to demean the controversial but incontestably brilliant Swales as not a "serious historian," and Roudinesco's claim that there is not "the slightest proof" for Freud's affair with Minna, like her reference to unspecified articles and books, is a strategy that allows her to create the illusion of scholarly mastery while in reality failing to engage with the substantial body of evidence that points strongly in the direction of an affair, although she repeatedly cites her own earlier work in which she purports to have offered the refutation that is missing here. She begins this same footnote by writing:

> Spread later on by Jung, over the years the rumor of an incestuous Freud became one of the major themes of psychoanalytic historiography in the English-speaking world, in particular after the publication in 1947 of Helen Walker Puner's book, *Sigmund Freud: His Life and Mind*.
>
> (p. 457*n*10)

It is, first of all, incorrect to say that Jung "spread" any sort of "rumor" about Freud's love life, since all he did was to share with a handful of trusted people what he had heard directly from Minna. But even more ill-advised is Roudinesco's slap at Puner, the only reference in her biography to this fountainhead of the revisionist tradition of Freud studies. For Puner (1947), contrary to Roudinesco's assertion, expressly denies that any "suspicion of slander" could "be breathed against 'the Jew's' personal life" and insists, on the contrary, that "Freud would never once swerve from the path of marital rectitude that grew from the seed of his general rigid morality" (p. 291). I have no clue where Roudinesco got the idea that Puner is aligned with those who believe in an "incestuous Freud." It suffices to know that she is simply making things up out of whole cloth and that her many blunders warrant the verdict that it is she, not Swales, who deserves to be castigated as not a "serious historian."

As a final illustration of the untrustworthiness of Roudinesco's (2014) entire narrative about Freud, I would cite her statements that "he condemned adultery" (p. 272) and "had a horror of adultery" (p. 301). One of Roudinesco's favorite tropes, as we have seen, is to accuse those with whom she disagrees of failing to offer "the slightest proof" of their claims. With what is by now a predictable irony, however, it is rather Roudinesco herself who feels under no obligation to corroborate her preposterous allegations about Freud's views on adultery. Not only did Freud time and again seek to bail his followers out of sexual hot water of one temperature or another without ever reproaching them on moral grounds, but he observed with equanimity in "'Civilized' Sexual Morality and Modern Nervous Illness" (1908) that married men "very frequently avail themselves of the degree of sexual freedom which is allowed to them . . . by even the strictest sexual code" (p. 195). Even more radically, he wrote in response to a questionnaire in 1905 that

> perhaps the only practical way in which to encourage morality would be the legalization of relations between the sexes outside of marriage, according a greater measure of sexual freedom and curtailing restrictions on that freedom. . . . Moreover, the existence of a marriage is in itself no grounds for sexual obligations when the marriage no longer fulfills the task of satisfying normal sexual instincts.
>
> (Boyer, 1978, pp. 91–92)

Needless to say, the essential article in which these quotations appear is nowhere to be found in Roudinesco's bibliography.

Again, I am unable to divine what gave rise to Roudinesco's fantasy that Freud had a "horror of adultery," other than her aversion to facing squarely anything that contradicts her idealized image of the founder of psychoanalysis. The same combination of intellectual laxity and willful blindness is evident in her treatment of Freud's early childhood. Roudinesco (2014) states that the incident in which he saw his mother naked as a boy took place "on a train trip from Freiberg to Leipzig" (p. 15), when a quick check of Freud's letter to Fliess of October 3, 1897, would have told her that it occurred on the later journey from Leipzig to Vienna; and she dismisses the probability that Freud was sexually abused by his nanny, whom he describes in the same indispensable letter as the "'prime originator'" of his neurosis who was his "teacher in sexual matters" and washed him in "reddish water" (Masson, 1985, pp. 268–69) as simply one of the "many rumors surrounding the private life" (Roudinesco, 2014, p. 16) of Freud that—far from offering a key to understanding his character—does not deserve to be taken seriously.

The field of Freud studies is notoriously contentious, united perhaps only by the conviction that Freud remains a figure of sufficient fascination and complexity to return to endlessly and to disagree about passionately. Many other reviewers have hailed this book by one of the most eminent and influential historians of psychoanalysis of our time; I have tried to spell out what are from my perspective its incurable defects. For a psychoanalyst to say, as Roudinesco does in her introduction, that she intends to "show that what Freud thought he was discovering was at bottom *nothing but* the product of a society, a familial environment, and a political situation" (p. 4; italics added) is puzzling indeed, as it seems to leave no room for the creative imagination or the inner life. The all-too-human Freud who undoubtedly masturbated and in all likelihood had sex with his sister-in-law is an entirely different man from the lifeless icon who is worshiped here.

Notes

1 Densely packed with biographical information about all manner of historical figures, Henri Ellenberger's *The Discovery of the Unconscious* (1970) is deservedly hailed as a classic for placing Freud in the larger context of dynamic psychiatry, and thus presciently recognizing the stature of Janet, while also giving even-handed treatment to Adler and Jung. Roudinesco (2014) commends Ellenberger for having been the first "to introduce *longue durée* into the Freudian adventure," as a consequence of which "Freud emerged stripped down and looking like a scientist torn between doubt and certainty" (p. 423).

2 On the dust jacket of Roudinesco's book, Mark Edmundson hails it for being "full of fresh facts about Freud's life," while Edmundson's own book, *The Death of Sigmund Freud* (2007), as Lacoursiere (2008) justly notes, fails to add "anything new to our factual knowledge of Freud's death" (p. 126n20).

3 I have documented the erroneousness of several of Roudinesco's assertions in the foregoing paragraphs in my own publications. On Freud's repeated destruction of his personal records and Sophocles' Theban plays not being a trilogy, see *Freud and Oedipus* (Rudnytsky, 1987, pp. 9, 275); on Stekel rather than Jung as the one who drew Freud's attention to *Gradiva*, see *Reading Psychoanalysis* (Rudnytsky, 2002a, p. 2;) and on the duration of Freud's cocaine use, see my entry on Freud (Rudnytsky, 2002b, p. 222) in *The Freud Encyclopedia*.

References

Adelman, Janet. 1992. *Suffocating Mothers: Fantasies of Maternal Origin in Shakespeare's Plays, "Hamlet" to "The Tempest."* New York: Routledge.
———. 1997. Iago's Alter Ego: Race as Projection in *Othello*. *Shakespeare Quarterly*, 48:125–44.
Andreas-Salomé, Lou. 1964. *The Freud Journal*. Trans. Stanley A. Leavy. New York: Basic Books, 1976.
Arlow, Jacob A. 1958. Freud, Friends, and Feuds. 2. Truth or Motivations? Toward a Definition of Psychoanalysis. *The Saturday Review*, June 14, pp. 14 & 54.
Aron, Lewis, and Adrienne Harris, eds. 1993. *The Legacy of Sándor Ferenczi*. Hillsdale, NJ: Analytic Press.
Auden, W. H. 1962. The Joker in the Pack. In *The Dyer's Hand and Other Essays*. New York: Random House, pp. 246–72.
Bair, Deirdre. 2003. *Jung: A Biography*. Boston: Little, Brown.
Balint, Michael. 1968. *The Basic Fault: Therapeutic Aspects of Regression*. New York: Brunner/Mazel, 1979.
Berman, Emanuel. 1981. Multiple Personality: Psychoanalytic Perspectives. *International Journal of Psycho-Analysis*, 62:283–300.
———. 2015. On "Polygamous Analysis." *American Journal of Psychoanalysis*, 75:29–36.
Berman, Jeffrey. 1987. *The Talking Cure: Literary Representations of Psychoanalysis*. New York: New York University Press.
———. 2007. Revisiting Philip Roth's Psychoanalysts. In *The Cambridge Companion to Philip Roth*. Ed. Timothy Parrish. Cambridge: Cambridge University Press, 2007, pp. 94–110.
Billinsky, John M. 1969. Jung and Freud (The End of a Romance). *Andover Newton Quarterly*, 10(2):39–43.
Blake, William. c. 1790. The Marriage of Heaven and Hell. In Noyes 1956, pp. 210–15.
Bloom, Claire. 1996. *Leaving a Doll's House: A Memoir*. Boston: Little, Brown.
Bloom, Harold. 1998. *Shakespeare: The Invention of the Human*. New York: Riverhead Books.

———. 2018. *Iago: The Strategies of Evil*. New York: Scribner.
Boehlich, Walter, ed. 1989. *The Letters of Sigmund Freud and Eduard Silberstein, 1871–1881*. Trans. Arnold J. Pomerans. Cambridge, MA: Harvard University Press, 1990.
Bollas, Christopher. 2007. *The Freudian Moment*. London: Karnac Books.
Bonomi, Carlo. 2015. *The Cut and the Building of Psychoanalysis, Volume 1: Sigmund Freud and Emma Eckstein*. New York: Routledge.
Boose, Lynda E. 1975. Othello's Handkerchief: "The Recognizance and Pledge of Love." *English Literary Renaissance*, 5:360–74.
Boyer, John W. 1978. Freud, Marriage, and Late Viennese Liberalism: A Commentary from 1905. *Journal of Modern History*, 50:72–102.
Brabant, Eva, Ernst Falzeder, and Patrizia Giampieri-Deutsch, eds. 1993. *The Correspondence of Sigmund Freud and Sándor Ferenczi: Vol. 1, 1908–1914*. Trans. Peter T. Hoffer. Cambridge, MA: Harvard University Press.
Bradley, A. C. 1904. *Shakespearean Tragedy: Lectures on "Hamlet," "Othello," "King Lear," and "Macbeth."* Harmondsworth, Eng.: Penguin Books, 1991.
Brandchaft, Bernard, Shelley Doctors, and Dorienne Sorter. 2010. *Toward an Emancipatory Psychoanalysis: Brandchaft's Intersubjective Vision*. New York: Routledge.
Breger, Louis. 2000. *Freud: Darkness in the Midst of Vision*. New York: Wiley.
Brennan, B. William. 2015a. Decoding Ferenczi's *Clinical Diary*: Biographical Notes on Identities Concealed and Revealed. *American Journal of Psychoanalysis*, 75:5–18.
———. 2015b. Out of the Archive/Unto the Couch: Clara Thompson's Analysis with Ferenczi. In *The Legacy of Sándor Ferenczi: From Ghost to Ancestor*. Ed. Adrienne Harris and Steven Kuchuck. London: Routledge, 2015, pp. 77–95.
Brenner, Ira. 2016. A Psychoactive Therapy of DID: A Multiphasic Model. In Howell and Itzkowitz, 2016, pp. 210–20.
Breuer, Josef, and Sigmund Freud. 1893–1895. Studies on Hysteria. In *The Standard Edition of the Complete Psychological Works of Sigmund Freud*. 24 vols. Ed. and Trans. James Strachey et al. London: Hogarth Press, 1953–1974. Vol. 2.
Bromberg, Philip. 1998. *Standing in the Spaces: Essays on Clinical Process, Trauma, and Dissociation*. New York: Psychology Press, 2001.
———. 2006. *Awakening the Dreamer: Clinical Journeys*. New York: Routledge, 2011.
———. 2011. *The Shadow of the Tsunami and the Growth of the Relational Mind*. New York: Routledge.
Brown, Norman O. 1959. *Life Against Death: The Psychoanalytical Meaning of History*. Middletown: Wesleyan University Press.
Bryson, Michael. 2004. *The Tyranny of Heaven: Milton's Rejection of God as King*. Newark: University of Delaware Press.
Burke, Kenneth. 1961. *The Rhetoric of Religion: Studies in Logology*. Berkeley: University of California Press, 1970.

Burston, Daniel. 1991. *The Legacy of Erich Fromm*. Cambridge, MA: Harvard University Press.
Cassullo, Gabriele. 2014. Splitting in the History of Psychoanalysis: From Janet and Freud to Fairbairn, Passing through Ferenczi and Suttie. In *Fairbairn and the Object Relations Tradition*. Ed. Graham S. Clarke and David E. Scharff. London: Karnac Books, 2014, pp. 49–58.
———. 2018. Ferenczi before Freud. In *Ferenczi's Influence on Contemporary Psychoanalytic Traditions: Lines of Development—Evolution of Theory and Practice over the Decades*. Ed. Aleksandar Dimitrijević, Gabriele Cassullo, and Jay Frankel. New York: Routledge, 2018, pp. 18–24.
———. 2019. On Not Taking Just One Part of It: Janet's Influence on Object Relations Theory. In *Rediscovering Pierre Janet: Trauma, Dissociation, and a New Context for Psychoanalysis*. Ed. Giuseppe Craparo, Francesca Ortu, and Onno van Hart. New York: Routledge, pp. 66–74.
Cinthio, Giovanni Battista Giraldi. 1566. Selections from *Gli Hecatommithi*. Trans. Geoffrey Bullough. In *Narrative and Dramatic Sources of Shakespeare: Vol. 7. Major Tragedies*. Ed. Geoffrey Bullough. New York: Columbia University Press, 1973, pp. 239–52.
Coleridge, Samuel Taylor. 1817. *Biographia Literaria, or Biographical Sketches of My Literary Life and Opinions*. Ed. George Watson. New York: Dutton, 1971.
———. 1822–1827. On *Othello*. In *Coleridge on Shakespeare: A Selection of the Essays, Notes, and Lectures of Samuel Taylor Coleridge on the Poems and Plays of Shakespeare*. Ed. Terence Hawkes. Harmondsworth, Eng.: Penguin Books, 1969, pp. 186–96.
Coltart, Nina. 1986. Slouching towards Bethlehem . . . or Thinking the Unthinkable in Psychoanalysis. In *Slouching towards Bethlehem . . . And Further Psychoanalytic Explorations*. London: Free Association Books, 2002, pp. 1–14.
Cooper, Arnold M. 1986. What Men Fear: The Façade of Castration Anxiety. In *The Quiet Revolution in American Psychoanalysis: Selected Papers*. Ed. Elizabeth L. Auchincloss. New York: Brunner-Routledge, 2005, pp. 150–62.
Cortina, Mauricio. 1996. Beyond Freud's Instinctivism and Fromm's Existential Humanism. In Cortina and Maccoby 1996, pp. 93–131.
———. 2015. The Greatness and Limitations of Erich Fromm's Humanism. *Contemporary Psychoanalysis*, 51:388–422.
Cortina, Mauricio, and Michael Maccoby, eds. 1996. *A Prophetic Analyst: Erich Fromm's Contributions to Psychoanalysis*. Northvale, NJ: Aronson.
Crews, Frederick. 2017. *Freud: The Making of an Illusion*. New York: Metropolitan Books.
Davies, Jody Messler. 1998. Repression and Dissociation—Freud and Janet: Fairbairn's New Model of Unconscious Process. In *Fairbairn Then and Now*. Ed. Neil J. Skolnick and David E. Scharff. Hillsdale, NJ: Analytic Press, 1998, pp. 53–69.

Davies, Jody Messler, and Mary Gail Frawley. 1994. *Treating the Adult Survivor of Childhood Sexual Abuse: A Psychoanalytic Perspective.* New York: Basic Books.

de Forest, Izette. 1942. The Therapeutic Technique of Sándor Ferenczi. *International Journal of Psycho-Analysis*, 33:120–39.

———. 1954. *The Leaven of Love: A Development of the Psychoanalytic Theory and Technique of Sándor Ferenczi.* New York: Da Capo Press, 1984.

Deutsch, Helene. 1937. Absence of Grief. *Psychoanalytic Quarterly*, 6:12–22.

Dickens, Charles. 1861. *Great Expectations.* Ed. Angus Calder. Harmondsworth, Eng.: Penguin Books, 1978.

Dupont, Judith, ed. 1985. *The Clinical Diary of Sándor Ferenczi.* Trans. Michael Balint and Nicola Zarday Jackson. Cambridge, MA: Harvard University Press, 1988.

Durkin, Kieran. 2014. *The Radical Humanism of Erich Fromm.* New York: Palgrave Macmillan.

Edmundson, Mark. 2007. *The Death of Sigmund Freud: The Legacy of His Last Days.* New York: Bloomsbury.

Eisold, Kenneth. 1997. Freud as Leader: The Early Years of the Vienna Society. In *The Organizational Life of Psychoanalysis: Conflicts, Dilemmas, and the Future of the Profession.* New York: Routledge, 2018, pp. 5–31.

Eissler, K. R. 1994. *Three Instances of Injustice.* Madison, CT: International Universities Press.

Ellenberger, Henri F. 1970. *The Discovery of the Unconscious: The History and Evolution of Dynamic Psychiatry.* New York: Basic Books.

Empson, William. 1961. *Milton's God.* Cambridge: Cambridge University Press, 1981.

Evans, J. Martin. 1968. *"Paradise Lost" and the Genesis Tradition.* Oxford: Clarendon Press.

Fairbairn, W. Ronald D. 1929. Dissociation and Repression. In *From Instinct to Self: Selected Papers of W. R. D. Fairbairn.* 2 vols. Ed. Ellinor Fairbairn Birtles and David E. Scharff. Northvale, NJ: Aronson, 1994. 2:13–79.

———. 1949. Steps in the Development of an Object-Relations Theory of the Personality. In Fairbairn 1952a, pp. 152–61.

———. 1952a. *Psychoanalytic Studies of the Personality.* London: Routledge and Kegan Paul, 1986.

———. 1952b. The Repression and Return of Bad Objects. In Fairbairn 1952a, pp. 59–81.

Falzeder, Ernst, and Eva Brabant, eds. 2000. *The Correspondence of Sigmund Freud and Sándor Ferenczi: Volume 3, 1920–1933.* Trans. Peter T. Hoffer. Cambridge, MA: Harvard University Press.

Fanon, Frantz. 1952. *Black Skin, White Masks.* Trans. Richard Philcox. New York: Grove Press, 2008.

Felman, Shoshana. 1980. On Reading Poetry: Reflections on the Limits and Possibilities of Psychoanalytic Approaches. In Muller and Richardson 1988, pp. 133–56.

Ferenczi, Sándor. 1912a. Exploring the Unconscious. In Ferenczi 1955, pp. 308–12.

———. 1912b. The Symbolic Representation of the Pleasure and Reality Principles in the Oedipus Myth. In *Sex in Psycho-Analysis*. Trans. Ernest Jones. New York: Dover, 1956, pp. 214–27.

———. 1913a. Belief, Disbelief, and Conviction. In *Further Contributions to the Theory and Technique of Psycho-Analysis*. Ed. J. Rickman. Trans. J. I. Suttie et al. New York: Brunner/Mazel, 1980, pp. 437–50.

———. 1913b. Kritik der Jungschen "Wandlungen und Symbole der Libido." In *Bausteine zur Psychoanalyse*. 4 vols. Bern: Verlag Hans Huber, 1964. 1:243–68.

———. 1917. My Friendship with Miksa Schächter. Trans. Borisz Szegal. *British Journal of Psychotherapy*, 9(1993):430–33.

———. 1924. *Thalassa: A Theory of Genitality*. Trans. Henry Alden Bunker. New York: Norton, 1968.

———. 1927. Review of *Technik der Psychoanalyse: I. Die Analytische Situation*, by Otto Rank. *International Journal of Psycho-Analysis*, 8:93–100.

———. 1929. The Unwelcome Child and His Death Instinct. In Ferenczi 1955, pp. 102–7.

———. 1930. The Principle of Relaxation and Neocatharsis. In Ferenczi 1955, pp. 108–25.

———. 1933. Confusion of Tongues between Adults and the Child: The Language of Tenderness and Passion. In Ferenczi 1955, pp. 156–67.

———. 1955. *Final Contributions to the Methods and Problems of Psycho-Analysis*. Ed. Michael Balint. Trans. Eric Mosbacher et al. New York: Brunner/Mazel, 1980.

Fish, Stanley E. 1967. *Surprised by Sin: The Reader in "Paradise Lost."* Berkeley: University of California Press, 1971.

Foehl, John C. 2014. A Phenomenology of Depth. *Psychoanalytic Dialogues*, 24:289–303.

Fortune, Christopher. 1993. The Case of "RN": Sándor Ferenczi's Radical Experiment in Psychoanalysis. In Aron and Harris 1993, pp. 101–20.

———. 1994. A Difficult Ending: Ferenczi, "R.N.," and the Experiment in Mutual Analysis. In *100 Years of Psychoanalysis: Contributions to the History of Psychoanalysis*. Ed. André Haynal and Ernst Falzeder. *Cahiers Psychiatriques Genevois*, special issue, 1994, pp. 217–23.

———. 1996. Mutual Analysis: A Logical Outcome of Sándor Ferenczi's Experiments in Psychoanalysis. In *Ferenczi's Turn in Psychoanalysis*. Ed. Peter L. Rudnytsky, Antal Bókay, and Patricia Giampieri-Deutsch. New York: New York University Press, 1996, pp. 170–87.

———, ed. 2002. *The Sándor Ferenczi—Georg Groddeck Correspondence, 1921–1933*. Trans. Jeannie Cohen, Elisabeth Petersdorff, and Norbert Ruebsatt. New York: Other Press.

Fox, Alice. 1979. Obstetrics and Gynecology in *Macbeth*. *Shakespeare Studies*, 12:127–41.

Freud, Sigmund. 1896. The Aetiology of Hysteria. In *The Standard Edition of the Complete Psychological Works* [= *S.E.*]. 24 vols. Ed. and trans. James Strachey et al., London: Hogarth Press, 1953–1974. 3;191–221.

———. 1900. *The Interpretation of Dreams. S.E.*, vols. 4 and 5.

———. 1901. *The Psychopathology of Everyday Life. S.E.*, vol. 6.

———. c. 1905. Psychopathic Characters on the Stage. S.E., 7:305–10

———. 1908. "Civilized" Sexual Morality and Modern Nervous Illness. S.E., 9:181–204.

———. 1910. "Wild" Psycho-Analysis. S.E., 11:221–27.

———. 1914a. *On the History of the Psycho-Analytic Movement. S.E.*, 14:7–66.

———. 1914b. On Narcissism: An Introduction. S.E., 14:67–102.

———. 1929. Some Dreams of Descartes': A Letter to Maxime Leroy. S.E., 21:203–4.

———. 1937. Analysis Terminable and Interminable. S.E., 23:216–53.

Friedman, Lawrence J., with Anke M. Schreiber. 2013. *The Lives of Erich Fromm: Love's Prophet*. New York: Columbia University Press.

Fromm, Erich. 1934. The Theory of Mother Right and Its Relevance for Social Psychology. In Fromm 1970b, pp. 110–35.

———. 1935. The Social Determinants of Psychoanalytic Therapy. Trans. Ernst Falzeder, with Caroline Schwarzacher. *International Forum of Psychoanalysis*, 9(2000):149–65.

———. 1941. *Escape from Freedom*. New York: Avon Books, 1969.

———. 1947. *Man for Himself: An Enquiry into the Psychology of Ethics*. London: Routledge and Kegan Paul, 1960.

———. 1955a. The Human Implications of Instinctivistic "Radicalism": A Reply to Herbert Marcuse. *Dissent*, 2:342–49.

———. 1955b. *The Sane Society*. New York: Holt, Rinehart and Winston, 1990.

———. 1956a. *The Art of Loving*. New York: Harper and Brothers.

———. 1956b. A Counter-Rebuttal to Herbert Marcuse. *Dissent*, 3:81–83.

———. 1958a. Freud, Friends, and Feuds. 1. Scientism or Fanaticism? *The Saturday Review*, June 14, pp. 11–13 & 55.

———. 1958b. Psychoanalysis—Science or Party Line? In *The Dogma of Christ and Other Essays on Religion, Psychology and Culture*. New York: Holt, Rinehart and Winston, 1963, pp. 131–44.

———. 1959a. On Being *Centrally* Related to the Patient. In Funk 2009, pp. 7–37.

———. 1959b. *Sigmund Freud's Mission*. New York: Grove Press, 1963.

———. 1961. Afterword to 1984, by George Orwell. New York: Signet Classic, 1964, pp. 257–67.

———. 1962. *Beyond the Chains of Illusion: My Encounter with Marx and Freud*. New York: Simon and Schuster.

———. 1964a. *The Heart of Man: Its Genius for Good and Evil*. New York: Harper and Row.

———. 1964b. Humanism and Psychoanalysis. *Contemporary Psychoanalysis*, 1:69–79.

———. 1968a. Marx's Contribution to the Knowledge of Man. In Fromm 1970b, pp. 62–75.

———. 1968b. The Oedipus Complex: Comments on the Case of Little Hans. In Fromm 1970b, pp. 90–100.

———. 1970a. The Crisis of Psychoanalysis. In Fromm 1970b, pp. 12–41.

———1970b. *The Crisis of Psychoanalysis: Essays on Freud, Marx, and Social Psychology*. Greenwich, CT: Fawcett Premier, 1971.

———. 1973. *The Anatomy of Human Destructiveness*. New York: Picador, 1992.

———. 1980. *Greatness and Limitations of Freud's Thought*. London: Jonathan Cape.

———. 1992a. The Alleged Radicalism of Herbert Marcuse. In Fromm 1992c, pp. 111–29.

———. 1992b. The Dialectic Revision of Psychoanalysis. In Fromm 1992c, pp. 11–80.

———. 1992c. *The Revision of Psychoanalysis*. Ed. Rainer Funk. Boulder, CO: Westview Press.

Funk, Rainer. 1998. Erich Fromm's Concept of Social Character. *Social Thought and Research*, 21:215–29.

———. 1999a. *Erich Fromm: His Life and Ideas: An Illustrated Biography*. Trans. Ian Portman and Manuela Kunkel. New York: Continuum, 2000.

———. 1999b. Erich Fromm's Role in the Foundation of the IFPS: Evidences from the Erich Fromm Archives in Tuebingen. Electronic Version, 13 pp.

———, ed. 2009. *The Clinical Erich Fromm: Personal Accounts and Papers on Therapeutic Technique*. Amsterdam: Rodopi.

Gabbard, Glen O. 1997. Letter: Glen O. Gabbard Replies [to Emanuel Berman]. *Journal of the American Psychoanalytic Association*, 45:571–72.

Garber, Marjorie. 2004. *Shakespeare After All*. New York: Pantheon.

Gay, Peter. 1988. *Freud: A Life for Our Time*. New York: Norton.

Giefer, Michael, ed. 2008. *Briefwechsel Sigmund Freud—Georg Groddeck*. In collaboration with Beate Schuh. Frankfurt: Stroemfeld.

Goethe, Johann Wolfgang von. 1795. *Wilhelm Meister's Apprenticeship*. Trans. Thomas Carlyle. New York: Collier Books, 1962.

Goodhart, Sandor. 1978. Ληστὰς Ἔφασκε: Oedipus and Laius' Many Murderers. *Diacritics*, 8(Spring):55–71.

Graf, Max. 1942. Reminiscences of Professor Sigmund Freud. *Psychoanalytic Quarterly*, 11:465–76.

Green, Maurice R., ed. 1964. *Interpersonal Psychoanalysis: The Selected Papers of Clara M. Thompson*. New York: Basic Books.

Grene, David, ed. and trans. 1954. *Oedipus the King*. In *Sophocles I*. Chicago: University of Chicago Press, 1970.

Groddeck, Georg. 1902. Ein Frauenproblem. In *Ein Frauenproblem/Hin zu Gottnatur*. Ed. Otto Jägersberg. Frankfurt: Stroemfeld, 2018.

———. 1909. Hin zu Gottnatur. In *Ein Frauenproblem/Hin zu Gottnatur*. Ed. Otto Jägersberg. Frankfurt: Stroemfeld, 2018.

———. 1913. *Nasamecu: Der gesunde und kranke Mensch gemeinverständlich dargestellt*. Ed. Michael Giefer. Frankfurt: Stroemfeld, 2014.

———. 1923. *The Book of the It*. [Trans. V. M. E. Collins.] Mansfield Center, CT: Martino Publishing, 2015.

———. 1925. Birthdays. In Groddeck 1949, pp. 13–19.

———. 1926a. Bowel Function. In Groddeck 1949, pp. 81–110.

———. 1926b. The It in Science, Art and Industry. In *The Unknown Self*. Trans. V. M. E. Collins. London: Vision Press, 1989, pp. 147–64.

———. 1926c. Speech. In Groddeck 1949, pp. 118–25.

———. 1927. Goethe's *Faust*. In Groddeck 1949, pp. 179–207.

———. 1933. The Body's Middleman. In Groddeck 1949, pp. 53–81.

———. 1949. *Exploring the Unconscious*. Trans. V. M. E. Collins. London: Vision Press, 1989.

———. 1951. *The World of Man*. Trans. V. M. E. Collins. London: Vision Press, 1967.

Grossman, Carl M., and Sylva Grossman. 1965. *The Wild Analyst: The Life and Work of Georg Groddeck*. New York: Braziller.

Grünbaum, Adolf. 1984. *The Foundations of Psychoanalysis: A Philosophical Critique*. Berkeley: University of California Press.

Grunes, Dorothy T., and Jerome M. Grunes. 2014. *What Psychoanalysis Teaches Us about Shakespeare: A Local Habitation and a Name*. London: Karnac Books.

Guasto, Gianni. 2014. Trauma and the Loss of Basic Trust. *International Forum of Psychoanalysis*, 23:44–49.

Guex, Germaine. 1950. *The Abandonment Neurosis*. Trans. Peter D. Douglas. London: Karnac Books, 2015.

Guntrip, Harry. 1971. The Promise of Psychoanalysis. In *In the Name of Life: Essays in Honor of Erich Fromm*. Ed. Bernard Landis and Edward S. Tauber. New York: Holt, Rinehart and Winston, 1992, pp. 44–55.

H.D. [Hilda Doolittle]. 1956. *Tribute to Freud*. New York: New Directions, 1974.

Hainer, Margaret L. 2016. The Ferenczi Paradox: His Importance in Understanding Dissociation and the Dissociation of His Importance in Psychoanalysis. In Howell and Itzkowitz 2016, pp. 57–69.

Harris, Adrienne. 2014. Encountering Erich Fromm. Review of *The Lives of Erich Fromm: Love's Prophet*, by Lawrence J. Friedman. *Journal of the American Psychoanalytic Association*, 62:503–19.

Harris, Adrienne, and Lewis Aron. 2017. The Work of Elizabeth Severn: An Appreciation. In Severn 1933, pp. xii–xviii.

Haynal, André E., and Ernst Falzeder. 1991. "Healing through Love"? A Unique Dialogue in the History of Psychoanalysis. In *Psychoanalytic Filiations: Mapping the Psychoanalytic Movement*, by Ernst Falzeder. London: Karnac Books, 2015, pp. 3–18.

Heidegger, Martin. 1927. *Being and Time*. Trans. John Macquarrie and Edward Robinson. Oxford: Blackwell, 2001.

Herman, Peter C. 2005. *Destabilizing Milton: "Paradise Lost" and the Poetics of Incertitude*. New York: Palgrave Macmillan.

Herman, Peter C., and Elizabeth Sauer, eds. 2012. *The New Milton Criticism.* Cambridge: Cambridge University Press.

Hirsch, Irwin. 2000. Interview with Benjamin Wolstein. *Contemporary Psychoanalysis*, 36:187–232.

Hoffer, Peter T. 2010. From Elasticity to the Confusion of Tongues: A Historical Commentary on the Technical Dimension of the Freud/Ferenczi Controversy. *Psychoanalytic Perspectives*, 7:90–103.

Horney, Karen. 1924. On the Genesis of the Castration Complex in Women. In *Feminine Psychology.* Ed. Harold Kelman. New York: Norton, 1973, pp. 37–53.

———. 1942. *Self-Analysis.* New York: Norton, 1970.

Hornstein, Gail A. 2000. *To Redeem One Person Is to Redeem the World: The Life of Frieda Fromm-Reichmann.* New York: Free Press.

Howell, Elizabeth F. 2005. *The Dissociative Mind.* New York: Routledge.

Howell, Elizabeth F., and Sheldon Itzkowitz, eds. 2016. *The Dissociative Mind in Psychoanalysis: Understanding and Working with Trauma.* New York: Routledge.

Hughes, Merritt Y., ed. 1957. *John Milton: Complete Poems and Major Prose.* Indianapolis: Bobbs-Merrill.

Hunter, W. B. 1971. The War in Heaven: The Exaltation of the Son. In *Bright Essence: Studies in Milton's Theology.* Ed. W. B. Hunter, C. A. Patrides, and J. H. Adamson. Salt Lake City: University of Utah Press, 1973, pp. 115–30.

Hyman, Stanley Edgar. 1970. *Iago: Some Approaches to the Illusion of His Motivation.* New York: Atheneum.

Irigaray, Luce. 1974. *Speculum of the Other Woman.* Trans. Gillian C. Gill. Ithaca: Cornell University Press, 1985.

Jones, Ernest. 1913. The God Complex: The Belief that One Is God, and the Resulting Character Traits. In *Essays on Applied Psychoanalysis.* 2 vols. London: Hogarth Press, 1964. 2:244–65.

———. 1953. *The Life and Work of Sigmund Freud: Vol. 1. The Formative Years and the Great Discoveries, 1856–1900.* New York: Basic Books.

———. 1955. *The Life and Work of Sigmund Freud: Vol. 2. Years of Maturity, 1901–1919.* New York: Basic Books.

———. 1957. *The Life and Work of Sigmund Freud: Vol. 3, The Last Phase, 1919–1939.* New York: Basic Books.

Jung, C. G. 1963. *Memories, Dreams, Reflections.* Rev. ed. Ed. Aniela Jaffé. Trans. Richard and Clara Winston. New York: Vintage Books, 1989.

Kakutani, Michiko. 2018. *The Death of Truth: Notes on Falsehood in the Age of Trump.* New York: Tim Duggan Books.

Karpf, Fay B. 1953. *The Psychology and Psychotherapy of Otto Rank: An Historical and Comparative Introduction.* New York: Philosophical Library.

Kaufmann, Walter, ed and trans. 1954. *The Portable Nietzsche.* New York: Viking Press, 1967.

Khoury, Gérard D. 2009. A Crucial Encounter. In Funk 2009, pp. 161–68.

Kirsch, Arthur. 1978. The Polarization of Erotic Love in *Othello. Modern Language Review*, 73:721–40.

Klein, Melanie. 1930. The Importance of Symbol-Formation in the Development of the Ego. In *The Writings of Melanie Klein*. Ed. Roger Money-Kyrle, Betty Joseph, Edna O'Shaughnessy, and Hanna Segal. 4 vols. New York: Free Press, 1984. 1:219–32.

Kleinschmidt, Hans J. 1967. The Angry Act: The Role of Aggression in Creativity. *American Imago*, 24:98–128.

Knights, L. C. 1933. How Many Children Had Lady Macbeth? In *Explorations: Essays in Criticism Mainly on the Literature of the Seventeenth Century*. Westport, CT: Greenwood Press, 1975, pp. 15–54.

Kohut, Heinz. 1972. Thoughts on Narcissism and Narcissistic Rage. *Psychoanalytic Study of the Child*, 27:360–400.

———. 1982. Introspection, Empathy, and the Semi-Circle of Mental Health. *International Journal of Psycho-Analysis*, 63:395–407.

Krugman, Paul. 2018. The G.O.P.'s Climate of Paranoia. *The New York Times*, August 21, p. A22. www.nytimes.com/2018/08/20/opinion/trump-republican-truth-climate-change.html?emc=edit_th_180821&nl=todaysheadlines&nlid=296777500821

Lacan, Jacques. 1949. The Mirror Stage as Formative of the Function of the I. In *Écrits: A Selection*. Trans. Alan Sheridan. New York: Norton, 1997, pp. 1–7.

———. 1956. Seminar on "The Purloined Letter." Trans. Jeffrey Mehlman. In Muller and Richardson 1988, pp. 28–54.

Lachmann, Frank M. 1996. How Many Selves Make a Person? *Contemporary Psychoanalysis*, 32:595–614.

Lacoursiere, Roy B. 2008. Freud's Death: Historical Truth and Biographical Fictions. *American Imago*, 65:107–28.

Landis, Bernard. 2009. When You Hear the Word, the Reality Is Lost. In Funk 2009, pp. 137–40.

Laplanche, Jean. 1970. *Life and Death in Psychoanalysis*. Trans. Jeffrey Mehlman. Baltimore: Johns Hopkins University Press, 1976.

Lewis, C. S. 1942. *A Preface to "Paradise Lost."* London: Oxford University Press, 1971.

Ludwig, Emil. 1947. *Dr. Freud: An Analysis and a Warning*. New York: Hellman, Williams.

Maccoby, Michael. 1996. The Two Voices of Erich Fromm: The Prophetic and the Analytic. In Cortina and Maccoby 1996, pp. 61–92.

Mahler, Margaret. 1974. On the First Three Subphases of the Separation-Individuation Process. *Psychoanalysis and Contemporary Science*, 3:295–306.

Marcel, Mary. 2005. *Freud's Traumatic Memory: Reclaiming Seduction Theory and Revisiting Oedipus*. Pittsburgh: Duquesne University Press.

Marcuse, Herbert. 1955. *Eros and Civilization: A Philosophical Inquiry into Freud*. New York: Vintage Books, 1961.

Martynkewicz, Wolfgang. 1997. *Georg Groddeck: Eine Biographie*. Frankfurt: Fischer.

Masson, Jeffrey M. 1984. *The Assault on Truth: Freud's Suppression of the Seduction Theory.* New York: Farrar, Straus & Giroux.

———, ed. and trans. 1985. *The Complete Letters of Sigmund Freud to Wilhelm Fliess, 1887–1904.* Cambridge, MA: Harvard University Press.

May, Rollo. 1950. *The Age of Anxiety.* New York: Ronald Press.

McGuire, William, ed. 1974. *The Freud/Jung Letters: The Correspondence between Sigmund Freud and C. G. Jung.* Trans. Ralph Manheim and R. F. C. Hull. Princeton: Princeton University Press.

———, ed. 1989. *Analytical Psychology: Notes of the Seminar Given in 1925*, by C. G. Jung. Princeton: Princeton University Press.

McLaughlin, Neil. 1998a. How to Become a Forgotten Intellectual: Intellectual Movements and the Rise and Fall of Erich Fromm. *Sociological Forum,* 13:215–46.

———. 1998b. Why Do Schools of Thought Fail? Neo-Freudianism as a Case Study in the Sociology of Knowledge. *Journal of the History of the Behavioral Sciences,* 34:113–34.

Medawar, P. B. 1969. *Induction and Intuition in Scientific Thought.* London: Methuen.

Meyer-Palmedo, Ingeborg, ed. 2014. *Correspondence 1904–1938: Sigmund Freud and Anna Freud.* Trans. Nick Somers. Malden, MA: Polity Press.

Miller, Alice. 1979. *The Drama of the Gifted Child: The Search for the True Self.* Trans. Ruth Ward. New York: Basic Books, 1981.

Morgann, Maurice. 1777. Essay on the Dramatic Character of Sir John Falstaff. In *Eighteenth Century Essays on Shakespeare.* Ed. D. Nichol Smith. Glasgow: MacLehose, 1904, pp. 278–364.

Muller, John P., and William J. Richardson, eds. 1988. *The Purloined Poe: Lacan, Derrida, and Psychoanalytic Reading.* Baltimore: Johns Hopkins University Press.

Nietzsche, Friedrich. 1888. Ecce Homo. In *On the Genealogy of Morals* and *Ecce Homo.* Trans. Walter Kaufmann. New York: Vintage Books, 1969.

Noyes, Russel B., ed. 1956. *English Romantic Poetry and Prose.* New York: Oxford University Press.

Orange, Donna M. 2011. *The Suffering Stranger: Hermeneutics for Everyday Clinical Practice.* New York: Routledge.

———. 2018. Multiplicity and Integrity: Does an Anti-Developmental Tilt Still Exist in Relational Psychoanalysis? In *Decentering Relational Theory: A Comparative Critique.* Ed. Lewis Aron, Sue Grand, and Joyce Slochower. New York: Routledge, pp. 148–72.

Orwell, George. 1943. Looking Back on the Spanish War. In Orwell 1954, pp. 193–215.

———. 1944. Raffles and Miss Blandish. In Orwell 1954, pp. 139–54.

———. 1947. Why I Write. In Orwell 1954, pp. 313–20.

———. 1952. "'Such, Such Were the Joys . . .'" In Orwell 1954, pp. 9–55.

———. 1954. *A Collection of Essays*. Garden City, NY: Doubleday Anchor.
Paris, Bernard J. 2010. *Heaven and Its Discontents: Milton's Characters in "Paradise Lost."* New Brunswick, NJ: Transaction.
Parsons, Michael. 2014. *Living Psychoanalysis: From Theory to Experience*. London: Routledge.
Partridge, Simon. 2007. Trauma at the Threshold: An Eight-Year-Old Goes to Boarding School. *Attachment: New Directions in Psychotherapy and Relational Psychoanalysis*, 1:310–12.
———. 2011. British Upper-Class Complex Trauma Syndrome: The Case of Charles Rycroft, Psychoanalyst and Psychotherapist. *Attachment: New Directions in Psychotherapy and Relational Psychoanalysis*, 5:154–63.
Paskauskas, R. Andrew, ed. 1993. *The Complete Correspondence of Sigmund Freud and Ernest Jones, 1908–1939*. Cambridge, MA: Harvard University Press.
Peláez, Miguel Gutiérrez. 2009. Trauma Theory in Sándor Ferenczi's Writings of 1931 and 1932. *International Journal of Psychoanalysis*, 90:1217–33.
Peter, John. 1960. *A Critique of "Paradise Lost."* New York: Columbia University Press, 1961.
Polmear, Caroline. 2012. The Basic Fault and the Borderline Psychotic Transference. In Williams, Keene, and Derman, pp. 361–86.
Poster, Mark F., Galina Hristeva, and Michael Giefer. 2016. Georg Groddeck: The "Pinch of Pepper" of Psychoanalysis. *American Journal of Psychoanalysis*, 76:161–82.
Prince, Morton. 1906. *The Dissociation of a Personality: A Biographical Study in Abnormal Psychology*. 2nd ed. New York: Longmans, Green, 1913.
Puner, Helen Walker. 1947. *Freud: His Life and His Mind*. New York: Howell, Soskin.
Pyles, Robert L. 2018. Authoritarianism—Part II. Posting on Members List. *American Psychoanalytic Association*, February 10.
Rabaté, Jean-Michel. 2014. *The Cambridge Introduction to Literature and Psychoanalysis*. New York: Cambridge University Press.
Rachman, Arnold W. 2018. *Elizabeth Severn: The "Evil Genius" of Psychoanalysis*. New York: Routledge.
Richards, I. A. 1934. *Coleridge on Imagination*. New York: Routledge, 2001.
Ricoeur, Paul. 1965. *Freud and Philosophy: An Essay on Interpretation*. Trans. Denis Savage. New Haven: Yale University Press, 1970.
Roazen, Paul. 1975. *Freud and His Followers*. New York: New American Library, 1976.
———. 2001. The Exclusion of Erich Fromm from the IPA. *Contemporary Psychoanalysis*, 37:5–42.
Rosenberg, Samuel. 1978. *Why Freud Fainted*. Indianapolis: Bobbs-Merrill.
Ross, Lawrence J. 1960. The Meaning of Strawberries in Shakespeare. *Studies in the Renaissance*, 7:225–40.
Roth, Philip. 1969. *Portnoy's Complaint*. New York: Vintage Books, 1994.

———. 1975. *My Life as a Man*. New York: Vintage Books, 1993.
Roudinesco, Élisabeth. 2014. *Freud in His Time and Ours*. Trans. Catherine Porter. Cambridge, MA: Harvard University Press, 2016.
Rudnytsky, Peter L. 1985. The Purloined Handkerchief in *Othello*. In *The Psychoanalytic Study of Literature*. Ed. Joseph Reppen and Maurice Charney. Hillsdale, NJ: Analytic Press, 1985, pp. 169–90.
———. 1987. *Freud and Oedipus*. New York: Columbia University Press.
———. 1988. "Here Only Weak": Sexuality and the Structure of Trauma in *Paradise Lost*. In *The Persistence of Myth: Psychoanalytic and Structuralist Perspectives*. Ed. Peter L. Rudnytsky. New York: Guilford, 1988, pp. 153–76.
———. 1991. *The Psychoanalytic Vocation: Rank, Winnicott, and the Legacy of Freud*. New Haven: Yale University Press.
———. 2002a. *Reading Psychoanalysis: Freud, Rank, Ferenczi, Groddeck*. Ithaca: Cornell University Press.
———. 2002b. Freud, Sigmund (1856–1939). In *The Freud Encyclopedia: Theory, Therapy, and Culture*. Ed. Edward Erwin. New York: Routledge, 2002, pp. 219–29.
———. 2011. *Rescuing Psychoanalysis from Freud and Other Essays in Re-Vision*. London: Karnac Books.
Rumrich, John P. 1987. *Matter of Glory: A New Preface to "Paradise Lost."* Pittsburgh: University of Pittsburgh Press.
Sachs, Hanns. 1944. *Freud: Master and Friend*. Cambridge, MA: Harvard University Press, 1945.
Sander, Lewis W. 1995. Identity and the Experience of Specificity in a Process of Recognition: Commentary on Seligman and Shanok. *Psychoanalytic Dialogues*, 5:579–93.
Schacht, Lore, ed. 1977. *The Meaning of Illness: Selected Psychoanalytic Writings*, by Georg Groddeck. Trans. Gertrud Mander. London: Maresfield Library, 1988.
Schore, Allan. 2011. Foreword to Bromberg 2011, pp. ix–xxxvii.
Schröter, Michael, ed. 2004. *Sigmund Freud Max Eitingon: Briefwechsel 1906–1939*. 2 vols. Tübingen: edition diskord.
———. 2015. Neue Details über die psychoanalytische Ausbildung von Erich Fromm (und Frieda Fromm-Reichmann). *Fromm Forum* (Deutsche Ausgabe), 19:112–15.
Severn, Elizabeth. 1913. *Psycho-therapy: Its Doctrine and Practice*. 2nd ed. London: Rider and Son, 1914. University of California Library Reprint.
———. 1917. *The Psychology of Behavior: A Practical Study of Human Personality and Conduct with Special Reference to Methods of Development*. New York: Dodd, Mead. Kessenger Legacy Reprints.
———. 1933. *The Discovery of the Self: A Study in Psychological Cure*. Ed. Peter L. Rudnytsky. New York: Routledge, 2017.
———. 1952. Interview with Kurt R. Eissler. Sigmund Freud Archives, Manuscripts Division, Library of Congress, December 20. Washington, DC, 24 pp.

Shakespeare, William. 1601. *Hamlet*. Ed. Harold Jenkins. Arden Shakespeare—Second Series. Walton-on-Thames, Eng: Thomas Nelson, 1997.

———. 1604. *Othello*. Ed. E. A. J. Honigmann. Arden Shakespeare—Third Series. New York: Bloomsbury, 2016.

———. 1605. *King Lear*. Ed. R. A. Foakes. Arden Shakespeare—Third Series. Walton-on-Thames, Eng.: Thomas Nelson, 1997.

———. 1606. *Macbeth*. Ed. Sandra Clark and Pamela Mason. Arden Shakespeare—Third Series. New York: Bloomsbury, 2016.

———. 1611. *The Winter's Tale*. Ed. John Pitcher. Arden Shakespeare—Third Series. London: Methuen, 2010.

Shapiro, Sue A. 1993. Clara Thompson: Ferenczi's Messenger with Half a Message. In Aron and Harris 1993, pp. 159–73.

———. 2000. The Unique Benjamin Wolstein as Experienced and Read. *Contemporary Psychoanalysis*, 36:301–41.

Shaw, Daniel. 2014. *Traumatic Narcissism: Relational Systems of Subjugation*. New York: Routledge.

Shelley, Percy Bysshe. 1821. *A Defence of Poetry*. In Noyes 1956, pp. 1097–112.

Smith, Nancy A. 1998. "Orpha Reviving": Toward an Honorable Recognition of Elizabeth Severn. *International Forum of Psychoanalysis*, 7:241–46.

———. 1999. From Oedipus to Orpha: Revisiting Ferenczi and Severn's Landmark Case. *American Journal of Psychoanalysis*, 59:345–66.

Soreanu, Raluca. 2019. Michael Balint's Word Trail: The "Ocnophil," the "Philobat," and Creative Dyads. *Psychoanalysis and History*, 21:53–72.

Spivack, Bernard. 1958. *Shakespeare and the Allegory of Evil: The History of a Metaphor in Relation to His Major Villains*. New York: Columbia University Press.

Stanton, Martin. 1991. *Sándor Ferenczi: Reconsidering Active Intervention*. Northvale, NJ: Aronson.

Stern, Donnel B. 1997. *Unformulated Experience: From Dissociation to Imagination in Psychoanalysis*. Hillsdale, NJ: Analytic Press.

———. 2010. *Partners in Thought: Working with Unformulated Experience, Dissociation, and Enactment*. New York: Routledge.

———. 2015. *Relational Freedom: Emergent Properties of the Interpersonal Field*. New York: Routledge.

Stern, Jeffrey. 2016. "Loving Not Wisely But Too Well": Envy, Jealousy, and Narcissistic Rage in *Othello*. Unpublished manuscript.

Stevens, Wallace. 1942. Notes Toward a Supreme Fiction. In *Collected Poems*. London: Faber and Faber, 1971, pp. 380–408.

Strindberg, August. 1887. *The Father*. In *Seven Plays*. Trans. Arvid Paulson. New York: Bantam Books, 1972, pp. 6–56.

Sullivan, Harry Stack. 1950. The Illusion of Personal Individuality. In *The Fusion of Psychiatry and Social Science*. Ed. Helen Swick Perry. New York: Norton, 1971, pp. 198–226.

———. 1953. *The Interpersonal Theory of Psychiatry*. New York: Norton.

Swales, Peter J. 1982. Freud, Minna Bernays, and the Conquest of Rome: New Light on the Origins of Psychoanalysis. *New American Review*, 1(Spring/Summer):1–23.
Taft, Jessie. 1958. *Otto Rank: A Biographical Study*. New York: Julian Press.
Tauber, Edward S. 2009. Words Are Ways. In Funk 2009, pp. 131–34.
Thompson, Clara M. 1933. Ferenczi's Relaxation Method. In Green 1964, pp. 67–71.
———. 1943. "The Therapeutic Technique of Sándor Ferenczi": A Comment. *International Journal of Psycho-Analysis*, 24:64–66.
———. 1944. Ferenczi's Contributions to Psychoanalysis. In Green 1964, pp. 72–82.
———. 1952. Interview with Kurt R. Eissler. Sigmund Freud Archives, Manuscripts Division, Library of Congress, June 4. Washington, DC, 24 pp.
Tillyard, E. M. W. 1930. *Milton*. London: Chatto and Windus, 1951.
Trilling, Lionel. 1940. Freud and Literature. In Trilling 1950, pp. 32–54.
———. 1946. The Function of the Little Magazine. In Trilling 1950, pp. 89–99.
———. 1950. *The Liberal Imagination: Essays on Literature and Society*. Garden City, NY: Anchor Books, 1953.
Van der Hart, Onno. 2016. Pierre Janet, Sigmund Freud, and Dissociation of the Personality: The First Codification of a Psychodynamic Depth Psychology. In Howell and Itzkowitz 2016, pp. 44–56.
Van der Hart, Onno, Ellert R. S. Nijenhuis, and Kathy Steele. 2006. *The Haunted Self: Structural Dissociation and the Treatment of Chronic Traumatization*. New York: Norton.
Van der Kolk, Bessel. 2014. *The Body Keeps the Score: Brain, Mind, and Body in the Healing of Trauma*. New York: Penguin Books, 2015.
Waldock, A. J. A. 1947. *"Paradise Lost" and Its Critics*. Cambridge: Cambridge University Press, 1966.
Webster, Richard. 1995. *Why Freud was Wrong: Sin, Science, and Psychoanalysis*. New York: Basic Books.
Wheeler, Richard P. 1981. *Shakespeare's Development and the Problem Comedies: Turn and Counter-Turn*. Berkeley: University of California Press.
Wilde, Oscar. 1891. *The Picture of Dorian Gray*. Ed. Peter Ackroyd. Harmondsworth, Eng.: Penguin Books, 1985.
Willbern, David. 1997. *Poetic Will: Shakespeare and the Play of Language*. Philadelphia: University of Pennsylvania Press.
Williams, Paul, John Keene, and Sira Derman. eds. 2012. *Independent Psychoanalysis Today*. London: Karnac Books.
Wilson, Edward O. 1975. *Sociobiology: The New Synthesis*. Cambridge, MA: Harvard University Press.
———. 1978. *On Human Nature*. Cambridge, MA: Harvard University Press.
———. 1984. *Biophilia*. Cambridge, MA: Harvard University Press.
———. 1998. *Consilience: The Unity of Knowledge*. New York: Knopf.
Winnicott, D. W. 1949. Hate in the Counter-Transference. In Winnicott 1958, pp. 194–203.

———. 1953. Transitional Objects and Transitional Phenomena. In Winnicott 1971, pp. 1–25.

———. 1955. Withdrawal and Regression. In Winnicott 1958, pp. 255–61.

———. 1958. *Through Paediatrics to Psycho-Analysis: Collected Papers.* New York: Basic Books, 1975.

———. 1960. The Theory of the Parent-Infant Relationship. In Winnicott 1965, pp. 37–55.

———. 1965. *The Maturational Processes and the Facilitating Environment: Studies in the Theory of Emotional Development.* New York: International Universities Press, 1966.

———. 1967. The Location of Cultural Experience. In Winnicott 1971, pp. 95–103.

———. 1971. *Playing and Reality.* New York: Tavistock Publications, 1984.

Wolff, Larry. 1988. *Child Abuse in Freud's Vienna: Postcards from the End of the World.* New York: New York University Press, 1995.

Wolstein, Benjamin. 1992. Resistance Interlocked with Countertransference—R. N. and Ferenczi, and American Interpersonal Relations. *Contemporary Psychoanalysis,* 28:172–89.

Wulff, Mosche. 1946. Fetishism and Object Choice in Early Childhood. *Psychoanalytic Quarterly,* 15:450–71.

Index

abandonment 96, 161, 174, 177, 182–84, 186*n*11; and Oedipus 8, 16
Abraham, Karl 60
Addison, Joseph 40–41
Adelman, Janet 168, 174, 177, 196, 198
Adler, Alfred 69*n*7, 153–54, 213*n*1
Adorno, Theodor 76, 106, 112
adultery 174, 180, 212
Afterword to *1984* (Fromm) 98
aggression 10, 100, 102, 197
Ainsworth, Mary 13
American Institute for Psychoanalysis 82, 114
American Psychoanalytic Association 82, 114
Anatomy of Human Destructiveness, The (Fromm) 2, 11, 99–100, 103*n*5, 111, 194–203
Andreas-Salomé, Lou 67*n*7, 205
Anna O. 139, 141
"applied" psychoanalysis 4, 167, 184
Arlow, Jacob A. 103*n*1, 104, 120
Aron, Lewis 137
Art of Loving, The (Fromm) 91, 103*n*4
Asch, Joseph 123
attachment 13–14, 62, 95–96, 113, 161; Freud's insecure 69*n*8, 87
Auden, W. H. 189, 195, 204*n*3
Augustine, St. 48, 56, 188
authoritarian character 102, 104–5, 110–14; Freud as 77–79, 85–86, 90, 92, 96, 103*n*6, 105, 113; God as 54, 59; as sadomasochistic structure 85, 93, 107–8, 113; *see also Escape from Freedom*
authoritarian ethics 97, 193
authoritarianism 3–4, 81; and humanism 98; and narcissism 54

Bachofen, Johann Jakob 87
Bair, Deirdre 209, 211
Balint, Michael 4, 92, 96, 100–1, 113, 123; and borderline pathologies 168–70, 181, 185*n*3, 186*n*11; *see also* ocnophilia; philobatism
Beebe, Beatrice 12
Benjamin, Walter 88
Berman, Emanuel 144, 150*n*3
Berman, Jeffrey 186*n*12
Bernays, Eli 206
Bernays, Martha *see* Freud, Martha
Bernays, Minna 30–31, 59–60, 146, 209–11, 213
Beyond the Chains of Illusion (Fromm) 87–88
Billinsky, John M. 210–11
biophilia 99, 198–99; *see also* necrophilia
Bismarck, Otto von 207
Blake, William 39–40, 43, 68*n*2
Bloom, Claire 184
Bloom, Harold 185*n*8, 187–88, 195, 197, 202, 204*n*2
Boehlich, Walter 208
Bollas, Christopher 6, 155
Bone, Harry 71
Bonomi, Carlo 139
Book of the It (Groddeck) 70, 78, 152–63 *passim*
Boose, Lynda 185*n*5
Bowlby, John 13–14, 100–1

Boyer, John W. 216
Bradley, A. C. 185*n*8, 188–89, 196
Brandchaft, Bernard 113
Breger, Louis 205–6
Brennan, B. William 118, 120, 122, 144
Breuer, Josef 138–39, 141
Bromberg, Philip 6, 8, 11–16, 34, 138–39, 142, 148–49; *see also* dissociation
Brown, Marcus M. 136*n*2
Brown, Norman O. 70
Burke, Kenneth 46–49, 51
Burston, Daniel 84, 194
Butler, Christopher 18

Caligula 202
Cassullo, Gabriele 140, 150*n*5
castration 66, 155, 175, 180, 183
Cavitch, Max 28–29
Charcot, Jean-Martin 140, 150*n*4
Christian Doctrine, The (Milton) 46, 50, 69*n*6
Cinthio, Geraldi 180, 190
Clinical Diary (Ferenczi) 3, 66, 69*n*9, 70, 80, 107, 109–10, 117–35 *passim*, 138, 142, 145, 147, 150
Clinton, Bill 15
Coleridge, Samuel Taylor 187–89, 202
Coltart, Nina 70
"Confusion of Tongues" (Ferenczi) 80, 86, 105, 129, 137, 145, 160
consilience 102
constructivism 11, 18, 23, 30, 34; *see also* objectivism; social constructionism
Conway, Kellyanne 18
Cooper, Arnold M. 175, 183
Cortina, Mauricio 95–96, 140
Crews, Frederick 205
"Crisis of Psychoanalysis, The" (Fromm) 91–93

Darwin, Charles 45
Davies, Jody Messler 138, 150*n*4
de Forest, Izette 71–72, 86, 104–5, 119, 123
Derrida, Jacques 18, 72
Descartes, René 125
Deutsch, Helene 161
dialogue 4, 16–17, 33–34, 150*n*4; and enactment 147–50; concerning Freud 206; in Shakespeare 179, 199; supposed between Freud and Ferenczi 149; with texts 31, 156

dichotomy: between authoritarian and humanist ethics 97, 193; between benign and malignant regression 4; between creativity and compliance 111; between latent and manifest content 30; between maternal and paternal love 87; false in Fromm 97; false rejected by Fromm 103*n*7
Dickens, Charles 25–26
Dickinson, Emily 28
Dilthey, Wilhelm 21, 31–32
Discovery of the Self, The (Severn) 3, 117–18, 120, 123–25, 128–29, 131–34, 137–38, 143, 147–48, 150; as mutual publication 126
dissociation 137–51 *passim*, 150*n*4; by Bromberg 28–29; by God in *Paradise Lost* 54–55; by Groddeck 157; interpersonalization of 146; by Lady Macbeth 180; and multiple self 8, 12, 17, 140; and repression 6, 8, 25, 138–40; Stern and Bromberg on 13–17, 139, 146; and trauma 3, 6, 14–17, 34, 35*n*7, 129, 132–33; *see also* Breuer, Josef; Fairbairn, W. R. D.; Ferenczi, Sándor; Janet, Pierre; Prince, Morton; Van der Kolk, Bessel
Dissociative Identity Disorder 12, 139
Dormandi, Olga 136*n*2
Dostoevsky, Feodor 188
dreams 125, 179; Eve's 46; Freud on 6, 17, 29–30, 33; Jung's 209; in *Macbeth* 176; in *Othello* 190; and Severn 132–35; *see also Interpretation of Dreams, The*
drive theory *see* libido theory
Durkin, Kieran 72

Edmundson, Mark 213*n*2
Eichholz, David 185*n*3
Eisold, Kenneth 103*n*6
Eissler, Kurt R. 82, 89, 92, 119, 121, 124, 126, 210–11
Eissler, Ruth 82–83, 89, 92
Eitingon, Max 75
Eliot, T. S. 5
Ellenberger, Henri 213*n*1
Empson, William 41–45, 49–52, 54, 66
Enlightenment, the 2, 159, 162
enactment 16, 110, 145–50
environmental factors 63, 71, 111–12, 123, 160, 170
Erikson, Erik 12

Escape from Freedom (Fromm) 2, 9, 11, 70–74, 83, 85–86, 95, 98–99, 106, 108, 194; reviewed by Menninger 73
Evans, J. M. 57

Fairbairn, W. R. D. 55, 100, 139–42, 150*n*4
Fanon, Frantz 183–84
Felman, Shoshana 167
femininity 62, 66, 145, 168, 173, 177, 179–80
feminism 62, 67
Fenichel, Otto 76
Ferenczi, Gizella 122–23, 128, 208
Ferenczi, Sándor 2–4, 6, 11, 34, 68*n*5, 69*n*9, 76, 86–87, 96–97; 100, 205, 209; and dissociation 138–40, 142–47, 149; on Freud, 66–68, 69*n*9, 79–80, 85, 107, 109, 124, 126–27; and Groddeck 78, 122, 145, 154, 159–60, 162–63, 208; and Janet 140–43; and "kissing technique" 120, 144; misogyny of 128, 147, 149; and mother 127, 130–31, 134; "Principle of Relaxation and Neo-Catharsis, The" 80, 139, 142; and relational turn 72, 102; on Rank 111; self-diagnosis of schizophrenia 127; *Thalassa* 67, 109–10; Thompson on 108–10, 144; and trauma 56, 128, 130, 137, 141, 147–48; and unwelcome child 130; as "wise baby" 129; *see also Clinical Diary*; "Confusion of Tongues"; Fromm, Erich; Jones, Ernest; mutual analysis; *Thalassa*
fetishism 180
field theory 10–11, 23, 25–27, 34, 34*n*2, 144
Fingarette, Herbert 5
Fish, Stanley E. 40–45, 48–49, 51, 53, 55, 63, 65–66
Fliess, Wilhelm 69*n*8, 208, 213
Fluss, Emil 208
Fluss, Gisela 208
Foehl, John C. 34*n*2
Fortune, Christopher 117, 126, 137, 139
Foucault, Michel 18
Fox, Alice 181
Frankfurt School *see* Institute for Social Research
Frawley, Mary Gail 138
Freud, Anna 137, 150*n*2, 209
Freud, Martha 59–60, 209

Freud, Sigmund 3–4, 9–10, 22, 32, 35*n*10, 70, 73–74, 87, 96–97, 99, 102; on adultery 212; "Analysis Terminable and Interminable" 146; and archaeology 17, 35*n*10; and borderline pathologies 175; and character-types 192, 198; "'Civilized' Sexual Morality" 212; cocaine use of 208, 214*n*3 ; disregard of evidence by 100; and Dora 33; dualism of 59; and Groddeck 103*n*3, 153–58, 160, 162, 163*n*1; on Hamlet 35*n*9, 185*n*8; and Iago 201; and Janet 138–43; legacy of 2; and Little Hans 69*n*7, 71; and masturbation 210, 213; need for fame of, 63, 65–66; *On the History of the Psycho-Analytic Movement* 125, 153; on *Oedipus Rex* 6–8, 24, 29–33, 35*n*9; and *Othello* 190; and *Paradise Lost* 46, 56–60, 62–68, 69*n*7, 69*n*8, 71; *Psychopathology of Everyday Life* 30–31; relationship to mother 87, 90, 105, 145, 219; and Severn 118–20, 123–28, 132–33, 135, 136*n*4, 144–45; sexuality of 4, 30–31, 209–10, 212–13; topographical model of 16; and trauma 144–50, 150*n*1, 150*n*2, 150*n*4, 213; trip to American 209; urinary incontinence of 209; *see also* attachment; authoritarian character; dreams; Ferenczi, Sándor; Fromm, Erich; *Interpretation of Dreams*; Jung, C. G.; libido theory; narcissism; seduction theory
Friedman, Lawrence 1, 70, 84–85, 90, 103*n*3, 106
Frink, Horace 206
Fromm, Annis Freeman 87
Fromm, Erich 1, 3, 4, 103*n*1, 103*n*2, 103*n*3, 202, 206; and Auden 195, 204*n*3; and authoritarianism 2, 73, 81, 90, 97, 104, 109–10, 112–14; blind spots of 73, 79, 84, 87–88, 91, 96; on central relatedness 84; and Ferenczi 76–78, 84, 90, 92–93, 97, 100, 102, 104–5, 111–13, 205; and Freud piety 84, 91; and Groddeck 70–72, 76–78, 84, 86–87, 96, 102, 103*n*3, 157, 160, 163*n*2; and homosexuality 91; and humanistic psychoanalysis 2, 34, 193; and literary psychoanalysis 4, 28, 73, 96, 157, 167; and Marxism, 72, 97; narcissism of 89; as object relations psychoanalyst 81, 94, 100–2, 111–12; relationship to mother

89–90, 96; 88–89; and Stalinist history 84, 89, 104, 106, 114; and Donnel Stern 8; and Sullivan 8–11, 20, 72–73, 82, 100, 106, 111; and transference 94; *see also* Horney, Karen; humanism; Jones, Ernest; magic helper; necrophilia; Oedipus complex; pathology of normalcy; revisionism in psychoanalysis; social character; titles of works
Fromm, Henny Gurland 88
Fromm, Rosa Krause 89
Fromm-Reichmann, Frieda 74–77, 88, 100
"Fundamental Positions of Psychoanalysis" (Fromm) 90–91
Funk, Rainer 71, 90, 103*n*2

Gabbard, Glen 149
Gadamer, Hans-Georg 16, 31–33
Garber, Marjorie 202
Garnet, Henry 176
Gay, Peter 205–6
Genesis 45–47
German Psychoanalytic Society 74–76, 82
Giuliani, Rudy 18
Goethe, Johann Wolfgang von 110, 159–60, 185*n*8, 189
Goodhart, Sandor 8, 24
Golz, Else von der 162
Graf, Max 69*n*7
Greatness and Limitations of Freud's Thought (Fromm) 91, 93–94
Green, Maurice R. 120–21
Groddeck, Barbara 162, 163*n*3
Groddeck, Georg 2–3, 6, 185*n*5, 207–8; absence of grief in 161–62; and birthdays 152, 158; blind spots of 153, 158–62; as psychoanalyst 153–54, 156; and Severn 122–23, 145; siblings of 157, 162; traumas of 157–58, 160–62, 185*n*5; as "wild" analyst 154–55; and Winnicott 159; *see also Book of the It*; Ferenczi, Sándor; Fromm, Erich
Grossman, Carl, and Sylva Grossman 71, 76, 86, 154, 157, 161–62, 163*n*2
Grünbaum, Adolf 17
Grunes, Dorothy, and Jerome Grunes 184
Guasto, Gianni 68*n*5, 136*n*5
Guex, Germaine 183, 186*n*11
Guntrip, Harry 11, 100–2, 103*n*8

Harris, Adrienne 1, 70, 136*n*6, 137
Haynal, André, and Ernst Falzeder 149

H.D. (Hilda Doolittle) 145
Heart of Man, The (Fromm) 194, 197–98, 201
Heidegger, Martin 12, 18, 99
hermeneutics 18, 20, 23, 26, 29, 31, 102, 148; of suspicion and trust 33–34
Heywood, Charles Kenneth 136*n*2
Hirsch, Irwin 34*n*6
Hitler, Adolf 202
Hoche, Alfred 125
Hoffer, Peter 150*n*1
Horkheimer, Max 73–74, 76, 106, 112
Horney, Karen 62, 118, 154; and Fromm 72–74, 77, 82, 88, 100, 106, 111–12, 114
Hornstein, Gail A. 75
Howell, Elizabeth 138
humanism 8, 20, 27, 34, 198; Fromm and 72, 81, 88, 97–98, 102; normative 193, 202
"Humanism and Psychoanalysis" (Fromm) 2
Hunter, William B., Jr., 69*6*
Hyman, Stanley Edgar 216*n*2

Inhofe, Jim 22
Institute for Social Research 72–73, 75–76, 82, 106, 112
International Federation of Psychoanalytic Societies 90
International Psychoanalytical Association 58, 75, 82–83, 90, 111, 113–14
Interpretation of Dreams, The (Freud) 6, 59, 64, 145, 185*n*8
Irigaray, Luce 67

Jackson, Edith 120, 144
Janet, Pierre 13, 16, 35*n*7, 138–43, 150*n*4, 150*n*5, 213*n*1
Jay, Martin 112
Jelliffe, Smith Ely 123
Jensen, Wilhelm 207, 214*n*3
Jones, Ernest 82, 124, 144–45; on Freud 59, 70, 85, 104–5, 205; Fromm on 71, 75, 85–86, 89, 92, 96, 100–1, 103*n*1, 105–6, 114, 119; on God complex 65; and sanity of Rank and Ferenczi 71, 83–84, 86, 92, 104, 114, 119, 124, 136*n*4, 145
Jung, C. G. 213*n*1, 214*n*3; Ferenczi on 111, 146; Freud and 58–60, 67, 145, 153–54, 208–11

Kakutani, Michiko 18, 20
Kandel, Eric 21
Karpf, Fay B. 71–72
Keyserling, Hermann 152, 158
Khoury, Gérard D. 70, 98
Kirsch, Arthur 174
Klein, Melanie 11, 101, 178–79, 196
Kleinschmidt, Hans 183–84, 186*n*12
Knights, L. C. 178, 185*n*8
Kohut, Heinz 54, 56, 118, 123–24, 188, 197; *see also* narcissistic rage
Krugman, Paul 22

Lacan, Jacques 10, 167, 175
Lachmann, Frank 12
Lacoursiere, Roy B. 208, 213*n*2
Laing, R. D. 100
Landauer, Karl 74–76
Landis, Bernard 87, 101
Laplanche, Jean 46
Leroy, Maxime 125
Levinas, Emmanuel 33
Lewis, C. S. 40–41, 43–45, 48, 51, 63
libido theory 91, 100, 106, 109, 112, 154, 192
Lidz, Theodore 100
Lorenz, Konrad 99–100
Ludwig, Emil 205
Luther, Martin 12

Macbeth (Shakespeare) 4, 175–81, 184; birth imagery in 168–69, 172–73, 176–78, 185*n*6; menstruation in 180–81; as philobatic tragedy 171–72, 175, 177–78; Porter scene in 175–76, 179, 199; weaning in 169, 172, 185*n*6
Maccoby, Michael 94
magic helper 2, 105, 107–9, 113
Mahler, Margaret 95, 171
Main, Mary 14
Man for Himself (Fromm) 81, 89, 97, 192–93, 195
Marcel, Mary 68*n*5
Marcuse, Herbert 100, 112–13
Martynkewicz, Wolfgang 152–54, 159, 162, 163*n*1, 163*n*3
Marvell, Andrew 5
Marx, Karl 33, 72, 97, 202
"Marx's Contribution to the Knowledge of Man" (Fromm) 97
masochism 93, 98, 106; *see also* sadism; authoritarian character

Masson, Jeffrey M. 117, 136*n*2
May, Rollo 204*n*3
McGuire, William 209
McLaughlin, Neil 72
Medawar, Peter B. 101, 103*n*8
Meier, Carl A. 211
Meigs, Kathleen 117, 136*n*1
Menninger, Karl 73
Meyer, Adolf 100
Miller, Alice 64
Milton, John 1; and Arianism 69*n*6; *see also* Christian Doctrine, The; Paradise Lost
Möbius, August Ferdinand 140
Morgann, Maurice 185*n*8
mutual analysis 136*n*3; between Ferenczi and Severn 3, 6, 71, 117, 121, 126–29, 131, 138, 147–50; Bromberg on 148; desired by Thompson 119, 121–22; fee arrangement for 122; Ferenczi on 111, 121, 128, 134, 146; Gabbard on 149; Severn on 121–22, 126, 138

narcissism 113, 145, 175, 183, 197, 200; and borderline pathologies 172, 175, 183; of Freud 3, 66, 93; Freud on 61–62, 66, 113; of Groddeck 161; and necrophilia 198, 201; *see also* Fromm, Erich; Kohut, Heinz; *Paradise Lost*; Shaw, Daniel
narcissistic rage 54, 68*n*3, 172, 188, 197
necrophilia 4, 198–99, 201; *see also* biophilia
neo-Freudianism 72–73, 112
neuropsychoanalysis 100
New York Psychoanalytic Society 82
Nietzsche, Friedrich 18–19, 23, 32–33, 157

objectivism 17–23, 34, 41, 44, 98, 206; *see also* constructivism
object relations theory 11, 81, 100–2, 112, 140, 159
ocnophilia 4, 169–72, 174–75, 178, 181, 183, 186*n*11; *see also* philobatism
Oedipus complex 7–8, 16, 24, 61, 68*n*5, 110, 155, 186*n*11; Fromm and 88, 100; and original sin 56, 63
Oedipus Rex (Sophocles) 6–8, 16, 24–27, 34*n*3, 35*n*8, 47, 56, 61, 214*n*3
Orange, Donna 12, 33, 56
Orwell, George 72, 97–98, 185*n*5; Orwellian 18, 20, 22

Othello (Shakespeare) 4, 54, 182, 185*n*7, 202–3; allegory in 189, 203; anal imagery in 190, 192, 196–201; birth imagery in 196–97, 201; blackness and whiteness in 174, 204*n*4; and capitalism 191–92, 199–200, 202; Clown in 199–201; handkerchief in 171, 173–75, 177, 179–80, 183, 185*n*9; Iago's motives in 189–93, 196–97, 203, 204*n*2; misogyny and racism in 193, 197, 204*n*4; and morality play tradition 189; narcissistic rage in 173, 188; and negative transcendence 187, 193–95, 197–98, 201–2; as ocnophilic tragedy 171–74, 176; sadism in 192, 196, 201

Paddock, Stephen 203
Palmer, Richard 31
Pálos, Elma 128, 208
Pálos, Gizella *see* Ferenczi, Gizella
Paradise Lost (Milton) 3, 162, 187–89, 204*n*2; allegory in 61; deferred action in 46; dichotomy in 51, 59; double bind in 53–54, 56–57, 59, 71, 77; the Fall in 40, 45–49, 51–52, 55–57, 61, 66–67, 68*n*2; and Freud as God 58–60, 62–65, 68, 71, 77; glory in 50–54, 57, 63–65, 67; Golden Scepter and Iron Rod in 53–54, 59, 66; narcissism in 45, 51, 53–55, 57, 60–63, 65–66; rabbit—duck paradigm in 48, 50, 55; theological vs. logological perspectives on 46–49, 51; theological vs. Romantic readings of 39–45, 49, 57, 68; *see also Christian Doctrine, The*; dissociation; Freud, Sigmund; Milton, John; patriarchy; trauma
Paris, Bernard J. 51–56, 62, 64
Parsons, Michael 151*n*7
Partridge, Simon 185*n*5
pathology of normalcy 20, 193–94
patriarchy 3, 71, 77, 79, 84; *Paradise Lost* and 57–58, 60–62, 67
Paul, St. 22–23, 195
Peláez, Miguel Gutiérrez 150*n*1
Peter, John 42
philobatism 4, 169–72, 175, 177–78, 181, 183, 186*n*11; *see also* ocnophilia
Pitcher, John 185
Poe, Edgar Allan 167, 175
Polmear, Caroline 4, 167–72, 174, 177–78, 181; 185*n*1

postmodernism 2, 18, 20, 23, 98, 167
Prince, Morton 142–44
"Psychoanalysis: Science or Party Line?" (Fromm) 83–84, 86, 89, 96, 103*n*1
Puner, Helen Walker 205–6, 211–12
Putnam, Frank 12
Pyles, Robert 145–46

Rabaté, Jean-Michel 35*n*10
Rachman, Arnold W. 4, 118, 136*n*2, 144
Radó, Sándor 75
Rank, Otto 2, 60, 71–72, 84, 86, 92, 102, 104–5, 111, 114, 119, 136*n*4; as analyst of Severn 123; and Groddeck 154; *see also* Jones, Ernest
regression 4, 99, 129, 138; Balint on 4; Fromm and Winnicott on 95–96
Reichmann, Frieda *see* Fromm-Reichmann, Frieda
revisionism in psychoanalysis 5, 56, 63, 205–6, 209, 211; and Fromm 71–73, 83, 100, 103*n*6, 105, 112
Revision of Psychoanalysis, The (Fromm) 71, 103*n*7
Richards, I. A. 25
Richardson, Jonathan 41
Ricoeur, Paul 33
Roazen, Paul 75, 82, 113–14, 205–6
Rosenberg, Samuel 60
Ross, Lawrence 185*n*9
Roth, Philip 184, 186*n*12
Roudinesco, Élisabeth 4, 31, 206–13 *passim*, 213*n*1, 213*n*2, 214*n*3
Rudnytsky, Peter L. 1, 5, 10, 21, 34*n*3, 35*n*8, 46, 68, 71–72, 102, 152, 175, 214*n*3
Rumrich, John 51, 55, 57, 59, 65, 69*n*6
Rycroft, Charles 185*n*5

Sachs, Hanns 74–76, 89
sadism 11, 43, 49, 85, 98, 106; *see also* authoritarian character; masochism; *Othello*
Sander, Lewis 12
Sane Society, The (Fromm) 9, 20, 187, 191–93, 202
Sartre, Jean-Paul 99
Schächter, Miksa 140
Schleiermacher, Friedrich 31–33
Schopenhauer, Arthur 32, 110
Schore, Allan 34
Schröter, Michael 75–76, 89

Schumann, Hanneliese 156
Schur, Max 208
Schweninger, Ernst 207
"Scienticism or Fanaticism?" (Fromm) see "Psychoanalysis: Science or Party Line?"
Secret Committee 111, 162
seduction theory 56, 68n5, 125, 137–39, 145, 160
self, sense of 8, 11–12, 14, 27, 33, 81, 88, 97, 194–95, 201–2; pseudo 11, 74, 112; see also dissociation
Severn, Elizabeth 3–4, 130–35, 136n2, 136n3, 136n7; as "evil genius" 125; on Ferenczi 122, 126–31; and Fromm 71; and Groddeck 159; meets Freud 124; and Orpha 117–18, 133; on psychoanalysis 123–24; *The Psychology of Behavior* 118, 143; *Psycho-therapy* 142–43; and Stern 6; as Queen 122; and trauma 131–32, 139–41, 144–45, 149; see also Freud, Sigmund; *The Discovery of the Self*; mutual analysis
Severn, Margaret 122, 126, 136n2, 136n3
sexual abuse 14, 26–27, 56, 68n5, 69n8, 118–20, 128, 131, 137–39, 143, 150n1, 160, 213
sexuality 33, 46, 56, 62, 67, 77, 85, 102, 107, 154, 158, 176–77, 179, 198, 209; see also Freud, Sigmund
sexual symbols 153, 155–56, 173, 180
Shakespeare, William 23, 32; *Antony and Cleopatra* 172; *Coriolanus* 172; *Hamlet* 185n4, 187–88, 199, 203; *Henry IV, Part 1*, 28, 185n8; *King Lear* 54, 60, 68n3, 172, 199; *Timon of Athens* 172; *The Winter's Tale* 173, 185n4; see also Freud, Sigmund;; *Macbeth*; *Othello*
Shapiro, Sue A. 35n6, 119
Shaw, Daniel 113
Shelley, Percy Bysshe 39, 43, 49
Sigmund Freud's Mission (Fromm) 1, 71, 75, 82, 84–86, 88–92, 96, 105, 205
Sigray, Harriot 122
Silberstein, Eduard 208
Simmel, Ernst 154
Skinner, B. F. 100
Smith, Nancy A. 117–18
social character 2, 4, 10, 68n3, 80–81, 85, 93, 103n2, 106, 160, 190, 194–95, 197, 202

social constructionism 2, 6, 12; see also constructivism
"Social Determinants of Psychoanalytic Therapy, The" (Fromm) 74, 76–82, 84–86, 89–90, 92, 104
Sophocles 207, 214n3; see also *Oedipus Rex*
Soreanu, Raluca 185n3
Spinoza, Baruch 97, 202
Spivack, Bernard 189
Stanton, Martin 117
Stekel, Wilhelm 58, 207, 214n3
Stepansky, Paul 207
Stern, Daniel 12
Stern, Donnel 1, 5–9, 11–20, 22–24, 27–28, 30–34, 34n1, 34n5, 138, 144, 146–50, 151n6; see also dissociation; enactment; field theory; hermeneutics
Stern, Jeffrey 172
Stevens, Wallace 29
Strindberg, August 127, 129–31, 148
Stross, Josephine 208
Sullivan, Harry Stack 12, 15, 27, 139, 142, 145; see also Fromm, Erich
Suttie, Ian 150n5
Swales, Peter J. 30, 210–12

Taft, Jessie 71–72
Tauber, Edward S. 87, 101
Thompson, Clara 71, 82, 104, 108–10, 118–23, 144; see also mutual analysis
Tillyard, E. M. W. 68n2, 68n4
trauma 27, 33, 79, 81, 119, 121, 127–28, 137–39, 141–45, 147–48, 150, 150n1, 150n2; and borderline pathologies 168–70, 172–3, 178, 181, 183, 185n5, 186n12; reality of 125–26, 132; Freud—Ferenczi disagreement as 113; intergenerational 136n3; Oedipus and 16, 24, 26–29, 33–34; *Paradise Lost* and 46, 56, 63, 66, 68n5; Post-Traumatic Stress Disorders 12–13, 25; and Severn 118, 121, 124–25, 127–30, 133–34; see also dissociation; sexual abuse
Trilling, Lionel 112
Trump, Donald 18, 22, 98, 202

Van der Hart, Onno 35n7, 139
Van der Kolk, Bessel 13–14, 16–17, 26–27, 29
Vienna Psychoanalytic Society 69n7
Voigt, Emmy von 156, 163n1
Voltaire 50

Waldock, A. J. A. 41–45, 47–51, 68n2, 68n4
Weber, Alfred 103n2
Webster, Richard 63–65
Weil, Simone 198
Wheeler, Richard P. 172
Wiesbaden Congress 86, 105, 137
Wilde, Oscar 1, 21
Willbern, David 167–69, 176, 179–80
William Alanson White Institute 6, 82, 114
Wilson, Edward O. 99–100, 102

Winnicott, D. W. 9–10, 14, 29, 74, 81, 94–95, 100, 185n7; and antisocial tendency 123; and Groddeck 159–60; "Hate in the Counter-Transference" 87; *Playing and Reality* 70; and Severn 123; and transitional objects 26, 175, 185n7; and True Self 6, 11, 111
Wittels, Fritz 206–7
Wittenberg, Wilhelm 74–75
Wolff, Larry 68n5
Wolstein, Benjamin 11–12, 34–35n6, 117
Wulff, Mosche 175